Web Design For Dumm...

Cheat Sheet

Web Graphic Design Tips

- Design the Web page interface to fit within the first 600 × 350 pixels so that the important content is visible when the page first loads.

- Achieve a balanced layout by designing no more than three focal points: Use the "big, medium, small" strategy.

- Break the page into a few functional areas to maximize page real estate.

- Use colored areas to break up the page visually.

- Avoid using fonts set smaller than 12 point (depending on the font).

- Use standard computer system fonts for all HTML text.

- Create style guides for each Web site project. This ensures a consistent look throughout the site and allows multiple designers to build it.

Building Site Maps

- Develop a wish list of content to include in the site and then organize it into a standard outline form with no more than three levels if possible: Main idea, topic, and sub-topic.

- Avoid navigation problems in the site by keeping the outline to just five to seven main ideas.

- Convert the outline into a site map. Make a horizontal row of boxes for each main idea. Below that, make a row of boxes for each topic.

- Choose a standard set of symbols for the site map. Use boxes to represent pages, cylinders to represent databases, and then connect everything together with lines and arrows.

- Build a professional-looking site map with an illustration program like Adobe Illustrator, Macromedia Freehand, or Inspiration (see the free trials on the CD included with this book).

Tips for graphic production

- Build all Web graphics in 72 dpi, the standard display resolution of the Web.

- Don't bother creating high-resolution graphics — the browser automatically displays all graphics at 72 dpi.

- Save graphics that have a mix of text, flat-colored graphics, and photos as GIF files.

- Save all purely photographic images as JPEG files.

- Always display anti-aliased graphics on the correct background color; otherwise, they develop an ugly halo around them.

- Use Web safe colors for all text and flat-colored graphics.

- Slice graphics into pieces and save each piece in either GIF or JPEG files to optimize performance. String them back together using an HTML table.

Designing a Client Presentation

- Create three to four different design ideas for the client to choose from.

- Create a set of two graphical mockups for each design idea that show the home page and one sub-page. This enables the client to see how the design works throughout the site.

- When presenting to clients, don't include a design idea that you can't live with. Clients have a knack for picking the ugliest design.

- Create both an online and an offline presentation for the final client presentation. Mount prints of the design ideas on boards and create an online *click-through* in HTML so the client can see how they look in a Web browser.

For Dummies: Bestselling Book Series for Beginners

Web Design For Dummies®

Navigation Design

- Don't overuse real-world metaphors. For example, design buttons to look like those on a camera instead of making the whole interface look like one.

- Leave a *breadcrumb trail* for users — a trail of text links that traces a user's path through a site like this: Home⇨Category⇨Subcategory⇨Story.

- Use a *cross-navigation* button scheme, with one button for each main category of your Web site.

- Differentiate the visual design of non-clickable and clickable elements: Don't use the same graphic as a button on one page and a headline on another.

- Use rollover animation on buttons to enhance interaction and usability.

- Always place buttons in the same location on the page and don't change their appearance: Consistency is key.

- Always label icons and buttons by their function.

User Testing

- Always conduct a user test before you get entrenched in production.

- To prepare for testing, identify a specific task to test, such as "Find and purchase a book called *Web Design for Dummies*." Build a working HTML prototype to test those tasks only.

- Test at least five to seven people for best results.

- Don't ask leading questions during a user test. This points out issues that users should be able to judge for themselves and expresses doubt about its design.

HTML Layout Tricks

- Use individual HTML tables to organize a page into modular areas: This strategy makes the page easy to update.

- Let HTML do the design work with background colors, background tiles, and colored tables.

- Use non-breaking spaces and transparent GIF *shims* to add extra space around objects in your layout.

Copyright © 2001 Wiley Publishing, Inc.
All rights reserved.

Item 0823-7.

For more information about Wiley Publishing, call 1-800-762-2974.

For Dummies: Bestselling Book Series for Beginners

Web Design

FOR

DUMMIES®

by Lisa Lopuck

Wiley Publishing, Inc.

Web Design For Dummies®

Published by
Wiley Publishing, Inc.
909 Third Avenue
New York, NY 10022
www.wiley.com

Copyright © 2001 Wiley Publishing, Inc., Indianapolis, Indiana

Published simultaneously in Canada

For general information on our other products and services or to obtain technical support, please contact our Customer Care Department within the U.S. at 800-762-2974, outside the U.S. at 317-572-3993, or fax 317-572-4002.

Wiley also publishes its books in a variety of electronic formats. Some content that appears in print may not be available in electronic books.

Library of Congress Cataloging-in-Publication Data:

Library of Congress Control Number: 2001086259

ISBN: 0-7645-0823-7

Manufactured in the United States of America

10 9 8 7 6 5

1B/SV/QY/QS/IN

About the Author

In 1988, **Lisa Lopuck** got her first glimpse of multimedia while still at UCLA pursuing her degree in Design. She saw a tiny, black-and-white, interactive HyperCard stack designed by The Voyager Company and immediately knew her career path.

Her first job out of school was working at the Apple Multimedia Lab in San Francisco. She then moved on to Skywalker Ranch, working with George Lucas to design educational CD-ROMs. The rest has been interactive history — working with everyone from Kaleida to eBay, writing best-selling books, teaching, and speaking at conferences along the way.

In 1996, she co-founded Electravision, an award-winning Web design agency in San Francisco with clients such as Twentieth Century Fox, National Geographic, Microsoft, and Mall of America. Electravision's work won awards, including Yahoo!'s Best of the Year, Site of the Day, and Best of the Web. In 1997, Electravision founded and hosted Kidskamp, the Web's first virtual summer camp, in which 1,000 kids from all over the world participated. Electravision also created the highly acclaimed online murder mystery series, *Suspect*, one of the Web's first online entertainment series.

In 1998, Lisa founded eHandsOn.com, an Internet company that provides expert-led online training for professional Web developers. Lisa can be reached at lisa@lopuck.com.

Dedication

For my husband, Matt Gunnell, who is my chief evangelist, and for my daughter, Jasmine, who passed up many a Barbie play session so I could write this book.

For Sheryl Hampton, with whom I shared a few great years in the Web design trenches — and I have 1,000 Polaroids to prove it!

And for Mark Grilli, my new partner in crime at eHandsOn.com.

Author's Acknowledgments

Thanks to the many people who helped make this book possible: To the team at eHandsOn who worked hard to assemble the free training trials; to Diana Smedley at Macromedia who makes sure I always have the latest software; to Linda Morris, my editor, who kept everything on track; and to the folks who granted rights to include screenshots of their Web sites in this book.

Publisher's Acknowledgments

We're proud of this book; please send us your comments through our online registration form located at www.dummies.com/register/.

Some of the people who helped bring this book to market include the following:

Acquisitions, Editorial, and Media Development

Project Editor: Linda Morris

Acquisitions Editor: Tom Heine

Copy Editor: Rebekah Mancilla

Proof Editor: Sarah Shupert

Technical Editor: Dennis Short

Senior Permissions Editor: Carmen Krikorian

Media Development Specialist: Brock Bigard

Media Development Coordinator:
Marisa E. Pearman

Editorial Manager: Kyle Looper

Media Development Supervisor:
Richard Graves

Editorial Assistant: Jean Rogers

Production

Project Coordinator: Regina Snyder

Layout and Graphics: John Greenough, Jackie Nicholas, Jacque Schneider, Rashell Smith, Jeremey Unger

Proofreaders: Valery Bourke, Susan Moritz, Angel Perez, Marianne Santy, York Production Services, Inc.

Indexer: York Production Services, Inc.

Publishing and Editorial for Technology Dummies

   Richard Swadley, Vice President and Executive Group Publisher
   Mary C. Corder, Editorial Director
   Andy Cummings, Vice President and Publisher

Publishing for Consumer Dummies

   Diane Graves Steele, Vice President and Publisher
   Joyce Pepple, Acquisitions Director

Composition Services

   Gerry Fahey, Vice President of Production Services
   Debbie Stailey, Director of Composition Services

Contents at a Glance

Cartoons at a Glance

By Rich Tennant

page 183

"Just how accurately should my Web site reflect my place of business?"

page 263

page 213

"I have to say I'm really impressed with the interactivity on this car wash Web site."

page 71

"I can't really explain it, but everytime I animate someone swinging a golf club, a little divot of code comes up missing on the home page."

page 7

Cartoon Information:
Fax: 978-546-7747
E-Mail: richtennant@the5thwave.com
World Wide Web: www.the5thwave.com

Table of Contents

Introduction

Designing professional Web sites is not just about making pretty pages: It's about planning the site, creating easy-to-understand user interfaces, working with a team of people, understanding technologies, and managing client relationships. Creating a Web site is a process, and Web designers are involved every step of the way.

The field offers so much to learn: You can build a rewarding career and spend years mastering all the little things, from the oodles of graphics and HTML software programs to figuring out how to organize hundreds of Web pages into a usable interface. (Egads! That's a specialty by itself.)

Over the course of the next 300 or so pages, I show you how to transform your creative self into a full-fledged Web designer — ready to undertake the creation of a major Web site. You still need years of practice and experience to turn out the good stuff, but this book gives you the solid foundation that you need and can serve as a reference as you build your Web design career.

About This Book

This book is written for the creative professional or soon-to-be creative professional who's looking to get into the world of Web design. I'm not talking about building personal Web sites with frilly fonts, loud background patterns, and silly pictures of your baby's first birthday. I'm talking about building large, serious business Web sites for real-world clients — clients ranging from established companies to start-up "dot-coms" that need high-powered Web sites to function as an integral part of their business.

Whether you are, or are looking to be, an independent creative consultant or work in the in-house creative department for a company or design agency, you'll find that the processes, tips, and techniques covered in this book are essential to every project.

By the end of this book, you'll know how to

- Work as part of the team of people required to build a Web site
- Work with a client to assemble a winning proposal
- Turn a wish list of content into a working site map
- Build a killer design presentation and wow your clients

- ✔ Choose software programs for building Web graphics
- ✔ Design graphics that download quickly and look great across platforms and browsers
- ✔ Design a user-friendly navigation system for a site
- ✔ Organize and conduct user tests
- ✔ Make technology choices

This book gives you the know-how it takes to walk the walk and talk the talk with the best Web designers. After you know all that stuff, you can raise your hourly rate enough to buy that house in the hills. Perhaps that's an exaggeration, but you'll certainly enjoy yourself. (And if you do get that house in the hills, make sure you have a guesthouse for me!)

Conventions Used in This Book

Throughout this book, I use conventions in the text to make things easier to understand. For example, if I'm introducing a new term, I put it in *italics* and then define it. When I first use an industry-specific term such as *site map*, I make it italic and then give you the scoop on what it means. Usually, these terms are also accompanied by a Web Speak icon (see the section "Icons Used in This Book" later in this Introduction).

Code listings and Web addresses are set in a monospaced font like this: `www.dummies.com`. If I want to call your attention to a particular line or section of the code, you'll see it set in bold like this: `<body>`.

Foolish Assumptions

Every chapter in this book is aimed at seasoned designers and artists in other fields such as print design and architecture who now want to apply their creative talents to Web design. But even if you don't have a creative background, many of the chapters in this book can still be a great help to you. If you've built your own personal Web site, but now want to polish up your act and start building Web sites professionally, this book is also for you.

You don't need to know HTML, the coding language of the Web, or high-tech programming languages in order to get the most out of these 19 chapters. In this book, you can find everything you need to know about the people, the planning processes, user interface design, graphic design, and the technologies to start on your journey as a professional Web designer. This book doesn't give you magical creative powers. It will, however, help you channel the creative juices that you have into building better-looking, user-friendly, and efficient Web sites.

What You Shouldn't Read

Whatever you do, don't let the technical stuff in this book lead you astray. Throughout this book, and especially in the later chapters, I include some pretty hairy code examples and explain the basics of how they work. As a Web designer, you don't have to be a crack programmer; you just need to be familiar with the underlying technologies and their capabilities. The more you get into Web design, the easier it is to understand the technical stuff, and it doesn't look so scary.

Whenever you see the Technical Stuff icon in the margin like this, you can choose to turn a blind eye and know that you won't miss out on too much. After all, this book is geared toward the creative professional looking to apply their skills to designing Web sites, not building laser-guided satellites.

How This Book Is Organized

This book is organized to follow the basic workflow of a major Web site design project. Part I starts out with the planning procedures — from your initial meetings with the client to developing a site map. From there, Parts II and III move into graphic and user interface design tips and techniques. Part IV covers the ghastly but essential techno-babble, and finally, Part V sums everything up in a handy reference guide. Whew! Let me break it down:

Part I: The Web Design Kick-Off

Just like a football game, a lot of planning and preparation goes on before the start of a Web site project. The site map of a Web site is kind of like your game plan, and the Web production team you assemble sort of your starting line-up. In this part, you find out what kind of team you need to build a site, how to work with a client, and how to gather a wish list of all the content needed for a site. You also learn how to build a site map that serves as the blueprint of an entire Web site.

Part II: Designing Web Graphics

Designing the actual graphics for a Web site is the fun part — you get to apply your creative talents and get busy with the mouse. Chapters 5 through 10 discuss graphic design issues and techniques according to how they relate to the Web, along with all the technical color theory and palette stuff that you need to know. You also learn graphic production techniques and how to prepare a knock-em-dead client presentation.

Part III: Creating a User-Friendly Face

After you learn how to push pixels around in style to build Web graphics, the next layer to conquer is designing a graphical interface that enables people to navigate around in a site. After all, what good is a Web site if people can't figure out how to use it? In this part, I discuss techniques for designing effective navigation schemes and how to conduct user tests to see if your designs actually work.

Part IV: Producing the Final Web Site

After you determine the graphic and user interface design, the real work begins — assembling the designs into a working Web site. Here's where the scary technical stuff comes in. Don't worry — Chapters 13 and 14 give you a friendly tour of the inner workings of HTML, the basic language of the Web. You even find out how to can manipulate HTML for your own page design and layout purposes. Chapter 15 takes you a little further and illuminates the technologies that really turn Web sites into movin', groovin' business machines.

Part V: The Part of Tens

True to the *For Dummies* style, Chapters 16 through 19 sum up the contents of the book into Top Ten lists that you can use as handy reference guides. Rip these chapters out and stick them under your desk at work where you can easily access them without anyone ever knowing. Your boss will be impressed with the fountains of knowledge that you suddenly possess. (Then, of course, you'll have to buy a second *Web Design For Dummies* book that's undamaged.)

Icons Used in This Book

To make this book user-friendly, I've tagged various sections with icons that point out cool ideas, things to look out for, or industry jargon. As you read, be on the lookout for these little guys:

In talking about Web design, it's impossible to avoid the techno-babble. That's why I like to give you a little advance warning with this icon so you can mentally prepare. The technical stuff is there to give you background, but if it makes your head spin, you can choose to ignore it guilt-free. I won't blame you.

The Web design landscape is littered with land mines that can get you into trouble. Pay special attention to the stuff marked with the little bomb icon.

I love a tasty morsel of advice. I use this icon whenever I've got some cool inside information to share with you.

This icon is not exactly a bomb threat warning, but it does mark things that you should keep in mind during the course of a Web site project.

Like any other industry, Web design is fraught with insider terms. To make sure you get a high-class education here, I've pointed out all the good ones so you can carry on an informed conversation and look like you've been designing Web sites since the dawn of time.

I'm Here if You Need Me!

You're probably not used to authors extending themselves for personal counseling and help, but don't-cha-know, I'm just that kind of person. I love teaching and talking with people around the world. You can also see my personal work at www.lopuck.com.

I get a lot of e-mail these days, but I try to respond to it all. Let me know what you think of the book (good or bad), if you have questions, or if you just have a good Web design war story to share. I'm all ears at lisa@lopuck.com.

You can also contact the publisher or authors of other *For Dummies* books by visiting the Dummies Web site at www.dummies.com. The snail-mail address is

Wiley Publishing, Inc.
10475 Crosspoint Boulevard
Indianapolis, IN 46256

Part I
The Web Design Kick-Off

The 5th Wave By Rich Tennant

"I can't really explain it, but everytime I animate someone swinging a golf club, a little divot of code comes up missing on the home page."

In this part . . .

Most of us grew up with the mantra "measure twice, cut once" drilled into our brains — and for good reason. It works for so many situations — from open-heart surgery to designing Web pages. And, like surgeons, we Web designers can do a lot of damage by just sort of goin' for it without taking time to plan. So, like many other things in life, a little bit of planning in the beginning goes a long way in saving you a lot of time, effort, and headache later on in your Web design process.

This part of the book is the Web design warm-up where you meet the team, learn how to organize and plan a Web site, and build a site map. In fact, so much pre-game activity goes into making a professional Web site that you won't push a single pixel of artwork until Chapter 5. By the end of this part, you'll know how to kick off a professional Web site so that when you get to Part II, you're ready to dig in and start production.

Chapter 1

So, You Want to Be a Web Designer?

In This Chapter

▶ Figuring out the Web site design process, from start to finish

▶ Setting team member roles and responsibilities

▶ Building a site map

▶ Creating design mock-ups

▶ Understanding HTML and programming languages

▶ Testing for usability and quality

*T*he Internet industry seems to have exploded overnight. Those who can claim that they've been designing Web sites since 1995 actually qualify as dinosaurs of the industry. This is great news for you if you're thinking about becoming a professional Web designer. The industry is so new that a lot of territory is uncharted, and exciting — albeit rapid — developments are around every corner.

Web design is not just about creating a single Web page that looks pretty. In this book, I show you how to design a whole collection of pretty Web pages that also link together in a way that makes sense to the user. Modern Web sites can consist of hundreds of pages. As a professional Web designer, it's your job to know how to integrate design and navigation using the myriad of technologies available to build an effective Web site.

Does this sound like a daunting task? Never fear, that's what teams are for! It's a rare and well-paid person who can do everything from HTML coding to programming to graphic design. If you want to be a Web designer, you simply need to understand enough about the entire process from start to finish, and the role that every team member plays, to enable you to focus on the fun stuff: design.

In this chapter, I walk you through the entire Web design process from initial concept to final execution and I discuss the roles that everyone must play to pull off a successful site.

From Concept to Execution

A lot of fancy Web design companies like to refer new clients to their patent-pending, proprietary "five-step design process" to educate them on the chronology of the Web creative process. The process isn't ultra-special or top-secret, it's just common sense nicely spelled out for the client:

1. **The concept.** The first step in designing a Web site is simply a discovery phase to define the concept. The most important things to nail down in this phase are

   - Who's the audience?

   - What's the site supposed to do?

   - How big a Web site does the client need and want?

2. **Architecture.** The next thing that you need to do is map out the site on paper. During this phase, you create what looks like a blueprint for the Web site and determine the kind of technologies you need to make everything work.

3. **Design.** Here's where the fun begins. Now that you have a good idea of the site's goals and structure and how the parts interrelate, it's time to put a face on it. In this phase, you assemble different visual and navigation ideas and present them to the client.

4. **Execution.** After the client chooses a design direction, production can begin. Graphic elements, HTML, programming, media elements, and content all come together to create the final site.

5. **Quality assurance and testing.** When all is said and done, combing through the site before it goes "live" on the Internet for all to see is a good idea. Carefully look for programming bugs, links that go to the wrong pages, spelling errors, and so on. Also make sure that the site works on different browsers. For example, the site in Figure 1-1 works just fine in Internet Explorer, but does some funky repeating action in Netscape. This is one of the things to watch out for during the quality assurance and testing phase.

Figure 1-1:
This background tile image looks fine in Explorer, but not in Netscape.

The page viewed in Explorer

The same page viewed in Netscape

Mind Garden® and MindGarden.com® are registered trademarks of Mind Garden, Inc.

The People Involved

Designing Web sites is such a huge undertaking that to do it right, you really need a team of people. In this section, I list the major players, their roles, and when you need 'em.

Marketing folks: Those with the big idea

In the old dinosaur days, you could get away with sticking a Web site up on the Internet and expect to get reasonable traffic without much further effort. In the crowded Internet highways of today, however, you really need a marketing plan. The marketing folks must be involved with the Web site from the very beginning. They are in charge of the following responsibilities:

✔ **Creating the content of the Web site.** The Web site needs to say the right things. Nothing's worse than your visitors missing the point of the Web site.

You've got, at most, about three to four seconds to get your main message across with words and graphics to hook your visitor. If visitors don't get it, they're off to the competition. After all, it's just as convenient to type in their URL as it is to type in yours.

✔ **Reeling in the visitors.** The marketing folks' biggest task is to figure out how to steer Web surfers to your site. In the Internet business, "getting eyeballs" (fun industry jargon for getting people to look at your site) is probably second in priority to making money hand over fist. For these reasons, marketing folks need to get crackin' on their marketing plan right away.

Project management

Kelly Goto

Creative Director, www.Idea.com

Successful project management is keeping the members of the Web development team "on the same page" throughout the project. Balancing the needs of the client, the goals of the site, and the reality of scope and budget is a challenging task. Establishing clear means of communication means understanding the needs of the client and individual team members. Following a process and understanding the overall goals and objectives of the site from the onset is also critical to the success of a project. The goal is to maintain clear objectives through each phase of development, to manage *scope creep* (the tendency of projects to expand in size), and to predict the future.

Producer folks: For the reality check

After you get clients excited about a Web project, their eyes tend to get bigger than the budget. Among many other responsibilities, it's the producer's job to set and manage client expectations so the project stays on track. The producer must keep the project, the team members, the client, and the resources on track from start to finish.

Designers

The designer is one of the most important people on the team. The designer crafts not only the site's architecture, but also the navigation and user interface design. What's more, the designer is in charge of the appearance of the site — integrating text, graphics, and animation to create a unique approach that suits the client's goals and branding.

Many Web designers are actually print design expatriates. If you are transitioning from the print design world, the hardest thing you need to learn is how to maximize the technologies and navigation options at your fingertips. Many print designers first making the transition create graphically-heavy interfaces that certainly look cool, but are not very practical. They download slowly and are hard to automate or update. The Web page in Figure 1-2 is 8½ x 11inches and has huge graphics! This page has navigational choices at the bottom, but they aren't visible because the page is larger than the browser window. In addition, can you tell what's clickable on this page? The page contains no friendly buttons or underlined links to tell you what to click on. As a print designer, you already have creative skills: You just need to focus on the technologies under the hood.

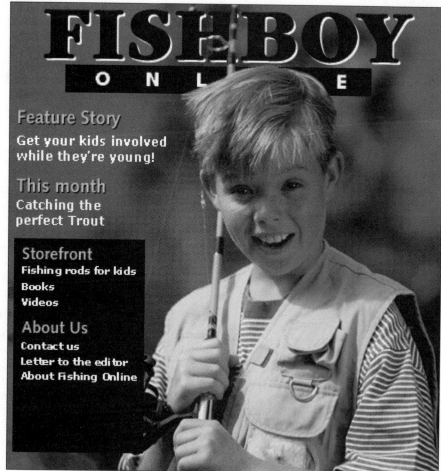

Figure 1-2:
This doesn't
work well as
a Web
interface; it
has no
buttons or
links to
guide users.

Media specialists

With the emergence of specialized media technologies like MP3 audio, Flash, and RealMedia, the opportunities to create cool spinning logos that sing and dance are endless. That's why it's best to leave sound design, complex animation, and streaming video production to a separate professional. This is especially true for Flash development. Flash is a software application that can create highly interactive, game-like applications, and animation. To get an idea of Flash's capabilities, look at the free trial of Macromedia's Flash 5 on the CD that accompanies this book.

HTML slingers

I first heard the term *HTML slingers* while working at an online auction company. The amusing title made sense because the folks who specialize in this stuff are creative programmers who have hands that can type out HTML faster than you can say "draw."

Although HTML is a coding language, being able to use it well involves a lot of creativity. For one reason, different browsers interpret code differently, which can really screw up your page layout. Good HTML slingers are great at finding workarounds for these browser incompatibilities — all the while maximizing a page's download performance.

Programmers

Modern Web sites would not be complete without their programmers. These are the folks that can really give your Web site a turbo boost by making it dynamic. (In the industry jargon, the word *dynamic* refers to an automated Web site.)

A Web site often consists of hundreds of pages — well, that's only a half-truth. Programmers can help you build a few template Web pages that you can use again and again throughout your Web site. This way, you can quickly create a Web site consisting of hundreds of pages, as shown in Figure 1-3. An online database *populates* (industry term for "fills in") the template with different information to create each new page.

In addition to coding the template Web pages with techie software development packages like the scripting language PHP (short for *Hypertext Preprocessor* — go figure), Microsoft's ASP (Active Server Pages), and Allaire's Cold Fusion, programmers also create the online databases that house all the information. Building databases can be so complex that many times you need a specialized database dude or dudette for that task alone!

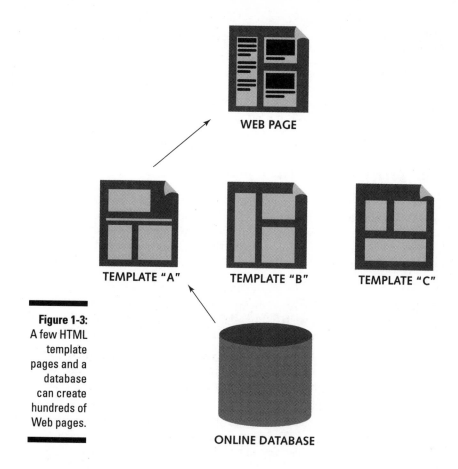

Figure 1-3:
A few HTML
template
pages and a
database
can create
hundreds of
Web pages.

The Blueprint for the Site

When you buy or receive toys labeled "some assembly required," you know you're in for a brain-twisting treat. Most people spend the first half-hour attempting the task without the aid of instructions. Not until they have pulled half of their hair out do they finally surrender to reading the manual.

This is a great metaphor for designing a Web site: Many people jump right in and start building Web sites without any sort of blueprint or *site map*, as it's called in the industry. Rushing into a job like this is flirting with disaster. For one thing, the team won't have any unified direction. Secondly, without a plan, you can't possibly anticipate all of the content, Web pages, and features that need to go into the site!

For example, imagine getting halfway through the design and then realizing that you forgot to include a critical feature like a member sign-in box. Now you find yourself re-doing pages that could have been done right the first time — if you'd only had a plan.

Spending a little time up-front creating a blueprint for the Web site saves you gobs of time and money down the road.

From outline to out-of-sight

Now that I've used cheap scare tactics to convince you that you need a site map before you begin designing a Web site, the question remains — how do you make one? The easiest way to make a site map diagram is to start with an old-fashioned outline. After you have an outline, it's fairly easy to turn it into a diagram, which is the beginning of a site map. Here are four easy steps to building an outline:

1. **Make a wish list.** During the concept stage, when you sit down with your client, jot down a wish list of all the content that the site will include. This gives you an idea of the size and scope of the project.

2. **Group content.** From the wish list, you can begin to organize the content into logical groups. For example, you can lump all the general company information together and all the product stuff together.

3. **Create categories.** After you have a few groups of content, you begin to see a pattern emerging. Some groups are similar and you can lump them together into categories. The key to a successful site map is precision: Try to identify the smallest amount of distinct categories as possible.

4. **Build an outline.** After you complete steps 1–3, the outline practically builds itself. The categories become the main ideas. Below the categories are the groups, and within the groups are lists of content. Figure 1-4 is a great example of how to create an outline from a well-organized list of content.

Converting your outline into a diagram

A completed outline is the equipment that you need to create the diagram of your Web site, which is the beginning of the site map. I say "beginning" because site maps can get pretty detailed, and they show a lot more than just a listing of pages and features. Site maps show how all the pages interrelate and how databases factor into the equation.

Horse Owner's Depot

I. **Selecting the Right Horse** —— Category
   A. **Breeds** —— Group
      1. **Ponies**
      2. **Horses** —— List of content
   B. **Riding Style**
      1. **English**
      2. **Western**

II. **Training and Showing**
   A. **A Horse's Ground Manners**
   B. **Riding**
   C. **Showing**

III. **Costs of Keeping a Horse**
   A. **Training**
   B. **Board**
   C. **Vet Care and Shoes**

IV. **Online Store**
   A. **Horse Care Products**
   B. **Saddles and Tack**
      1. **Saddles and Bridles**
      2. **Halters and Blankets**
      3. **Protective Wear**
   C. **Rider's Equipment**

Figure 1-4:
The first step to building a great site map is to create an outline.

Creating a diagram is easy. Simply draw a box to represent each page of your Web site. Starting at the top of a large piece of paper, draw one box to represent the home page. Below that, create one box for each main idea on your outline. The boxes for your main ideas are generally lined up side by side in a horizontal row as shown in Figure 1-5.

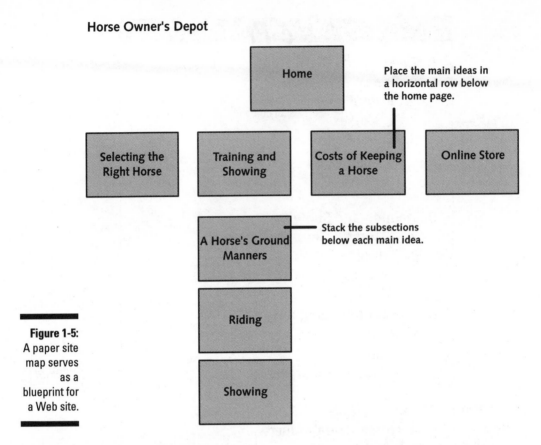

Horse Owner's Depot

Place the main ideas in a horizontal row below the home page.

Stack the subsections below each main idea.

Figure 1-5:
A paper site map serves as a blueprint for a Web site.

Below each main idea, draw a row of vertical boxes representing each subsection in your outline. In the end, your diagram should have about three to four rows of boxes showing the hierarchy of your outline. When you have a diagram that shows a box for each Web page, you can begin to design a navigation scheme that gets people from one page to the next. You can also sketch out the content of each page. By adding this level of detail, your diagram turns into a site map.

A good site map can also foreshadow usability problems before your site goes into production. If your map has too many main categories that are each a little thin on content, you end up with a site that overwhelms the user with choices and clutters the screen. Conversely, if your site map has just a few main categories that each have a ton of stuff, you end up with a site that takes forever to navigate — making people click too many times to drill down to the info they need.

A good number of main categories to shoot for is five to seven. Within each main category, try to keep it to no more than two levels of subcategories.

Design and Graphic Production

As you may have guessed, you have a lot of planning to do before you start pushing pixels around the screen. This is the part where you get to come up with a host of different creative ideas. After you and the client zero in on the design, you can prepare templates to make the production process easy.

Designing Web page mockups

The best way to decide on a design that everyone likes is to create a set of page mockups. These don't have to be working Web pages; they only need to convey the visual idea. In fact, you should mock up the Web page as one big picture. In the picture, render HTML elements as text fields and buttons. This way, the client gets a good idea of what the final page may look like. Figure 1-6 shows two different Web design ideas created by David Solhaug (sgraphik.com) for Propel for www.Propel.com. He created a few different design variations and posted them all to a private Web site for the client to view. As shown in Figure 1-7, the client can click on different links to see different design ideas.

Figure 1-6:
Always present a few different design ideas for the client to choose from.

The Web makes it extremely easy to conduct business with clients all around the world. In fact, I have clients whom, to this day, I've never met!

Generally, you should create two pages per design idea: A home page and one of the major *subpages* (a page that links off the home page). This is enough material for the client to see not only how the design looks on the home page, but also how it works throughout the site.

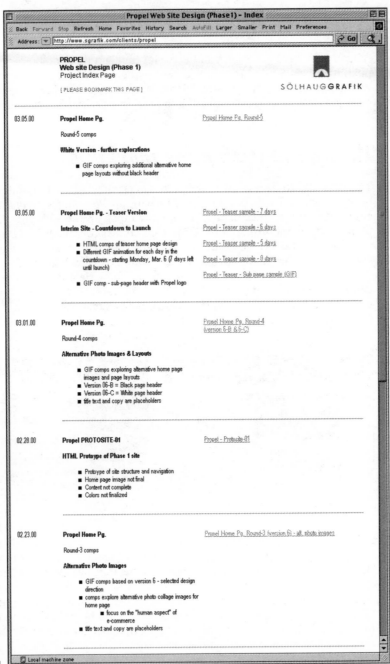

Producing final Web graphics

After the client chooses a design direction for the site, the grunt work can really begin. The most efficient way to produce the multitude of necessary graphics is to work from design templates. For example, most Web sites have a number of elements that are frequently repeated, such as buttons, headlines, and navigation bars. Using design templates ensures that your site doesn't appear to have multiple personalities and enables you to delegate graphic production to a team of people while maintaining design consistency.

Use a program like Photoshop or Fireworks to produce not only the template designs but also the final art for the site. Free trials of these programs are available on the CD that accompanies this book.

The Techie Stuff Under the Hood

After a lot of pixel-pushing, your Web site can begin to look really cool, but something has to hold it together and make it work. This is where the HTML slingers, media specialists, and programmers come in. Though you may feel like this project is your baby, don't look over their shoulders while they work. Just be glad that it's them doing it, and not you!

Holding it all together with HTML

Like the joke that says, "Duct tape holds the world together," *HTML* is certainly the glue that holds the World Wide Web together. HTML (HyperText Markup Language) is a simple coding language that tells your Web browser how to string formatted text, graphics, tables, and media elements together on the page.

Every page of every Web site, such as the one in Figure 1-8, is built with either HTML or some other programming language, which I discuss in the next section. You can write HTML code in any simple text editor — even Microsoft Word. After you finish, you can load it into a Web browser and see the results.

HTML is pretty limited in what it can do. For example, you can't build an `Amazon.com` shopping system with just raw HTML. For that, you need to bring out the big guns — those other programming languages, which I discuss in the next section.

Figure 1-8: Every Web page has two sides: the pretty exterior and the HTML code that makes it work.

Databases, programming, and things to make your head spin

If you're designing a Web site that's going to do anything beyond a simple show of nice text and graphics, you have to enlist the programmers. Web sites that show personalized messages, allow you to buy products with credit cards, or register for special events all require specialized programming. You can't build this sort of functionality with HTML alone.

Development software, such as Allaire's Cold Fusion, and programming languages, such as Microsoft's Active Server Pages (ASP), are actually integrated right into the HTML code for the page — making it a funky hybrid of coding languages. The HTML portion controls the page layout, whereas the programming language does all the cool stuff — such as linking to an online database to automatically display a "product of the day." Figure 1-9, for example, shows how the ASP code connects to an online database, where it can grab cool stuff like someone's name, weight, and annual salary. The HTML code then neatly formats the information for all to see.

Figure 1-9: The functions on this page are too complex to do with just HTML.

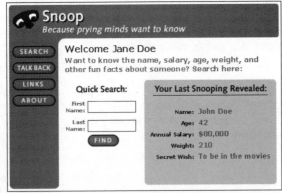

To build a page like this, you can either roll up your sleeves and type ASP code directly into the HTML page, or you can use tools like Dreamweaver UltraDev to do it for you.

So now that your head is spinning with all the technical to-dos, it's time to start working on the home stretch — a testing and launch plan for the site.

Test and Launch

Building a Web site requires so much detail-watching that you're bound to make mistakes along the way. User testing and "debugging" are crucial steps that you shouldn't put off until the end of the project: You should consider these elements throughout the design process. Imagine building an entire Web site that no one can figure out how to use except for you and the programmers! User testing helps you to know if you are on the right track, and helps you to identify any changes you can incorporate to make your site easier to use and understand.

Usability testing

User testing is probably the most overlooked step in the Web design process. Many designers have an ego problem that can become a bigger problem for you: They think that the site makes perfect sense because they designed it. I suggest getting a fresh eye to look at your designs early in the process; that is, before production begins!

Ask your family and friends to take a look at your early design directions. Without giving any hints, ask them to tell you what the site's about. Also ask them how they can do a certain task, such as buying a book, on your Web page.

These kinds of early tests help to shape your designs, but it's important to conduct "real" user tests. By "real," I mean that you must recruit any available human being that fits the site's target audience (men aged 40, for example) to sit down with you so you can ask them about your site. Don't miss Chapter 12 for an in-depth discussion on organizing and conducting user tests.

Quality assurance

Just because the Web is a flexible publishing medium, don't be tempted to just throw the site online and make on-the-fly changes to it. Before your site goes live on the Internet, check for misspellings and *bugs* — those pesky little broken links and programming errors that make you and your team look bad.

In addition, check your site on different platforms (Mac and PC) and different browsers (Netscape and Internet Explorer) to make sure that everything works the way you expect it to.

User testing and quality assurance are the crowning jewels of your Web site achievement: Don't overlook these final polishing steps. If you want to be a Web designer, it's important to be diligent every step of the way — from the initial client meeting to taking the site live on the Internet.

Chapter 2

Designing the Right Site for the Right Crowd

*L*ike life, there is a time and a place for everything in Web design. Just as you wouldn't break out your best comedy routine on a job interview, you also don't want to design an inappropriate Web site for your client — unless, of course, you're feeling reckless.

You need to determine what kind of person is going to be visiting and using the site. Then, you need to figure out how to market to this person. Only when you have these questions squared away should you begin to think about a content outline and a technology plan. After all, how can you make content and technology decisions unless you know something about the end user?

For example, imagine designing a hip, swingin' interface for a mutual fund company's Web site. Would you want to trust your hard-earned money with a company whose site looks like it doubles as a nightclub? Neither would the client! To avoid unnecessary embarrassment, your first priority is to figure out what crowd you're designing for. After you do, you can let the ideas start flowing and begin building the foundation of the Web site.

Figuring Out Who the Audience Is

Suppose that you're designing a Web site for a retirement home. The first thing that comes to mind may be old ladies playing bingo and eating stewed prunes, but what if your client is trying to shed that stereotypical image? Also, if you're not familiar with the assisted living industry, you may also mistakenly assume that the audience for the site will only be elderly people.

Unless you sit down with your client and ask a lot of questions, you would never know that the real audience for the site is people in their forties — the people who make plans for their aging parents. Whoa! This changes everything about your ideas for the Web site — from the graphical appearance to the content features.

This example illustrates an important point: Having structured conversations with your client and asking them many questions about both their industry and their intended audience is a critical step in the design process.

Question checklist for clients

The best way to extract all the vital information from your clients is to have a face-to-face chat with them and run through a list of previously prepared questions. This is your chance to play their shrink — to get into their heads. What sorts of questions should you ask? Table 2-1 is a generic list to get you started. You should ultimately create your own standard list and modify it for each new project.

Table 2-1	Checklist for Clients
Question	*Reason for Asking*
Why are you spending all this good money on a Web site?	Find out what they hope to achieve with the Web site. Is this going to be a marketing piece like a brochure or is the site a revenue-producing storefront?
Describe the ideal customer for this Web site.	Have the client describe this customer in detail. Is the customer male or female? Is he or she a professional? If so, in what kind of field? Do they have a lot of disposable cash, or are they looking for a convenient bargain? Are they technically inclined or do they need things spelled out for them?
What kind of things does the target customer buy and own?	This question is really for those considering commercial Web sites. The goal here is to find out if the customers care about brand names. This will help shape the visual design of the site.
How will this Web site help them?	Your Web site must provide value to the customer. This question goes a long way to help shape your content outline and technology needs.
Is this a Web site that people visit often or just when they need it?	This is an important question mainly for technical design reasons. For example, if people come back often, it's a good idea to have them register as a customer or join in Web boards. Otherwise, these efforts will be an expensive nuisance.

The creative brief

Armed with pages of notes about the client's plans, the audience, and the goals of the Web site, your next step is to distill this information into a *creative brief*. This document is, essentially, your game plan for the site. You use it to help focus your design, technology, and content decisions throughout production. The creative brief should contain three sections:

- ✔ **The Web site's purpose and goals.** This section should clearly state what the client expects from the Web site. Is the site simply an online marketing brochure, or is it a valuable revenue-generating tool for their customers? Will the site facilitate new business leads or automate current business practices?

- ✔ **The Web site's target audience.** In this section, describe the perfect customer and how this Web site will cater to the needs of this person. Also describe the not-so-perfect customer and why the site isn't designed for this person.

- ✔ **Content and design recommendations.** Based on what you know from the two previous sections about the site's audience and purpose, create a list of content and design ideas. For example, if the audience is mid- to upper-class professional people in their forties looking for a safe place for their parents to retire, the site's design should promote a safe, homey, and professional tone.

The creative brief doesn't have to be very long: One to three pages of information should suffice. After you've put it together, share it with the client to make sure everyone's on the same page. Some design firms even have the client "sign off" on the creative brief. Depending upon the size, scope, and the financial stakes, you may not need the client's signature, but you should certainly get his or her blessing.

Developing a Marketing Plan

Although marketing is not my professional focus, through the years, I've absorbed a lot of ideas and guerilla tactics for marketing Web sites. My greatest observation is that you shouldn't expect people to come flocking to your Web site all by themselves. The Internet simply has too many Web sites for anyone to find — or care about — your site unless you bring it to their attention.

Therefore, you or a dedicated marketing person on your team must sit down with the client and brainstorm a plan. Although some clients may not know the best way to market their Web site, they do know a lot about reaching their customers. Together your team and the client should develop a list of ideas, action items, and budgets. You have no time to waste either: You should begin marketing efforts almost immediately.

Offline marketing

The most effective way to market a Web site is to combine *online* and *offline* marketing campaigns. *Offline marketing* refers to all media that's not on the Web — radio, magazines, event sponsorships, trade shows, and so on. Here are some offline marketing ideas to consider:

- ✔ **Magazine articles.** Articles in trade magazines are highly effective marketing tools for a Web site. Recent statistics suggest that a magazine article is the second most motivating factor to visit a Web site (word of mouth is first).

  If your marketing plan includes getting exposure in magazine articles, remember that most magazines plan their editorial schedule a year in advance. You may miss the boat entirely. Enlist the help of a public relations specialist who is familiar with magazine schedules and who has the contacts to get your client's Web site into some headlines.

- ✔ **Radio.** Radio is a good way to focus on regional areas. You just need to keep in mind your target audience. Local news programs that feature the weather and traffic reports are great ways to capture the attention of the nine-to-five worker bees during commute hours. Advertising on "soft hits of the '80s" stations is good for targeting office workers, whereas the local hipster music station can attract the young and young at heart.

- ✔ **Trade shows and conferences.** Trade shows can be an expensive way to promote your Web site. Not only do you have to consider the price of the booth space, but also the cost of a nice display. Nevertheless, you may find that they work perfectly for your site's needs. In addition to trade shows, you should look into conferences. If possible, try to get a speaking gig at the show, or enlist one of the speakers to talk about your site.

Online marketing

Online marketing refers to a Web-based campaign (for example, buying those annoying banners at the top of Web pages). Here are some ideas for an online marketing campaign:

- ✔ **Online feature stories.** Every industry has its share of informational or resource Web sites that run feature articles. Snuggling up close to one of these sites is a great way to promote your site. For example, a feature story on WebMD.com is a perfect place to showcase an assisted living Web site.

- ✔ **Ad banners.** From the studies I've read, online banners are hit and miss in their effectiveness. Most advertising folks claim that online banner ads have a two percent "click-through" rate, meaning that two percent of people who see the ads actually click on them to visit the respective site. So if you're considering this option, be honest with yourself: When was the last time you clicked on one of these ads in your last 100 Web visits? I don't know about you, but unless a banner is flashing that I won $1,000,000, my eye totally misses them.

✔ **Search engines.** Most people find new Web sites by using one of the search engine sites such as Yahoo! or Google — my personal favorite. When you type a term in the Search field of one of these sites, up comes a listing of sites that match that keyword. The search engines look in the `<meta>` tags of each HTML page for such keywords. (`<Meta>` tags are special HTML tags that contain important words and phrases that describe a page's content.) You can also proactively register your site at various search engines. This helps to ensure that your site appears in the resulting list when people search for its keywords.

✔ **Link exchanges.** A cheap way to market your site is to swap links with a partner Web site that shares a similar audience. Exchanging links is a common practice: You link to the partner's site either with a mini button, a text link, or a banner, and your partner reciprocates with something similar linking to your site.

If you're going to run a series of ad banners, they are most effective when run consistently for at least three months and when you run them on sites that share your target audience. By some estimates, a user must see the same ad nine times before it sways him or her to pay attention. Something else to keep in mind is the design of your ad banners. In Figure 2-1, the banner's black coloring blends it into the page, making it hard to distinguish from the content of the site.

Figure 2-1: With all the stuff on this page, it's hard to find what you came for, let alone respond to the banner.

Photo courtesy of ScreamDesign.com

Building an Outline for Your Site

During your initial meetings with the client, work with them to develop a *wish list,* which itemizes all the possible elements they want to include on the Web site. Many clients may already have such a list in their *Request For Proposal (RFP)*, but you may have some unique ideas to add. This list is important because you use it to develop an outline for the site.

Making a wish list of content, bells, and whistles

To create your client wish list, brainstorm a list of content and feature ideas — it doesn't have to be in any particular order. So what's the difference between content and features? A *feature* is the "bells and whistles" part of a Web site. For example, this may be a virtual tour of the company's facility or a search function — basically, a feature is any activity for the user. *Content* is the more static stuff, such as investor relations and product info.

After you have a sprawling list of ideas, the work really begins. You need to pare this information down into a good old-fashioned outline like the ones you made for your fifth-grade papers. (You remember — the ones that have Roman numerals in front of the main ideas.) Building an outline is important because it forces you to categorize and prioritize the wish list, and it forms the basis of the Web site's structure.

You may be surprised to know that clients often expect you to create this outline *before* you even land the job! Most Web design firms include a draft outline of content and features in their initial proposal for the job. This helps the client decide which design firm to hire. The proposal in Figure 2-2 outlines a phased approach to the design and suggests various content ideas.

Categorizing and prioritizing information

The key to producing a successful outline is your ability to group similar items and prioritize ideas based on the needs of the site. As you become more familiar with the list of ideas, a pattern begins to emerge. Some items go together quite easily, whereas other ideas don't fit in at all. Here are three easy steps for converting your wish list into a workable outline.

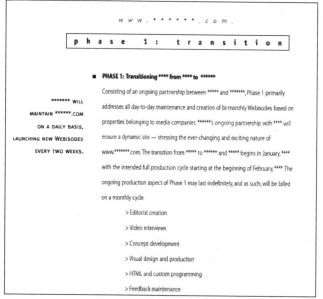

Figure 2-2:
This proposal for a high-tech firm's site contains an outline of schedule and content ideas.

1. **Group content ideas.** Find ideas that seem similar and place them next to each other. Use a computer to cut and paste them. For example, "contact information," "investor information," and "partner information" fit nicely together. Set these three aside and give them a temporary category title, such as "About the Company." As you go, you may find other items, such as "management team" that you can add to this group.

2. **Group feature ideas.** If the wish list contains features like a member sign-in area or a search function, set them aside in a "Resources" group. Some features, however, such as a virtual tour, may make more sense grouped in with the "Our Products" group.

3. **Assign a priority to each idea.** At this stage, the wish list begins to congeal into a chain of little islands — groups of similar information linked together in a logical way. The goal is to have as few groups as possible. To do this, you have to assign a priority to each group. If one group appears to be important, set it aside and give it an official category name. You can either toss less important groups out altogether or append them as subcategories to more important groups.

Following the five-to-seven rule

By prioritizing, combining, and excluding groups, your outline starts to take shape. This outline becomes the foundation of your site's structure. The hierarchy of information directly translates into a *site map* — a plan that shows how each of the Web pages interconnect and relate to each other.

For this reason, you must whittle away at your outline until you have about five to seven main categories or fewer. These categories often become your navigation links, and people have trouble navigating when they are bombarded by too many choices on the screen. Take a look at Figure 2-3. Four main categories are navigation buttons, but you can access more specific subcategories via the drop-down menu.

Figure 2-3:
The four main categories of this Web site become the standard navigation buttons.

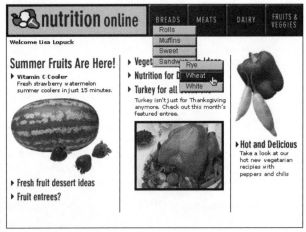

Modern Web sites are usually so big that it's impractical to always whittle them down to just five categories. If this is the case for your site, the solution is to create — you guessed it — groups of categories.

Take a look at the home page of Cooking.com in Figure 2-4. Across the top of the page you see a handful of main links, or categories. Down the left side you see another set of links. In Figure 2-5, you see yet another set of links placed at the bottom or *footer* of the page at Cooking.com. In each case, the set of links work well together. The groups also imply a hierarchy. The navigation group at the top is most important, the one at the left is next in importance, and the group in the page's footer is the least important.

Figure 2-4:
This Web
site relies
on groups of
links to get
you around
to all its
pages.

Photo courtesy of Cooking.com

Figure 2-5:
At the
bottom of
each page
is another
group of
links to help
you get
around.

Photo courtesy of Cooking.com

Creating the Technology Plan

Web sites are held together by HTML and programming code of all sorts, so it's probably a good idea to come up with a technology plan. For example, if your content outline calls for a virtual tour of the office, you need to make decisions about how you're going to pull that off. You can deliver virtual tours in many ways, and all affect the end user.

Decisions like these are all outlined in the *technology plan*, which is yet another document that the team can use as a guiding force throughout development. Generally speaking, the lead technology person on your team is responsible for defining the technology needs of the Web site. This plan should address the following issues:

- ✔ **Browser guidelines.** Not all browsers are created equal. This unfortunate fact forces you to choose which browser — even which browser version number — your Web site will support (not all features and interactivity will work on older browsers). If you think your audience is the casual Internet user, chances are they have older browsers. In this case, the technology plan should clearly state that the site supports Version 3.0 or above browsers. To avoid programming the site to the lowest common browser, you can use programming technologies to detect the end user's browser (type, version, connection speed, and so on) and automatically adapt the site for its capabilities.

- ✔ **Programming decisions.** If the Web site will have features that require database interaction, such as displaying a unique "product of the day," the lead technology person must determine what kind of database to build and what kind of programming can make it all work. In addition, the *server* — where the Web site actually "lives" on the Internet — affects database and programming choices. Not all servers are capable of running the same database or code. Such *server-side* (program runs on the server) and *client-side* (program runs from the Web page itself) programming applications can add a lot of functionality to a Web site like turning it into a customized shopping center.

- ✔ **Media decisions.** A virtual tour of the office may be a good idea, but not if viewing it crashes a person's computer or requires them to configure their browser in some weird way. Most people I know just open their browser and go. If you want to show cool media files, such as animations, 3D tours, and video, the best course is to use standard "plug-in" technologies, such as the Flash player, QuickTime, and RealPlayer. Most browsers are already set up to view these technologies. If the page requires any type of plug-in, however, providing a link to a site where the user can download and install it is a good idea. You can even design the Web page to automatically display the link if the browser doesn't detect the correct plug-in.

The great tables and frames debate

One technical side note that you should consider is whether your site will use *frames*. A Web page with frames is one that is divided into two or more independent sections. Each frame acts and scrolls independently, although links in one frame can load pages into another frame if you add the `<target>` attribute in the standard HTML link tag. For more on the hairy details of HTML coding, see Chapter 13.

The biggest complaint that most users have about frames is that after you start to drill down into one, you can't easily bookmark the spot. Some browsers just bookmark the frame set-up page with the original lineup of frames. Frames are also harder to maintain. They can lock you into a structure that forces you to redo a lot of stuff if you ever expand your site. To add insult to injury, older versions of browsers don't support frames.

Frames offer one big advantage: They enable you to keep frequently-used navigation items separate from the main content. This way, you can drill down into the main content frame and never have to reload the navigation frame, which saves users download time. As Figure 2-6 shows, you can scroll forever in the content frame while the navigation frame on the left stays put — even if the content area is a long scrolling list.

Because the advantages of frames are somewhat outweighed by the downsides, many designers have moved away from frames and turned to *tables* instead. Tables are basically spreadsheet-like structures that do a good job of organizing HTML, colors, and graphics on the page.

When used creatively, tables can provide the same download speed advantages as frames. For example, you can place the standard page navigational elements in one table and place all the content in another table. When you click to change pages, the standard navigation elements quickly redraw because they're still in your browser's memory. Without frames, the page is truly a single Web page and is easily bookmarked.

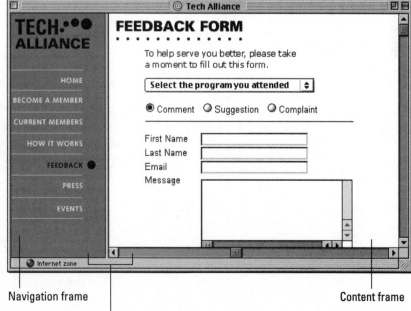

Figure 2-6: This Web page is actually two pages in one. Each page is inside a different frame.

Navigation frame   Content frame

Each frame is a different page

Tables make updating your site easy. If you put all the navigation stuff in one table, you can simply copy and paste the table onto every page of your site. Better yet, you can write some fancy programming code to do it for you automatically. Figure 2-7 shows a top navigation section in a separate table from the main content area. This makes it easy to update the navigation area with snowflakes for the holidays, for example, as shown in Figure 2-7.

Navigation area   Content area

Figure 2-7:
This home page has the navigation section and the content separated into two tables.

Wireless computing

In this day and age, you face growing pressure to make your client's Web site accessible to wireless devices, such as cell phones, pagers, and those little hand-held gadgets like PalmPilots. This is a big challenge because the screens on these little gizmos are so tiny. To handle this, many companies like AvantGo.com, whose Web site is shown in Figure 2-8, have specially designed content just for the wireless world. Users simply sign up at the main Web site using their desktop or laptop computer for the kind of content that they want delivered to their wireless gadget, as shown in Figure 2-9.

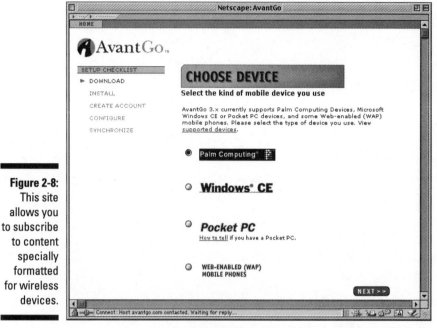

Figure 2-8:
This site
allows you
to subscribe
to content
specially
formatted
for wireless
devices.

AvantGo, the AvantGo logo, and AvantGo Enterprise are trademarks of AvantGo, Inc.

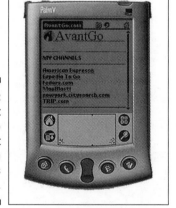

Figure 2-9:
Here's what
the Web
content
looks like on
a wireless
device.

AvantGo, the AvantGo logo, and AvantGo Enterprise are trademarks of AvantGo, Inc.

Chapter 3

Organizing and Navigating Web Content

In This Chapter

▶ Converting your outline into a diagram

▶ Integrating metaphors into your design

▶ Orienting people to your Web site

▶ Designing a navigation system for your Web site

The Web is a unique communication tool — it's not like the telephone, or TV, or books, or marketing brochures. People interact with Web sites differently than with other mediums. They click on buttons and links, access drop-down menus, fill out forms, and interact with animation, audio, and video media. For these reasons, to design Web user interfaces that simulate other media is to ignore the advantages of Web technology. Designing a Web site to look and function like a book, for example, is a waste of its capabilities.

As a budding Web designer, your biggest challenge is to design a unique Web page interface that maximizes the Web's abilities and allows users to quickly get from one page to the next. In this chapter, you find out how to build a diagram from your outline that represents each of the pages of your Web site. From the diagram, you can begin to design each page and think about how users will navigate between them.

After the Outline: The Site Map

The outline that you create for your Web site directly translates into a document called a site map, which is similar to a flow chart. A *site map* is a diagram that helps you visualize each page of a Web site before you build it. To create a site map, you translate each main idea and subcategory from your outline into a diagram of boxes connected by lines and arrows to show how the pages interconnect. A site map is critical to the construction of your Web site, and you'll refer to it often throughout the development process.

If you're a print designer, think of a site map as a sort of thumbnail sketch that you'd make for a brochure design.

After you've turned your outline into a collection of boxes arranged on paper, you have the beginnings of a site map. This site map gives you a good aerial view of the site so you can think about the specific design of each page. A good site map also helps you to create a navigation scheme that allows the site's visitors to easily maneuver from one page to the next. For even more details on how to create a great site map, see Chapter 4.

To transform your outline into beginnings of a site map, follow these simple steps:

1. **Start with a huge piece of paper.** I like to start on paper because you can quickly sketch out ideas and you have plenty of available design space. Find a large piece of paper and work in landscape orientation. (You'll find that you need a lot of horizontal space.) After you work out the map's details on paper, you can recreate it on the computer to make a nice, clean copy that you can distribute to both the client and the team.

When you're ready to transcribe your paper site map into a digital copy, try using a program like Engaging Minds' Inspiration. This software allows you to quickly build visual flowchart diagrams. Don't miss the free trial version on the CD included with this book.

2. **Draw a box for each Web page.** Starting with the home page, draw a box to represent each Web page of the site. Put the home page at the top of the paper. Then, as shown in Figure 3-1, start a new row beneath this box and draw a page for each of your main ideas.

Figure 3-1:
Draw a box
for the home
page and
place boxes
beneath for
each main
idea.

home page

Main idea 1	Main idea 2	Main idea 3	Main idea 4

3. **Draw the subcategories.** Begin a third row and draw a series of boxes for each page within the main sections. For space concerns, you may want to stack these pages vertically beneath their respective main idea boxes, as shown in Figure 3-2.

```
                        ┌──────────────┐
                        │   home       │
                        │   page       │
                        └──────────────┘

┌──────────┐  ┌──────────┐  ┌──────────┐  ┌──────────┐
│ Main idea│  │ Main idea│  │ Main idea│  │ Main idea│
│    1     │  │    2     │  │    3     │  │    4     │
└──────────┘  └──────────┘  └──────────┘  └──────────┘

┌──────────┐  ┌──────────┐  ┌──────────┐  ┌──────────┐
│Sub section│ │Sub section│ │Sub section│ │Sub section│
│    1A     │ │    2A     │ │    3A     │ │    4A     │
└──────────┘  └──────────┘  └──────────┘  └──────────┘

┌──────────┐  ┌──────────┐  ┌──────────┐  ┌──────────┐
│Sub section│ │Sub section│ │Sub section│ │Sub section│
│    1B     │ │    2B     │ │    3B     │ │    4B     │
└──────────┘  └──────────┘  └──────────┘  └──────────┘
```

Figure 3-2: After you've drawn the second row, space becomes a premium.

4. **Note any special functions and features.** In your outline, you have probably included features and functions that aren't really pages. Rather, they are interactive widgets that go *on* a page, or on a handful of pages. For example, you may want to put a member sign-in box on every page. The best way to represent items like this is to place a little symbol on each box where they should appear. Then, create a legend somewhere on the map that explains what the symbol represents. Figure 3-3 shows the symbol that I created for member sign-in boxes.

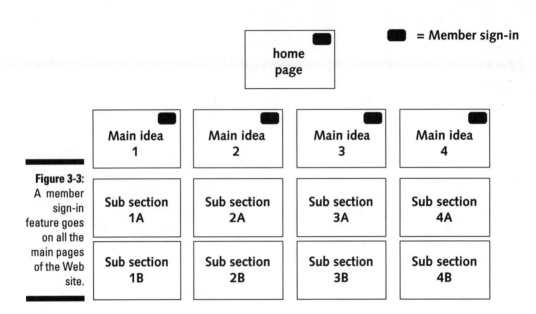

Figure 3-3:
A member
sign-in
feature goes
on all the
main pages
of the Web
site.

The Structural View from 35,000 Feet

With all the boxes in place, your site map is officially in the larval stage of development. At this point, you can't see the actual design and layout of each page, and you have no indication of how someone can jump from one page to the next. You do have a nice aerial view of the information structure — but that's it.

From this vantage point, however, you can begin to think of creative ways to present the content of each Web page. Remember, you're not limited to just text and graphics anymore. In this section, I pack your bag of tricks with some interesting ideas for content presentation. I talk about navigation ideas in the next section.

Presenting content on the page

You don't have to build each Web page as a collection of text and static graphics. Even if you do, the page doesn't have to be a particular size and orientation. You can create an interesting horizontal layout if it suits your content better than a vertically-scrolling list. A horizontal structure works great for a timeline interface, for example. In addition, many technologies — from animation to pop-up menus — are available to help you maximize your page space and present content in more interesting ways.

Maximizing your space

Most people have small computer monitors. If you hold up an 8½ x 11-inch piece of paper horizontally, you're looking at the size of most people's window to the World Wide Web. After you factor in the browser's interface with all its buttons across the top, favorites tabs, and scroll controls, the viewing space devoted to the Web is whittled down to practically nothing. This scrawny little window is your design canvas.

Glancing through your site map, you may notice that some categories are really crowded with content. Yuck! Here are some structural design techniques to help you better present your content, condense it, and, in many cases, combine multiple pages into one:

✔ **Scroll, baby, scroll.** This goes without saying — the designer is forced to get creative with this small broswer window space. You simply can't shove everything into the viewable area — the first 600 x 350 pixels of the browser window. However, you can maximize the scrolling nature of the page. When users see scrollbars and graphics that are cut off at either the bottom or side edges of the screen, they know that the page contains more content.

✔ **Put the important things front and center.** Always place the important content, headlines, or instructions in the viewable portion (about 700 x 450 pixels), and then entice people to scroll up and down or side to side for more stuff.

Take a look at the way content is organized in Figure 3-4. The 700 x 450-pixel viewing space is broken down into two frames. The top portion is a horizontal scrolling "room" with loads of things to click on. The bottom portion contains graphical menu choices that take you to different rooms. Talk about maximizing your space!

Figure 3-4:
On this page, a horizontally-scrolling panoramic interface maximizes the screen space.

✔ **Layer your content.** Another way to maximize the viewing space is to use pop-up graphics and menus to layer content on top of the screen. Interface devices like these hide content until the user does something on the screen, such as rollover (place the mouse pointer on top of) or click on a button. This is accomplished by using technologies such as JavaScript and DHTML (dynamic HTML). Look at Figure 3-5, from my site at `www.lopuck.com`, for a good example of layered content. When the mouse pointer rolls over one of the thumbnails, an "About the project" graphic appears.

Mouse rollover

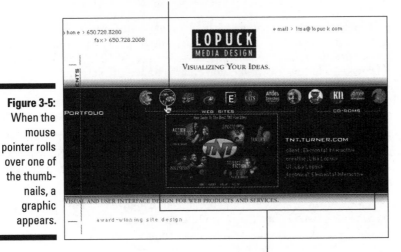

Figure 3-5: When the mouse pointer rolls over one of the thumbnails, a graphic appears.

"About the project" information

Designing a revolving door of content

Because Web page space is at a premium, another dimension that you need to consider is time. If you can't fit everything that you want inside the viewable area, you may want to think about animating the area. This way, you can cycle a lot of clickable links in and out over time in a relatively small space. Animation also works well with navigation choices. Take a look at Figure 3-6. In this example, a number of different movie icons appear and disappear so that the user never has more than three items to choose from at any one time.

Figure 3-6:
This animated interface for a movie studio can support up to 15 choices rotating in and out on the home page.

Keeping metaphors under adult supervision

Designers are commonly tempted to use real-world metaphors to organize and navigate Web content. In my experience, these kinds of metaphors can get ugly very quickly. They constrain your content and navigation options because you're forced to find things that make sense for the metaphor — not the content.

Creating flexible interfaces with animation

One client, a movie studio, wanted a Web site that showcased a variety of movies on the home page. Each month they wanted to show a different collection of movies. Some months, they wanted to showcase only four movies, and during other months, they wanted to feature as many as ten. This simple requirement, however, would result in an interface that looked sparse one month and overcrowded the next, which presented a big challenge for the design team.

The solution was a modular, animated interface that rotated through all the choices. The interface showed no more than three to four choices on the screen at any one time. In addition, the modular approach made updating easy. Each month, the client simply built icons for the new movies and put them into rotation. The client liked the approach and decided to create a similar animated interface to showcase their interactive games at a tradeshow.

For example, imagine that your client wants the Web page to look like an open book — complete with curled pages — even though the content of the Web site has nothing to do with literature or books. The book interface automatically locks you into a constrained set of navigation options. The curled pages automatically suggest that users must flip left to right through the content. The page metaphor also limits your content choices to items that make sense on the page of book, such as text and graphics — but no forms or pull-down menus. If you take metaphors too seriously, you can end up wasting time trying to match your content to the theme.

If you decide to use metaphors, stay in control! Don't let them carry you away to the point where they limit you, like the room metaphor, shown in Figure 3-7. Rather, use them sparingly, only to *suggest* a theme. See the difference that a subtle use of a room theme makes in Figure 3-8.

Figure 3-7:
Can you tell which object in this room interface takes you to the Games section?

Stay in control of your metaphors

A client once asked me to fix a project that was long overdue and way over budget. The project used a 3-D office interface to organize all the navigation choices — choices that had nothing to do with an office.

The 3-D artwork looked cool but it took up the entire screen — leaving no room for the actual content. The interface looked like an actual office — with desks, file cabinets, a phone, a computer, and so on. All the content choices were mapped on the various objects in the room. Not only did the office look have nothing

to do with the content choices, but the 3-D interface was also expensive to design, produce, and update.

User test after user test revealed that no one could correctly associate the navigation choices with the room objects. Even though the client was totally infatuated with the 3-D interface, it just wasn't working for the site. In less than 30 days, we chucked the 3-D interface and designed an elegant, straightforward solution that salvaged the project.

Figure 3-8:
A better
solution is
to use a
theme —
putting
labeled
icons in a
navigation
section.

(Content goes here)

How to Get Around in Style

Other than the graphical design, designing a user interface is one of the more challenging creative tasks that you face as a Web designer. The main goal is to make people feel in control of the site and capable of getting around quickly and efficiently. Nothing's worse than a user feeling lost in your site.

At this stage in development, the site map appears to be one big hierarchical structure, beginning with the home page. With this amount of content, it may appear to you that the user must click endlessly from page to page before they can finally drill down to the page that they're looking for — making them completely lose sight of where they are.

To help people get around and stay oriented, your navigation scheme must be a roadmap of the entire site, complete with "you are here" signs. In this section, I discuss a number of tips and standard design conventions to keep in mind when designing your interface.

For the jet set: Cross navigation

Remember the famous line from the '70s TV commercial: "How many licks does it take to get to the Tootsie Roll center of a Tootsie Pop?" With candy, the more licks, the better. On the Web, however, the opposite is true. Users won't find anything tasty about navigating through gobs of pages. Your goal is to get users from one page to the next in as few clicks as possible.

The best way to reduce the number of clicks is to provide the same set of navigation links on each page. This strategy, called *cross navigation*, enables people to quickly navigate from one main section to the next without needing to retrace any steps by clicking the Back button.

A cross-navigation system also gives people a sense of the Web site's size. For example, the screen in Figure 3-9 shows that you're in the Breads section and that you can explore three other main sections. Cross navigation also provides a mental anchor. Putting the same cross-navigation scheme in the same place on every page creates a point of reference that helps people stay oriented in your site.

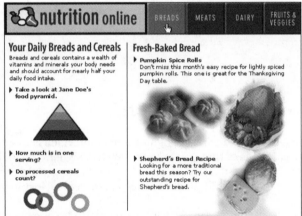

Figure 3-9: With this cross-navigation system in place, users can quickly traverse from one main section to the next.

For nature lovers: Leaving a trail of bread crumbs

If Hansel and Gretel can use a trail of bread crumbs to find their way back through the forest, just think of what a digital version of bread crumbs can do for visitors to your Web site. *Bread crumbs*, as they're called in the Web design industry, are literally a trail of text links that record your steps as you go, as shown in Figure 3-10.

As you dive deeper into a Web site, your trail gets longer and longer. Each link provides a quick way to retrace your steps back up the hierarchy. You don't have to follow the links in sequence; you can click on any link in the trail to quickly jump back to where you were. The trail also gives you a good idea of where you are in the site. Unlike with a cross-navigation scheme, however, you cannot jump across to *another* section; you can only jump back to one of your previous steps. Think of a bread crumb system as the browser's Back button on steroids. To implement a bread crumb trail, the site needs additional programming or you need to license or purchase such functionality from an outside source.

Bread crumb trail

Figure 3-10:
This bread crumb trail provides a convenient way for you to retrace your steps in a site.

Graphically, the design convention for a bread crumb interface is to show each previous step as an underlined, active text link followed by an arrow or a colon. The last link at the end of the trail is *not* underlined and represents the page that you are currently on. This last link is not clickable; it is merely a title announcing the current page.

When jets and nature lovers collide

Jets colliding with nature lovers sounds like a plot for a 1970's disaster flick — unless you're talking about Web site navigation. When you combine the jet power of a cross-navigation system with a bread crumb-style navigation trail, you have a flexible interface that's pretty close to foolproof, and one that's robust enough to handle large-scale sites with a lot of content.

Here's one way to using these two navigation devices together: Use the cross-navigation system to house links for the main sections. This lets people quickly bounce around to find the area that they're looking for. If your Web site has a lot of sections, use a pop-up menu to expand the cross-navigation options, as shown in Figure 3-11. Remember that you can use a few cross-navigation sets on the page, grouped by their function. For example, the standard footer links at the bottom of each page count as one cross-navigation set.

As people drill down within each section, provide a bread crumb navigation trail to help them stay oriented and able to back out of the section.

Figure 3-11: Combining a cross-navigation system with a bread crumb trail creates a powerful interface.

Chapter 4

Building a Great Site Map

In This Chapter

▶ Turning your diagram into a paper-drawn site map

▶ Building a digital site map

▶ Redesigning an existing Web site

*A*fter you've worked long and hard to create a basic diagram of your Web site, the next step is to turn the diagram into a *site map*. A site map is like a blueprint for a Web site. Each page of the site is displayed on the site map, which also shows each page's name, features, navigation scheme, and whether the page connects to an online database.

I know this is a ton of information to cram into your diagram, but it's crucial stuff. Every member of the team and the client will refer to this document throughout production, so the more details, the better.

The best way to represent all of this information is through a system of symbols — like those used by architects. No one set of standard symbols exists, but in this chapter, I introduce you to a number of symbols and software tools that many designers use to create a professional site map to share with clients and team members. You also get practice building a site map by deconstructing an existing Web site for the purposes of redesigning it.

Putting Your Ideas on Paper: The Site Map

The paper diagram that you create to build the site map tells only half of the story. The next level in constructing the site map is to show how the pages connect by drawing lines and arrows. In addition, you also need to sketch out the content plan for each page as much as possible. For example, here are some of the questions you need to address:

✔ Are you going to be using frames or tables?

✔ Will the page contain any rich media that requires a plug-in like a QuickTime or a Flash movie?

✔ Is the page connecting to a database?

After you've sketched your content plan into a diagram, it probably looks like a mess of lines going every which way, half-erased sketches, and lots of eraser droppings — proof that you've really put some thought into the ordeal. Take a look at Figure 4-1 and see if you can tell what's going on. When you've got most of the links and page content worked out on paper, you know you're ready to create a digital version of your site map.

Do-it-yourself digital site map tools

Creating a digital version of your site map allows you to make a clean copy that you can share with the team. A digital copy is not only easier to distribute to the team and the client; it's also your chance to wow the client with your professionalism and presentation skills. You can add the client's logo, your logo, and even mount the site map on a board to create a sizzling advertising agency-style presentation.

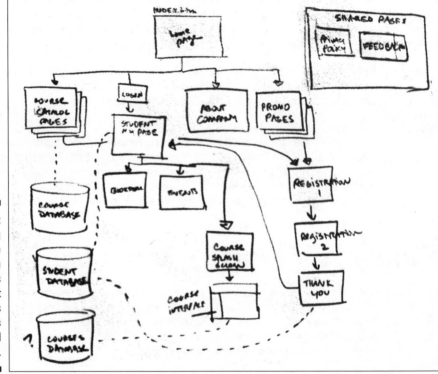

Figure 4-1: Sketching out a site map on paper first is faster, but not as readable as a digital copy.

You can use a number of software tools to create a digital version of your site map. Any vector-based illustration program will work just fine. Here are a couple of programs to consider:

- ✔ **Inspiration.** Inspiration is a software tool specifically designed for creating flowcharts for all sorts of business purposes. Inspiration's built-in tools are perfect for creating site maps for a Web site. You can purchase a copy of Inspiration on the Web at www.inspiration.com, or check out the free trial version on the CD included with this book.

- ✔ **Adobe Illustrator and Macromedia Freehand.** If you're a print designer, you're probably familiar with Adobe Illustrator and Macromedia Freehand as illustration tools used for creating fancy line art. These two tools are also great for creating highly customized site maps with your own unique design stamp. Figure 4-2 shows a sample site map that was created by Juxt Interactive (Juxtinteractive.com), a Web design firm.

Everyone's singing from the same songsheet

Establishing clear communication between you, the team, and the client should be a high priority throughout the Web design process. Sharing the initial site map with the client is an excellent way to make sure that you're on the right track and that the client knows exactly what they're buying.

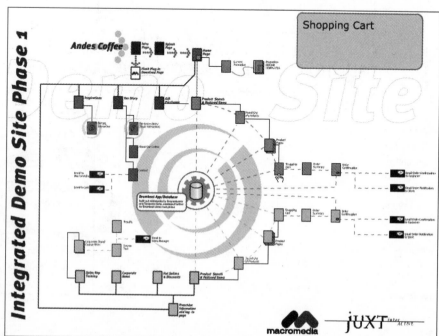

Figure 4-2:
This site map, created in Freehand, has Juxt Interactive's unique look.

Many Web design firms have the client sign off on the accepted site map in order to confirm and manage their expectations for the site. This way, the client can't come back to you in the future asking where the Founder's Bio page is. Armed with the client-approved site map, you can simply remind the client that the page in question was never part of the deal.

Although this sounds harsh, remember that the sign-off works both ways! Figure 4-3 shows a site map that includes a Founder's Bio page. In this case, the client has every right to wonder where the page is. In addition, an agreed-upon site map helps the design and HTML production teams anticipate and plan for all the pages of the site so nothing gets left out. Each production team member, working on the site, should have a copy of the site map that they can refer to throughout the project. Ultimately, a site map is a great tool to keep both sides singing from the same songsheet, so to speak.

Naming conventions

Another function of the site map is to establish the name of each Web page, or at least the naming convention used for each section of the site. Establishing the names of all the pages up front is important because every-one working on the site must know how to name the pages and how to link to other pages.

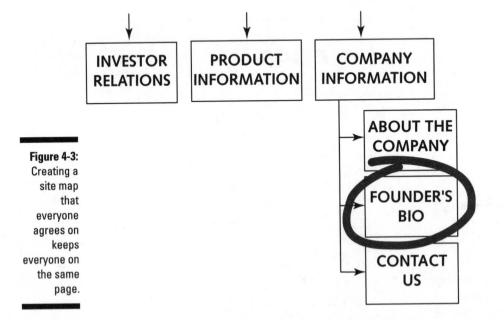

Figure 4-3:
Creating a site map that everyone agrees on keeps everyone on the same page.

If you are building a page with a set of links, for example, you must know the exact names of the pages that you are linking to. If a page's real name is "about.html" and you set up a link to reference "aboutus.html" — it's game over! In this situation, the link doesn't work and the user sees an ugly "page not found" error message.

On smaller-scale Web sites, you can write the name of the HTML page directly on its box in the site map, as shown in Figure 4-4. On large sites, it's not always possible to represent each page on the site map. For example, a store site may use one product page template over and over again to create hundreds of pages — one for each product in the store. For cases like this, you can come up with a naming scheme, such as "product001.html," as shown in Figure 4-5. Just remember to increment the number in the page's name for each different product.

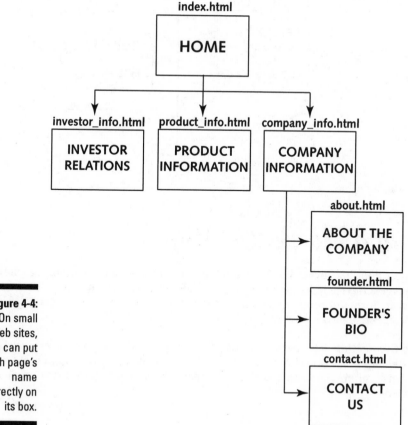

Figure 4-4: On small Web sites, you can put each page's name directly on its box.

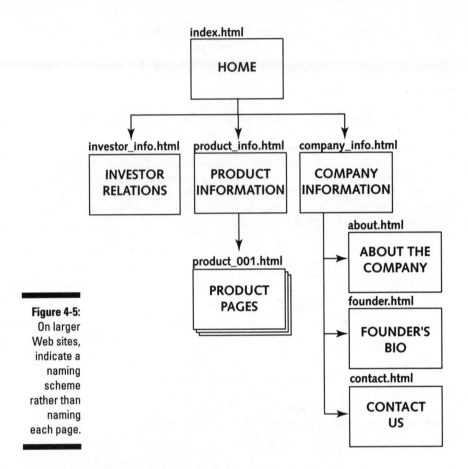

Figure 4-5:
On larger
Web sites,
indicate a
naming
scheme
rather than
naming
each page.

Building a Mo-Better Map

After doodling around on your diagram illustrating each page's design and how each page links together, you quickly discover that building a site map is an art form. Although no standard exists for drawing site maps, many Web designers' maps look remarkably similar.

In this section, you learn some tried-and-true design techniques for drawing a site map that everyone can read. In addition, you learn how to integrate your own symbol system to create a personalized map geared toward your client's needs.

Reading between the lines and boxes

To show how the pages on your diagram link together, you must draw a series of lines. This is literally a game of connect the dots, or in your case, boxes. You can also indicate specific content plans for each page by drawing symbols directly on the boxes. For example, you can show whether the page uses frames or tables by the way that you segment the box. The following is a list of some design conventions that many designers often use on their site maps to show both navigation and content plans for each page.

Showing how pages interconnect

Here are a few site map design techniques to show how pages link to each another:

  ✔ **Direct links.** The most basic way to show how two pages link together is to draw a line that connects them. Generally, all lines sprout forth from the home page's box and connect to each of the main section boxes, as shown in the left side of Figure 4-6. Considering the amount of boxes that you probably have on your diagram, this can get messy quickly. To keep the map clean, draw one line coming from the home page and then have it branch into individual lines that connect to each subpage, as shown in the right side of Figure 4-6.

Multiple lines connecting the home page to each sub page.

Clean up the map by combining the lines together.

Figure 4-6: To clean up the connecting lines, join them together.

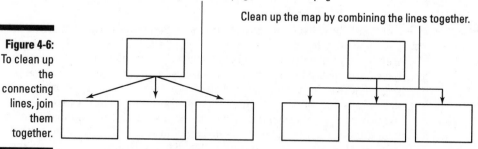

  ✔ **Cross-navigation system.** If your Web site uses a cross-navigation system, you can show this in your diagram by slightly modifying the linking lines. Rather than making one-way arrows like those in Figure 4-6, draw double-headed arrows and place them between the boxes, as shown in Figure 4-7. The double-headed arrows and the placement of the connecting lines implies that the user can quickly jump from one main section to the next.

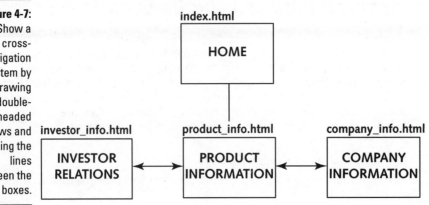

Figure 4-7:
Show a cross-navigation system by drawing double-headed arrows and placing the lines between the boxes.

- **Linking to a shared page.** In many cases, you have a few shared pages, such as a Credits or About the Company page, that many or even all the pages in the site link to. (In the Web industry, shared pages are sometimes called *global* pages.) In cases like this, drawing connecting lines from each page leading to the shared pages doesn't make sense, and it creates a big mess. Just as Alaska and Hawaii are traditionally shown pulled out on a U.S. map, you can create a special area on your site map just for the shared pages. Assign a symbol to each one, and then on your site map; place the symbol inside or next to the page that links to it, as shown in Figure 4-8.

- **Automatic flow from one page to the next.** Sometimes you want a Web page to display for a few seconds and then automatically flow to another page without requiring the user to click. For example, many Web sites these days have an animated intro sequence that plays before you get to the home page. Take a look at Figure 4-9, which is from www.oneworldjourneys.com/georgia. To accommodate situations like this on a diagram, I've developed my own squiggly line symbol to indicate an automatic flow-through. You can show automatic flow by drawing the beginning page directly on top of the page that it leads to. Then, draw a squiggly line with an arrow between the two pages, as shown in Figure 4-10.

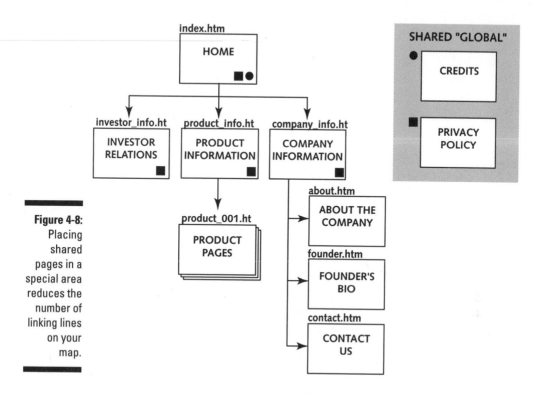

Figure 4-8:
Placing
shared
pages in a
special area
reduces the
number of
linking lines
on your
map.

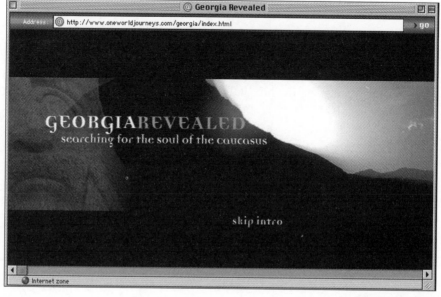

Figure 4-9:
This
animated
intro
sequence
plays before
you get to
the home
page of this
site.

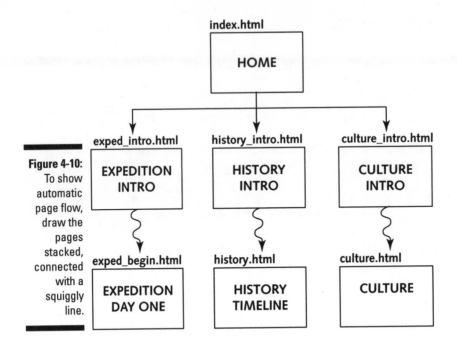

Showing page structure

Here are a few design techniques to show the specific content structure and features of each page:

> ✔ **Frame structure.** You need to know which pages require a frame structure because when a page uses frames, that page actually consists of a few pages packed into one. (Sort of an important detail for the development team to know!) To indicate that a page uses frames, draw lines to segment the box. If the page has three frames, for example, draw three segments, as shown in Figure 4-11.

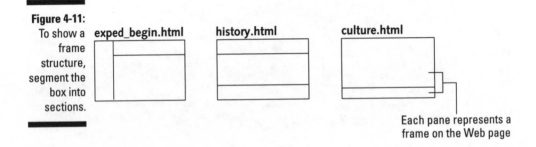

Each pane represents a frame on the Web page

Keep in mind that segmenting the box, which represents the page, to show a frame structure also implies a layout for the page. For example, you can segment the page into three horizontal frames just as easily as you can chop it up into two vertical ones. If you don't want the frame segmentation to be taken literally, say so on the map. Always slice a page with frames the same way so the design team knows how much flexibility they have on the page's layout.

✔ **Tables.** To show that a page is built with tables, draw a box or two inside the page, as shown in Figure 4-12. Each inset box represents one table. This scheme is useful, for example, to show that the navigation table is separate from the main content table. Again, remember that when you draw boxes to show a table structure, you can inadvertently imply a page layout.

Figure 4-12:
In this example, one box represents the navigation table, and the other the content table.

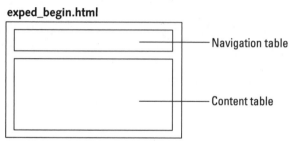

exped_begin.html

— Navigation table

— Content table

On the map, use a legend to show whether the table drawings are to be taken literally — suggesting an actual layout — or whether they merely indicate a general structure. Figure 4-13 shows a sample legend.

✔ **Features and tools.** Some tools, such as search boxes and sign-in functions, don't have their own pages; instead, they are features that go on a page or appear between two pages. For example, if you click on a login button, a special pop-up screen may appear for the user to log in before moving on to the next page. You can label these features using a symbol set like the one shown in Figure 4-14, or by drawing a small box on the connecting line between the two pages, as shown in Figure 4-15.

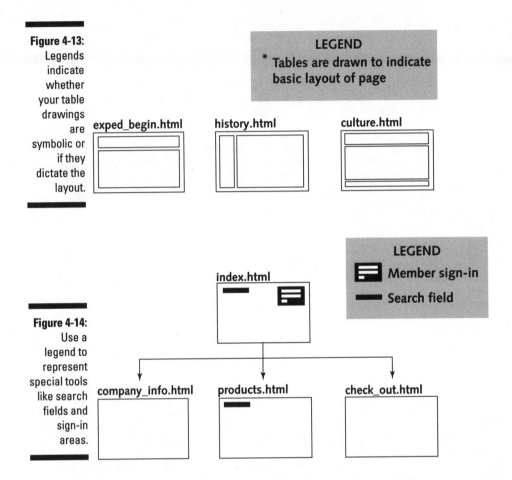

Figure 4-13:
Legends
indicate
whether
your table
drawings
are
symbolic or
if they
dictate the
layout.

LEGEND
* Tables are drawn to indicate basic layout of page

exped_begin.html

history.html

culture.html

LEGEND
Member sign-in
Search field

index.html

Figure 4-14:
Use a
legend to
represent
special tools
like search
fields and
sign-in
areas.

company_info.html

products.html

check_out.html

Drawing weird organizational structures

As your Web site grows in complexity, incorporating more technologies like database integration, you need to get a little more creative in your drawings. Again, no rules exist, but the following are some ideas and design conventions used throughout the Web industry

Representing unique user interfaces

Sometimes Web pages contain highly interactive, animated interfaces built with technologies like Flash or Java. These interfaces can have a lot of information and choices embedded within them. For example, you can build an entire application with one of these technologies — with its own collection of screens, links, and functions — and place it on just one Web page. Take a look at www.oneworldjourneys.com/georgia, a beautiful Web site about the nation of Georgia. A large portion of the experience happens in just one Web page with a Flash movie, as shown in Figure 4-16. Though the interface looks like a typical Web page, it is actually one of many screens contained in one Flash movie, playing on one Web page. By using Flash, you can optimize the page's performance because Flash is highly efficient at compressing and displaying graphics. The downside, however, is that users will need the Flash plug-in installed in their browsers to view Flash files.

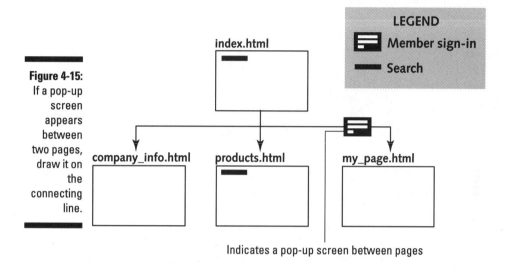

Figure 4-15: If a pop-up screen appears between two pages, draw it on the connecting line.

Indicates a pop-up screen between pages

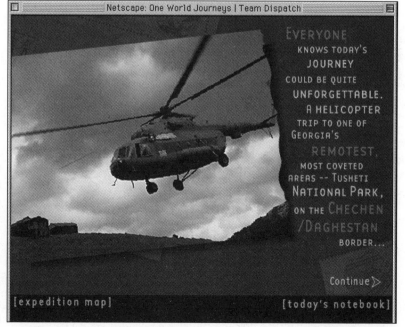

Figure 4-16: With Flash, you can create an entire interactive experience on just one Web page.

© OneWorldJourneys.com

You can indicate this sort of unique user interface on your site map in one of two ways:

✔ If the content on the Web page is a fully-interactive, self-contained application or a movie like the one in Figure 4-16, simply draw a box, fill it with gray, and place a symbol inside of it. In the legend, make reference to an appendix document that is a separate site map dedicated exclusively to the embedded media, as shown in Figure 4-17.

Figure 4-17:
To represent a highly interactive application or a movie, reference a separate site map document.

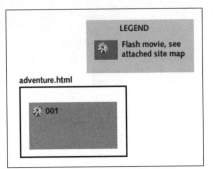

✔ If the animated interface is fairly simple, such as a 360° virtual tour, you can design an icon or symbol to place inside the Web page's box, as shown in Figure 4-18.

Figure 4-18:
To represent simpler interactive media, create an icon and place it inside the Web page's box.

Representing database integration

These days, designing a Web site that doesn't rely on a database for something is nearly impossible. Databases help your site work as a business tool. Databases can collect a user's information, display product and service offerings more efficiently, and personalize a page for each visitor.

To represent a database on a site map, most design firms use a cylindrical container symbol that looks like a can of soup. The database "soup can" can go anywhere on your site map, but most often I see it placed in the center or on the bottom — wherever it's most convenient to link multiple pages to. Pages that access the database have a dotted line connecting to it, as shown in Figure 4-19.

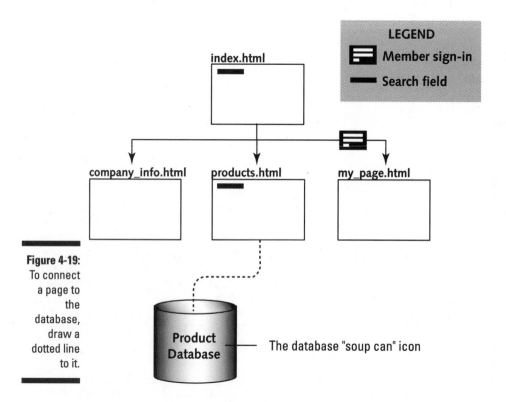

Figure 4-19: To connect a page to the database, draw a dotted line to it.

The database "soup can" icon

Developing your own set of symbols

As you blossom into a seasoned Web designer, you develop your own lexicon of symbols, lines, and shapes to represent various elements and interactions of a Web site. When creating your own symbols, the only rule is consistency. Regardless of the symbols or line art you decide to use on your site maps, just be sure to use them consistently and to clarify their meaning in a legend. A final word of advice: Keep your symbols simple.

Here are a few miscellaneous elements that you may encounter and some ideas for representing them on your site map:

✔ **Footers.** A lot of Web sites have a standard *footer* that goes at the bottom of each page. The purpose of the footer is to contain a redundant set of text links to the main areas of the Web site. (People with disabilities, such as the blind, sometimes use special input devices that rely on text links to get around a Web site.) Footers also contain legal information, such as a site's privacy policy. For these reasons, many designers put the footer in a separate table so it's easy to attach to each Web page and update in the future. On the site map, draw the footer as a skinny box at the bottom of each page, as shown in Figure 4-20.

Figure 4-20:
Draw standard footers as a skinny box at the bottom of the Web page.

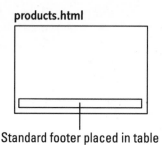

products.html

Standard footer placed in table

✔ **Flash movies.** Macromedia's Flash is a software application that creates highly interactive animated movies and game-like applications that you can place on a Web page. Because Flash movies can be fairly complex and require their own concentrated development, you should have a dedicated symbol to represent them on your site map. As I suggested earlier in this chapter, placing a symbol on the Web page that refers people to another site map or storyboard document is a common way to show Flash movies.

✔ **Template pages.** Sometimes designing a master template page is the most efficient way of building a large number of Web pages. An online database *populates* or fills the template with data, depending on the user's actions. For example, an online store may have hundreds of products that all use the same template page for display. To indicate a template page on your site map, draw it as a stack of pages — like the one shown in Figure 4-21— and remember to draw a dotted line to the database "soup can."

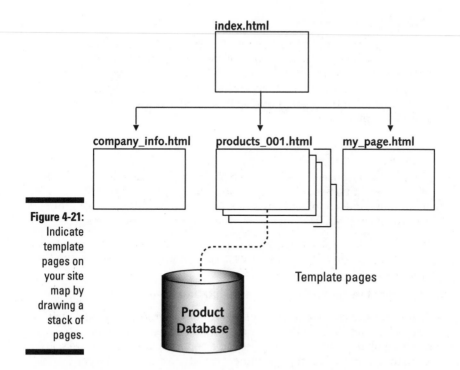

Figure 4-21:
Indicate
template
pages on
your site
map by
drawing a
stack of
pages.

Building a Map for a Site Redesign

Many people assume that Web design is always about creating a new Web site from scratch. The truth is that these days, almost every organization of any size already has a Web site. The primary need, therefore, is to keep the existing Web site fresh and evolving with the latest technologies and the changing needs of the company. Therefore, more often than not, clients approach you to *redesign* their Web site.

Site maps come in handy not only in the design process, but also in the redesign process. They allow you to see the current site in its totality and how the pages relate to each other. With a site map, you can see where the problems lie, and you can get ideas for a better design.

Deconstructing a Web site

So how do you create a site map for an existing Web site? You build it by picking the site apart (or *deconstructing,* as we say in the industry) to see how it's made. Here are three easy steps to get you started:

1. **Start with the home page.**

   Go to the home page of the Web site and look closely at all the links on the page. On a large piece of paper, draw a box at the top for the home page and, to the side, jot down a list of all the links you see. Keep them grouped as they are on the home page. For example, under a title of Footer, list all of the footer links. This list helps you stay oriented in the site as you pick it apart.

2. **Identify the main categories.**

   Click all the home page links and see where they take you. Your goal is to identify the purpose of each link and to distinguish the links that seem to be the most important main categories. You may be surprised to discover that some important content is hidden in a subtle link not grouped with the main links. This may be why you are redesigning the site!

   For each of the main categories you discover, draw boxes in a row below the home page. In a third row, draw boxes for all the content within the categories.

3. **Represent the global functions and database interactions.**

   Some links are consistent on each page. For example, each page may have a link to a Privacy Policy or a Contact Us page. Identify all the shared global pages and draw them in a separate area on the site map. Also, take a look at each page and notice which ones seem to rely on a database. For example, does the page greet you by name? If so, the page is getting your name either from a database or a *cookie* (a small piece of data stored on your computer). To represent these database or cookie-driven pages, draw a dotted line leading off the page's box to a note, as shown in Figure 4-22. Then, consult the client on all the database pages to find out which database should be referenced in each case. They may be using more than one database.

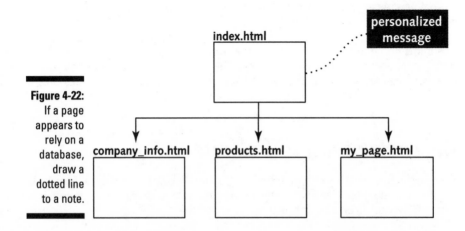

Figure 4-22:
If a page appears to rely on a database, draw a dotted line to a note.

Finishing the site map

Completing the site map for a redesign involves the same process as creating a site map for a brand new site — use your set of symbols and line art to fill in the detail of what's happening in the site. In a redesign process, you don't have to get too detailed in your deconstructed site map. The purpose of making a site map for the old site is to give you a better idea of the site's structure. The map is also a good point of discussion with the client — from here, you can ask a lot of questions and formulate ideas for the redesign. Here's a sample list of questions to ask the client:

- **What do you like least about the site now?** Find the root of the current site's problem by probing to see if the navigation or the content needs revising. Maybe both are fine and that the client just wants a new look to the site. Or, maybe the client wants to add new, more sophisticated features such as Flash and QuickTime movies.

- **Should any new content be added, or old content removed?** If a great deal of content must be added or removed, the site's navigation scheme may need a substantial redesign.

- **Has the site's purpose changed?** Many times a company has an existing Web site that was originally designed to act as a marketing piece, but now must act as a revenue-producing business machine. If so, you are faced with a substantial redesign of both content and navigation.

- **Has the company changed its focus or market positioning?** In such a case, the site's content and navigation, as well as its look and feel, may change drastically. When you design sites like these, you are almost starting over from scratch.

Part II
Designing Web Graphics

The 5th Wave   By Rich Tennant

"I have to say I'm really impressed with the interactivity on this car wash Web site."

In this part . . .

As a creative, soon-to-be Web professional, this is the part that you've been waiting for. This is the part where you get to flex some creative muscle and start building Web graphics from the ground up. If you've been a print designer or if you're new to the Web and need to know the tools, tips, issues, and techniques for designing Web graphics, this part is for you.

Chapters 5 and 6 walk you through the basic principles of graphic design and typography and discuss how they relate to the Web. As a Web designer, you must also be aware of the technical issues surrounding color palettes, image resolution, and file formats. Chapters 7 through 9 give you an in-depth understanding of these issues, as well as give you hands-on practice creating Web graphics with some of today's best software tools.

In Chapter 10, I show you how to put all of your skills together to create a set of design options for a Web site, and I discuss tips and ideas for presenting your ideas to the client.

Chapter 5

Web Graphic Design 101

● ●

● ●

*T*he same principles of balanced layout and use of text and graphics apply to designing Web sites as they do in media such as print and video, but a different set of constraints exist. In the Web design world, you've got to think small and efficient, readable and interactive. Plus, all sorts of pesky technical things can get in the way of your creativity.

If you're not a graphic designer, this chapter is really for you. I discuss basic graphic design principles of how to blend color, text, and images into a pleasing Web user interface that people don't mind coming back to again and again. If you are a designer already, this chapter covers some familiar design territory, but also shows how it all applies to Web site design.

Crafting the Visual Interface

The visual design of each Web page should accomplish two things: Make the page look cool and, more importantly, show people how to navigate around the site. These are big responsibilities for a humble graphic interface. The way you design buttons — even text links — and where you place them can make or break a Web page.

If a visitor can't find a button because nothing on the page *looks* like a button, they probably get confused and go off to the competition. Notice the difference between the two buttons shown in Figure 5-1. The button on the left looks like a mere heading, but the button on the right looks like a 3-D bubble that screams "Click me, please."

Figure 5-1:
Although
both are
buttons,
only the 3-D
one looks
clickable.

Aside from designing the interactive components to look interactive, you also need to be mindful of where you place them in the layout. If you change the location of a button from one page to the next, the user won't find it. The visual layout, therefore, must remain consistent and work throughout the entire site.

Generally speaking, the home page sets the *design direction* for the whole site and has more layout freedom than the rest of the pages. Each page beyond the home page, however, has a much more limited design layout because you have to keep the interface components consistently placed. In some ways, this makes your job easy — you need only to design a home page layout and a *sub-page* layout (in the industry, a subpage is everything past the home page).

The hard part of designing a subpage layout is that it must work for every page. Take a look at one of the subpages for www.propel.com, shown in Figure 5-2. This design is a simple framework across the top and left side. The middle portion can easily handle a bunch of different content elements — anything from forms to text and graphics.

Figure 5-2:
The
subpage
design of
this site is a
framework
that can
work for
many types
of pages.

Although your focus is designing just two main layouts — the home page and the subpage — a lot of design work goes into creating these two pages. To create an effective Web page, you have to follow basic design principles for blending color, type, and graphics. You must also use your page space efficiently to achieve a layout that's not too crowded and is flexible enough to display a lot of different media types, such as movies, text, and forms that users would fill out.

Blending color, type, and graphics

Color, type, and graphics are the three main ingredients that go into your Web design. Over-doing any one of these three can ruin the design, making it look slapdash. Here are some Web Graphic Design 101 rules for using color, type, and graphics effectively:

✔ **Choose colors that are appropriate to the subject matter.** For example, if the Web site is selling high-end executive homes, a palette of muted, "classic" colors works better than bright pink and green. Before you begin designing, create a few swatches (samples) of colors that you think will work well for the site and share them with the client.

✔ **Stick to a limited color palette.** You should use a limited palette of colors that all work well together, for two reasons:

- A limited color palette keeps your Web graphics lean and mean for speedier delivery over the Internet. The fewer colors you use, the smaller the file size. For example, if a file uses just eight colors rather than one hundred, it will be smaller. The smaller the file size, the faster the file can be downloaded.

- From a design perspective, a tight color palette looks better than a rainbow of colors. Create a color palette of no more than seven or so colors that you can use consistently throughout the site.

✔ **Use fonts to set the mood.** You have to be careful with fonts — they can have a lot of personality. Depending on the font you choose, type can make your Web site express happiness, sadness, professionalism, fun, and everything in between. Just as you choose an appropriate color scheme, you must also choose appropriate fonts for your Web site.

Generally, *serif* fonts (fonts that have little ledges on the tips of each letter, as shown in Figure 5-3) convey feelings of stability, security, professionalism, and longevity — perfect choices for a mutual fund Web site. Serif fonts are also better suited for large blocks of text. The body text of this book, for example, uses a serif font. *Sans serif* fonts (no ledges on the tips) convey feelings of forward thinking, cleanliness, and agility — great for a site selling advanced medical-imaging machines. Sans serif fonts are better for short blocks of text and headers.

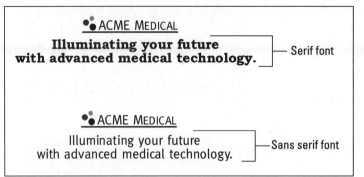

Figure 5-3:
Based on
the feel of
these fonts,
which
company
would you
rather have
giving you
an MRI?

✔ **Mix fonts wisely.** You aren't limited to using just one typeface for your entire Web site. In fact, using a few fonts for different situations is best: one for headings, another for subheadings, and yet another for the body text. More than three or four fonts, however, can be excessive. Choose a few different fonts and stick with them. Define a particular font style for each element and use it consistently. For example, always use the same font and the same point size for all main headings in the Web site.

Many designers use a mix of both serif and sans serif fonts for a Web site. You can create a nice look by using one style for a heading and the other style for the body text. For example, Figure 5-4 shows a sans serif heading and serif body text, and in Figure 5-5, the styles are reversed.

✔ **Use graphic elements efficiently.** Graphic elements consist of flat-colored areas and lines, photographs, and illustrations. In print design, you can use these elements rather freely, but in Web design, large photographs or complex graphics that take up the whole page are like lumbering elephants on your page. Big photos mean big file sizes that download slowly. When designing Web pages, try to use small graphic elements and combine them with HTML-generated graphics such as the colored tables and text shown in Figure 5-6. Such a combined approach keeps your page visually rich, yet more efficient.

✔ **Break up the page with graphics.** HTML and graphic elements are a great way to break up the page and draw the eye to the right places. In Figure 5-6, the colored heading and photo help draw the eye to the most important story on the page. The rule line separates the story from the heading, making the story easy to read. By the way, both the colored heading and the rule line in this example are HTML graphic elements.

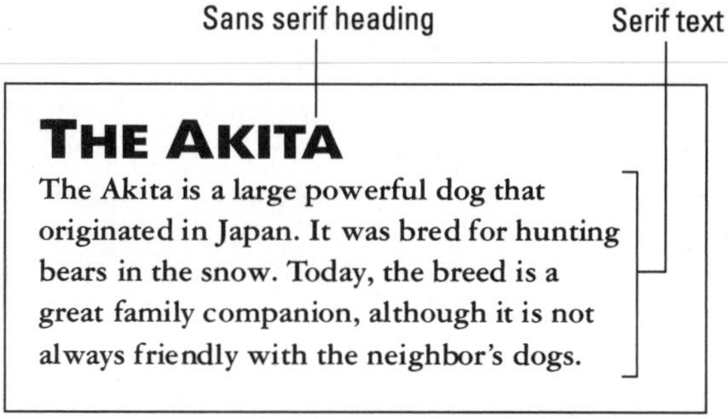

Sans serif heading   Serif text

Figure 5-4:
Use one
style for the
heading and
the other
style for the
body text.

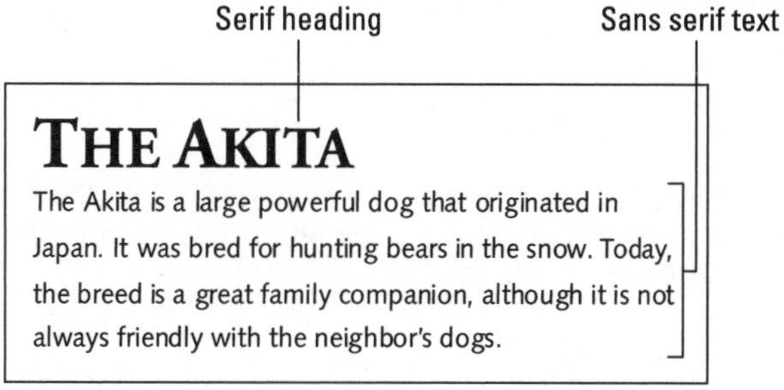

THE AKITA

The Akita is a large powerful dog that
originated in Japan. It was bred for hunting
bears in the snow. Today, the breed is a
great family companion, although it is not
always friendly with the neighbor's dogs.

Serif heading   Sans serif text

Figure 5-5:
In this
example,
the scheme
is reversed.

THE AKITA

The Akita is a large powerful dog that originated in
Japan. It was bred for hunting bears in the snow. Today,
the breed is a great family companion, although it is not
always friendly with the neighbor's dogs.

Graphic element created with HTML tags

Figure 5-6:
Graphic
elements
help to
segment the
page,
making it
easier for
viewers to
find items.

About Mind Garden

**Bringing out the best
in your employees**

Mindgarden.com uses proven techniques
for identifying each employee's strengths
and weaknesses. By identifying an
employee's unique characteristics, you can
employ better management techniques and
bring out the best of your employees.

*Mind Garden® and MindGarden.com® are
registered trademarks of Mind Garden, Inc.*

Using the ol' grid system

To help you lay out your Web page, set up a grid that you can align graphics, text, and HTML elements to. The grid can be anything you like — a three-column layout, two horizontal sections, or a page broken up into multiple sections, as shown in Figure 5-7.

Figure 5-7:
These two Web pages use a grid to divide the page into a few areas.

Unlike print design, where you can have an angled grid like the one in Figure 5-8, the very nature of frames, tables, and other constructs in HTML limit your Web page grid to horizontal and vertical lines.

Figure 5-8:
Angled grids, such as this print design, are rare in Web design.

One way to get around this is to place a Flash movie on the Web page that has an angled layout. The Flash movie is like a self-contained Web site complete with graphics, animation, and links. Flash, however, does not restrict you to a horizontal or vertical layout. For more information on how to use Flash, see *Flash 5 For Dummies* by Gurdy Leete and Ellen Finkelstein.

Grid systems are intended to impose a logical order on your Web page layout. Rather than randomly carving out a spot for everything that is to go on the page, align the elements with each another. Compare the two Web page sketches shown in Figure 5-9. In the example on the left, the elements look thrown on the page. In the example on the right, the elements are neatly presented.

Figure 5-9:
A grid system organizes the page and makes it more legible.

Figure 5-9:
A grid system organizes the page and makes it more legible.

Establishing Visual Priority

Clients are often so close to the subject matter that they have a hard time deciding which things are the most important on the page. Their inclination is to make everything big and include as much detail about each item as possible. As the designer, you have to help them create a descending order of importance. If you make everything the same size, everything competes for the user's attention — making nothing stand out.

Compare the two illustrations in Figure 5-10. In the drawing on the left, it's impossible to determine which section is the main point of the page. Because everything is the same size, no visual priority is established. No one particular element looks more important than another element. And because the layout is so tightly packed together, it looks like it has been subjected to a modern four-horsepower trash compactor. The viewer doesn't get any white space (sometimes referred to as *breathing space*) to take a break from all the information on the page.

Figure 5-10:
Which of these sketches establishes a clear priority for the content?

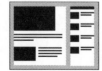

The key to achieving a balanced, well-prioritized layout is to focus on one thing at a time. Decide which elements are the most important and give them a larger share of the screen space. Also make sure that the important things are within the initial viewable portion of the screen: Don't make viewers scroll to reach the most important content. The next few sections offer a few design tips to help you make the most of your screen space without over-whelming your visitor.

Implementing the "big, medium, small" strategy

When designing a Web page, consider it as divided into three sections — a big section for the most important stuff, a medium-sized area for the next most important stuff, and the rest of the page for the less important stuff. By thinking of the page in terms of big, medium, and small areas, you automatically limit the amount of detail you can include for the less important things on the page. For example, if the "Founder's story" area is one of the least important items on the page, you may leave out a picture and just use a short heading and lead-in sentence.

Take a look at the home page in Figure 5-11. In this example, the big area has the fruit composition, the medium area on the right has a few specials and a log in. The third most important areas are the top navigation and the search function at the very bottom.

Figure 5-11:
This home page is an excellent example of the "big, medium, small" strategy.

Most important   Least important   Second most important

Using a "big, medium, small" strategy prevents you from giving the same visual priority to everything on the page and helps make the page easier to read and navigate.

Breaking up the page into manageable areas

Sometimes you can't avoid the fact that your Web page has a lot of stuff going on. For a news-oriented Web site, for example, breaking the page into a few different areas that you can design separately helps to organize your layout. By using color fields and rule lines to break up the page, you create the illusion of more space because each section operates independently. For example, the Web site `www.williams-sonoma.com`, shown in Figure 5-12, conveys a lot of information, but the three-column layout helps you get through it easily. Notice also how the "big, medium, small" strategy works for graphic images. The big graphic on top breaks out of the column so your eye goes to it first.

Figure 5-12: This Web site conveys a lot of information effectively by using rule lines to break up the space.

Designing around the fold line

If you are a print designer, *fold line* is probably a familiar term. The term refers to the spot where a brochure or other kind of printed item folds in half. Anything above the fold line is immediately visible; everything below it is hidden until the viewer unfolds the paper, or performs a similar action. On the Web, the immediately visible portion is pretty small because of the screen size. The point where your Web page gets cut off from view — requiring people to scroll — is called the *fold line*.

Another way that the Web differs from the print world is that the fold line is never quite the same from one computer to the next. Some people have large monitors; some have small ones. This means you have to design for the worst-case scenario or decide that your site will only support the larger monitors. The worst-case scenario is a viewing area of about 600 x 350 pixels when you consider shorter laptop screens, older 640 x 480 displays, and the browser's interface crowding the screen. This means that you must place the important stuff within the first 600 x 350 pixels. Otherwise, you run the risk that viewers might not see it, as shown in Figure 5-13. Most people today have the larger 800 x 600 pixel displays, so many sites are designed for 760 x 550 viewing to make room for the browser's interface buttons.

Figure 5-13: Be sure to place important stuff above the *fold line*. Otherwise, viewers may never know it's there.

First some pretty pictures

And now for an important message...

Beware of the evil "fold line"

Adding Breathing Space

Web pages that have tons of stuff packed into every nook and cranny make the page difficult to read and don't give the eye a chance to rest. When building a Web page layout, always plan for some open space around your design elements. The open spaces not only create a more inviting atmosphere that doesn't feel cramped, but also allow the eye to quickly identify all areas of the page — making it more legible. Here are a few design techniques to open up your layout and create more breathing room for the viewer:

✔ **Use white space wisely.** *White space* is exactly that — large areas of white or light-colored space around your design elements. The physiological effect is an open-air, comfortable feeling. A good goal is to leave at least 25 percent of the page clear of all graphics. Another tip is to leave larger chunks of white space around the most important area of the page, making it stand out like an island. Apple's Web site at `www.apple.com` is famous for its extensive use of white space.

Of course, the same principles apply when designing Web sites on a black or dark-colored background, but the feeling that a dark background conveys is somewhat different. A lot of space around objects on a dark background creates a sense of drama, excitement, and anticipation, as shown in the BMW Motorcycles Web site (`www.bmwusacycles.com`). Figure 5-14 is a good example of using dark space around graphics to create drama.

✔ **Let some elements float.** Web page layouts are, by nature, fairly geometric and boxy. Although it's normally a good idea to align all of your elements to a grid, your page can look too rigid if you follow this rule to the letter. To add visual interest, have some fun with only the most important element on the page. Allow an important element to break the rules a little by falling outside of the grid. This also helps it stand out from the rest. Look at the holiday image on Williams-Sonoma's Web page in Figure 5-15 — it cuts across two columns of the layout.

Figure 5-14:
This Web page creates excitement by leaving a lot of dark space around the text and graphics.

More computing power
at your fingertips

TECH·••
ALLIANCE

HOME   BECOME A MEMBER   CURRENT MEMBERS   HOW IT WORKS   PRESS   EVENTS

Figure 5-15:
The large image on this page breaks out of the grid to add visual interest to the page.

Panettone
Celebrate the holidays as the Italians do, with sweet, raisin-studded bread-delivered in a handsome gift tin.
$26.00

Assumption Abbey Fruitcake
Dark, spicy and laced with an ounce of rum, this incomparable fruitcake is a holiday favorite.
$34.00

✔ **Remember that less is more.** Of course, the less you have going on in the page, the easier it is to include white space and floating elements that break out of the rigid grid structure. Limit the amount of detail you include about the less important things on the page — save the detail for another page that focuses on that element.

Staying Consistent

A Web page is a really small window to view a lot of content. Viewing a Web page on a typical monitor is akin to using binoculars to enjoy a breathtaking 180° view — you can see only a small portion at one time. When looking through such a small window, it's easy to lose context and forget where you are in the big picture. That's why it's so important to provide viewers with a consistent user interface that anchors them in your Web site. Here are three rules for creating a consistent design to keep people oriented in your site:

✔ **Remember — location, location, location!** Always place interactive elements like buttons and links in the same relative location on each page. For example, create a standard Navigation bar and find a happy home for it on the page — and leave it there. After you "train" the user on how to get around, you don't want to make them search again for the buttons.

✔ **Keep the same graphic style.** Always draw interactive elements the same way. If they look like icons on one page and buttons on the next, the visual change throws people off — even if the elements are located consistently. Take a look at the buttons in Figure 5-16. Because the buttons look like icons on Page 2, the user may assume they are no longer active links.

Figure 5-16:
The links on
Page 1 look
like 3-D
buttons, but
those on
Page 2 look
like inactive
icons.

Page 1   Page 2

✔ **Group similar elements on the page.** Not all interface elements are created equal — some links take you to the main sections of the Web site,
whereas others take you to resource sections, such as "Contact Us"
areas or policy statements. Some interactive elements are tools, such as
search fields. In your Web page layout, group similar interface elements
together on the page and give them a similar graphic treatment. For
example, don't mix a Credits link in with the main navigation set.
Instead, set it off in its own area with its own look, along with similar
links, as shown in Figure 5-17.

Figure 5-17:
Main links
have a
different
graphic
treatment
and are
separated
from less
important
links.

Establishing Design Guidelines

After you design a layout for the home page and a layout that can work for all
the subpages, this basic design serves as a guideline for the production team.
Because a Web site can contain so many pages, however, these two layouts
cannot possibly contain enough design information for every possible page.
The team must know what fonts to use and in what situations, what color to
make the headings and body text, and so on. The team also needs graphic templates to create consistent buttons and correctly-sized images for each page.

To prepare the graphic production team, you must provide them with a set of style guides to cover font usage and a set of design templates that they can use to create consistent interface elements.

Type style guides

To cover all the possible text needs for both graphical and HTML text, you should establish a set of design style guides for the production team. These guidelines can be a simple text document that defines the fonts, point size, colors, and any special formatting and examples. Take a look at the sample set of text style guidelines in Figure 5-18.

Style:	Example:	Font settings:
Text links	About Us About Us	HTML text. Verdana size 1 Link color #333399 Visited link color #990066
Headlines	**Our Company**	Graphic text. Myriad bold condensed, 34 pt, #000066
Subheads	**This quarter's earnings**	HTML text. Arial Black size 2 Color #000066
Body text	This quarter, our company increased revenues by 25 percent.	HTML text. Georgia size 2 Color #333366
Captions	*This graph charts the company's growth over the past year.*	HTML text. Verdana size 1 Color #333366
Break-out text Used for pull quotes, etc.	Our company continues to meet or exceed customer expectations.	Graphic text. Myriad semi-bold Used for pull quotes, etc. Condensed, 16 pt, 125% leading Color #CC3333

Figure 5-18: Example of style guides for both graphical and HTML text for a Web site.

If your development team is using an HTML tool like Macromedia's Dreamweaver to assemble the Web pages, you can set up HTML text styles and share them with the team. This way, the team can automatically apply style settings to different text areas on the page.

Graphic templates

To ensure consistency throughout all of the graphical elements — from photographs and bullets to interactive buttons — you need to create a set of graphical templates. Use a program like Fireworks or Photoshop to make all the standard elements and save them in the software's native format, and not exported as a GIF or a JPEG.

By saving the templates in the native formats, you save all the layers, guides, and source art that create the graphics. This way, if the production team needs to change the color or size of a button as in Figure 5-19, they can work with the source art. They don't have to spend a lot of time rebuilding the graphic — a process that can introduce errors.

Figure 5-19:
When the production team has the source art, making all the buttons for a site is a snap.

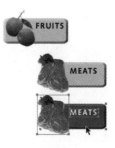

For more information on the GIF, JPEG, or native Fireworks and Photoshop file formats, see Chapter 6.

Chapter 6

Letter-Perfect Type Design

● ●

In This Chapter

▶ Choosing readable fonts for the Web

▶ Figuring out the difference between HTML and graphic text

▶ Understanding the browser font system

● ●

*P*erhaps more than any other detail, your font choices say a lot about the level of your graphic design skills. People who don't have any design training seem to gravitate toward the fun, frilly fonts and — like a kid in a candy store — try out every font on their system. You have to be careful with fonts, however, because they have a powerful effect on the look and feel of your Web site. Of all the graphic elements that go into a Web site, the fonts seem to make the biggest impression. Fonts have the uncanny ability to make people start listing off adjectives to describe your site like "cheerful" or "serious" or worse, "slapdash."

In Web design, you work with two different kinds of text, and if you aren't careful, they can cause double the trouble. The first kind is *HTML-generated text*, which comprises nearly 90 percent of all text in your Web site, and as such, is the one you work with most often. The second kind of text is *graphic text* — text that is actually an image you create in a graphics program such as Fireworks or Photoshop. In this chapter, I discuss basic typography design rules and techniques for creating great-looking HTML and graphic text for the Web. In addition, I discuss text readability issues, what fonts to choose for different purposes, and how to handle browser font display discrepancies. After reading this chapter, you will be able to wield fonts around your Web page with confidence and look like a seasoned pro.

Text That You Can Actually Read

Whether a Web site uses graphic or HTML-generated text, reading text on the computer screen is something akin to staring into the sun to watch the airplanes go by: You squint from the glare while trying to figure out the little letters. Reading a lot of text on a Web page is a mild form of torture. You can't avoid it, however, so it's your job as the designer to choose fonts and font sizes that are easy to read on a monitor.

Print designers have the luxury of working with all sorts of fonts and font sizes. This is because they can print with a high *resolution* (fine dot size) on paper — even if the text is very small, readers can still easily see the detail. Images displayed on a computer monitor, however, are a different story. The smallest dot of light on a monitor, called a *pixel*, is ¹⁄₇₂-inch wide, or 72 dots per inch — which, without making you get out your ruler, I can tell you is not that small when compared to the standard printing resolution of 300 dots per inch.

For example, take a look at the type sample in Figure 6-1. This text is 10-point Syntax in bold on the computer. It has been enlarged so you can see that only a few pixels make up each letter. Such a small number of pixels makes the text appear clunky and unreadable — especially when magnified like this. Ten-point type size is a common font on business cards, so as you can see, what works for a business card — a standard communication tool in the print world — doesn't fly as well on the computer screen. Of course, some fonts in this size work better than others on the Web, but you get the general idea.

Figure 6-1:
A monitor's pixels are too big to render 10-point text effectively.

In addition to fonts and font sizes, other factors contribute to text legibility on a Web page. You can do three things to make your text more readable (regardless of what font you choose):

- ✔ **Font colors.** Typically, dark text on a light background is more legible than the reverse. This rule holds true in Web design, so if your Web page has a lot of text that you want people to read, choose a light-colored background with dark text. Also, muted colors are more readable than neon green — or any other bright color, for that matter. Use bright colors only for headings or short subheadings, and use a muted palette for body text.

- ✔ **Leading.** If you are using a dark background for your Web page, you can widen the *leading*, or the space between the lines of text, to make the text more readable. Increasing the leading helps the eye to find the next line of text. Compare the visual effect of the three text blocks in Figure 6-2. The text in the left block is too cramped, whereas the middle block of text is much more readable — especially on the dark background. The leading in the right block gives an entirely different, more decorative feel to the text.

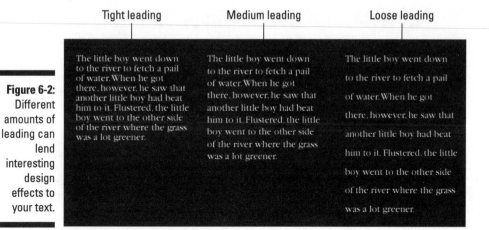

Tight leading   Medium leading   Loose leading

Figure 6-2:
Different
amounts of
leading can
lend
interesting
design
effects to
your text.

⚠ **WARNING!**

Using a significant amount of leading only works well for smaller blocks of text — not entire pages of body text. You can use a lot of leading to make a lead-in paragraph or a quote stand out from the main body, as shown in Figure 6-3.

Figure 6-3:
Using a lot
of leading
makes a
block of
text, such as
a caption or
a quote,
stand out.

The little boy went down to the river to fetch a pail of water. When he got there, however, that another little boy had beat him to it. Flustered, the little boy went to the other side of the river where the grass was a lot greener. The little boy went down to the river to fetch a pail of water. When he got there, however, he saw that another little boy had beat him to it. Flustered, the little boy went to the other side of the river where the grass was a lot greener. The little boy went down to the river to fetch a pail of water. When he got there, however, he saw that another little boy had beat him to it. Flustered, the little boy went to the other side of the river where the grass was a lot greener.

The little boy went down to the
river to fetch a pail of water.
When he got there, however,
he saw that another little boy
had beat him to it.

✔ **Column width.** Finally, the width of your column is an important detail to keep in mind. Because Web pages have more horizontal space than vertical space, you may be tempted to make each line of text run across the entire page to get as much "above the fold line" as possible. ("Above the fold line" means within the initial browser screen space — see Chapter 5 for more information on this concept.) The problem with this tactic, however, is that after your eyes get all the way across the page, you can't easily find the next line. (Plus, tracking your head from side to side like you're eating an ear of corn is a lot of work.) Try to limit each column's width to about five inches or so. That's narrow enough to help your eyes zig-zag down the page quickly and accurately.

Favorite and not-so-favorite fonts for the Web

So many fonts are floating around in the world today that it's impossible to provide you with a complete listing of which ones work for the Web and which ones don't. At the end of this section, however, I do provide a list of my personal favorites. Beyond my personal list, I can give you some general guidelines to help you select the right fonts for your situation.

For the most part, the rules and suggestions that I list here apply to graphic text that you create to embellish your page. When you use HTML-generated text, your choices are more or less limited to the standard set of fonts available on computers manufactured within the last few years.

Standard versus fancy fonts

In order to choose the right font for the job, you should be familiar with the different categories of fonts. Generally, you should use the standard fonts for pages of body text, and reserve the fancier fonts for short headings and subheadings, as shown in Figure 6-4.

Figure 6-4: When used together, fancy heading fonts and standard body text fonts create a nice look.

Decorative headline font   Standard body text font

The grass is always greener

The little boy went down to the river to fetch a pail of water. When he got there, however, he saw that another little boy had beat him to it. Flustered, the little boy went to the other side of the river where the grass was a lot greener.

By *standard fonts*, I mean fonts like Garamond, Times, Helvetica, and Verdana, which have limited personalities. The reader isn't distracted by the design of these simpler fonts, but can focus on the text at hand. Standard fonts are designed for easy reading — so they work well in the smaller point sizes. Fancier fonts, on the other hand, have a lot of detail and personality — ideal for larger-set headings and subheadings. These fonts grab people's attention, but they aren't designed for a long page of text, as Figure 6-5 demonstrates. You can often distinguish the decorative fonts just by their names, such as Kid Print, Comic Sans, Wingdings, and so on.

Figure 6-5:
The font on the left is designed for easy readability; the font on the right should be reserved for headings.

Easy to read font

The little boy went down to the river to fetch a pail of water. When he got there, however, he saw that another little boy had beat him to it. Flustered, the little boy went to the other side of the river where the grass was a lot greener.

Decorative font for headings

The little boy went down to the river to fetch a pail of water. When he got there, however, he saw that another little boy had beat him to it. Flustered, the little boy went to the other side of the river where the grass was a lot greener.

Through the thick and thin

The thickness of each individual letter (or line weight) contributes greatly to a font's readability. Because pixels on computers aren't comparatively very small, fonts that are too thin can fade away into oblivion — especially at smaller point sizes.

If you examine any font, you notice that the thickness varies in each letter. For example, take a look at the letter *m* in Figure 6-6. The letter is set in a few different typefaces for comparison. Some fonts, such as Kepel Bold (the example on the far left), change drastically between the thick and thin areas. At a small point size, all you see is a blob of bold strokes — the thin strokes disappear. When choosing fonts for small point size text, therefore, find versions that don't have a big variance in the stroke thickness — like the middle and right examples in Figure 6-6. Also, avoid the light editions of fonts — they are too thin to read at a small point size. (Most font families come in a variety of thicknesses, ranging from light for the thinnest of the set to bold, black, and ultra for a progressively heavier line weight.)

Figure 6-6:
The font on the left differs dramatically between the thick and thin areas.

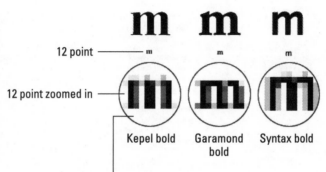

12 point

12 point zoomed in

Kepel bold

Garamond bold

Syntax bold

This font is difficult to read when small.

Figures 6-7 and 6-8 list some serif and sans serif fonts that read well on the Web. The fonts on the list all survived the "10 point test": They are all readable when set at just 10 points, which is the smallest font size for text that you should ever consider in Web design.

Font:	Example:	Comments:
Arial and Helvetica	Favorite San Serif **Favorite San Serif** Favorite San Serif	Works well for body text and headlines though can look a little generic
Meta	Favorite Serif **Favorite Serif**	Similar to Officina, works well for all situations
Myriad	Favorite Serif **Favorite Serif**	Clean modern font for all situations
Officina	Favorite Serif **Favorite Serif**	Modern san serif that works well for body text and headlines
Syntax	Favorite Serif **Favorite Serif**	Clean modern font for all situations
Verdana	Favorite Serif **Favorite Serif**	Designed specifically for the Web, Verdana works especially well as HTML text.

Figure 6-7: Sans-serif fonts for graphic or HTML text that pass the "10-point test."

Font:	Example:	Comments:
Bookman	**Favorite Serif**	Bookman is a more blocky serif, works well for headlines. Bold works best for the smaller font sizes
Century Schoolbook	**Favorite Serif**	The bold variety is readable but wider than other fonts the same point size
Copperplate	**FAVORITE SERIF**	Copperplate is usually all capital letters. Its formal nature works well for business headlines
Garamond and Goudy	**Favorite Serif** **Favorite Serif**	Beautiful old-style fonts for classic looks. Good for headlines or body text. Bold works better for small point sizes
Georgia	Favorite Serif	Like Verdana, Georgia was also specifically designed for Web legibility. The font works well for body text and headlines.
Times	**Favorite Serif**	To me, this font has less character than the other fonts listed here, but is a good stand-by for body and headline text.

Figure 6-8: Serif fonts that pass the "10-point test."

These two tables show fonts that pass the 10-point test ideal for graphic or HTML text. For graphic text, you can use whatever font works best for you. For HTML text, you should choose only fonts that are commonly available on most computers. For a list of these, see Figure 6-21.

Serif versus sans serif

Your font education won't be complete until you know the difference between serif and sans serif fonts. As Figure 6-9 illustrates, a *serif* is the little ledge that adorns the tips of a letter. *Sans serif* fonts, on the other hand, don't have these ledges. Some modern sans serif fonts do have a little curl on their tips, making you look twice, but they're still considered sans serif fonts.

Figure 6-9:
The letters of serif fonts have ledges on their tips. Sans serif fonts don't have ledges.

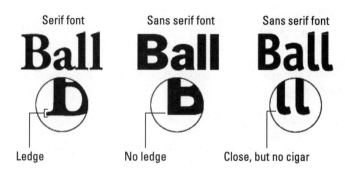

Serif font — Sans serif font — Sans serif font

Ledge — No ledge — Close, but no cigar

You can use either a serif or a sans serif font for both your body text and headings. Both styles work just as well for both purposes. The difference really comes down to the unique look you get from each type. Generally, a serif font conveys a more formal, business-like feel, whereas a sans serif font elicits a clean, modern look.

Try mixing serif and sans serif fonts together. For example, use one style for headings and the other style for the body text. Choosing a set of two to four fonts for your Web site — one for each different kind of type element — helps to add visual interest to the page.

Not too big; not too small

Unless you're going for a postmodern, unreadable artistic effect, avoid graphic text that is less than 12 points in size. Some fonts do work fairly well at 10 points, but most don't. On the flip side, don't make your text so big and horsey that your Web page looks like an eye chart. (By the way, *horsey* is a great, fussy designer term for large and clunky.)

A good rule of thumb: Keep your body text somewhere in the range of 10–12 points (some fonts are naturally larger than other fonts). Fourteen-point body text is way too big. For headings, use 14–24 point sizes. You have to use your judgment for each situation, but headings larger than 24 points approach the horsey territory.

Always use even-numbered point sizes like 10, 12, 14, 16, and so on — especially for sizes in this range. Computer fonts are crafted to look good on the screen in these specific sizes. If you specify an odd size, the computer must scale the font, which tweaks its appearance.

Text on background tiles

Many designers use *background tiles* to spice up the design of their Web page. A background tile is a repeating pattern that fills the entire Web page. The design elements are placed directly on top of the tiled pattern, just as they are on a solid-colored background. To make a background tile, create a graphic of any size. The Web page then repeats this graphic end-to-end across the entire page.

The problem with background tiles, however, is that their busy patterns and competing colors can adversely affect the visibility of your text. You can use background tiles; you just need to prepare them properly.

Here are some design techniques for creating background tiles that work well with text:

✔ **Create a background tile that is much larger than your Web page.**
Many people think of background tiles as a small, square 1-x-1-inch graphic like the floor tile in a house. This isn't necessarily true. You can create a background tile that is much larger than your Web page! This way, the single tile extends past the browser window, so the user won't see it repeat unless they do a lot of scrolling. By creating large tile, you can concentrate busier designs away from the main text areas.

✔ **Create a background tile that is a long and skinny horizontal strip.**
The pattern repeats *down* the page but the user will not see it repeat *across* the page unless they scroll, as shown in Figure 6-10. The net effect of this technique is the same as the "whole page" tile technique (discussed in the previous paragraph): You can control the placement of the busy and not-so-busy areas so they don't interfere with your text. If you use a large tile, keep the design simple (refrain from using photographic elements) and use as few colors as possible. This will help you reduce its file size and speed up its download time.

Long, thin tile

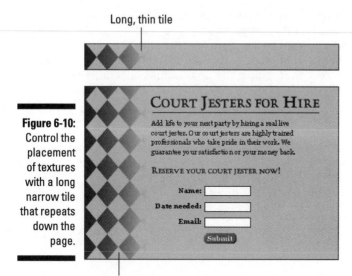

Figure 6-10:
Control the
placement
of textures
with a long
narrow tile
that repeats
down the
page.

Web page with tiled pattern

✔ **To make your background tiles download quickly, use as few colors as possible.** Using few colors reduces the file size. Try to keep the file size of your tile under 15 kilobytes, and ideally, closer to 10 kilobytes. This is possible even for the largest tiles if you use just a few solid-colored areas rather than intricate blends and designs.

✔ **If you do use a smaller tile, make sure that the pattern is subtle.** If you use a small tile with a pattern that repeats across the page, be sure that the colors you choose don't overpower the colors of the other text and graphics on the page. For example, make a tile with a subtle pattern of a few light colors and then choose a dark font for as much contrast as possible.

Graphic Text Versus HTML-Generated Text

Web pages contain two types of text: graphic text (which is really an image) and *live* HTML-generated text (which is generated with HTML tags). HTML-generated text is considered *live* because it is fully editable — just like the text in your word processor. You can apply various font and size settings to HTML-generated text and you can update it easily. Graphic text, however, is just an image. To make corrections to the text, you must re-do the graphic. In addition, graphic text has a larger file size than its equivalent in HTML-generated text, so it can take longer to download.

For these reasons, using more HTML-generated text than graphic text on your Web site is best. Because HTML-generated text is so much more efficient, you may be wondering why you should use graphic text at all. Together, these two types of text offer different levels of design flexibility. Because graphic text is an image just like a photograph, the possibilities are endless in terms of font, color, and even texture choices (such as placing an image of a sunset inside the letters).

Graphic text also allows you to achieve soft *anti-aliased* edges around the letters in your text, as shown in Figure 6-11. Because pixels are square, the rounded curves of graphics and graphic text look like stair steps. Anti-aliasing places a small gradient of color to softly blend the curved edges into the background. When you use a graphics program like Photoshop or Fireworks to create graphic text elements, the programs automatically anti-alias the text by default.

Figure 6-11:
Anti-aliasing
places a
gradient
around
curves to
softly blend
them into
the
background
color.

HTML-generated text, on the other hand, has *aliased* edges, so you get the stair step effect, as shown in Figure 6-12. Also, with HTML-generated text, your choices are much more limited because the fonts that you specify must be available on the end user's system. With so many different systems in use, you have about four fonts to choose from. In the HTML tags, you can specify first, second, and third choices for a font. For example, if you want a header to be Verdana, you can specify Arial and Helvetica as alternate font choices in case an end user doesn't have Verdana. I discuss this further later in this section.

A dash of graphic text, a pound of HTML-generated text

Most Web sites need constant revision, and yours is no exception. Making changes to HTML-generated text is a relatively easy process, but re-doing a whole slew of graphics is a grind. For this reason, you should use a ratio of about 90 percent HTML-generated text to 10 percent graphic text. Only use graphic text for small captions, headings, quotes, and other decorative text elements that you can sprinkle throughout your layout.

Figure 6-12:
Aliased
graphics
have no
blending
on their
edges —
making the
curved
areas look
like steps.

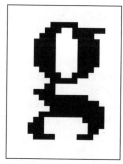

If you do create graphic text, you should always save the source art in the native format of the software. For example, if you create a heading in Photoshop and export it as a GIF for the Web, you should also save the original Photoshop file. After you export a file as a GIF, you can't change it — you have to re-do it. Software programs like Photoshop and Fireworks save text in an editable format — if you ever need to make changes to the GIF, you simply go back to the source file, make changes, and then re-export. For more information on GIF and other file formats, please see Chapter 10.

You should also keep graphic text to a minimum if you plan to *localize* (lingo for *translate*) your Web site for other countries. Translating HTML-generated text is far easier than rounding up all the sources of your graphic text and then re-doing them.

Graphic headings

After you get a good handle on where to use graphic text in your Web page layout, the next step is to dig in and create the graphic text. Graphic text is a cinch to make: Simply launch your favorite graphics program, wield the Text tool around a little, and then add some cool effects.

In this exercise, you use Fireworks to create a heading for a Web page, complete with drop shadow. I chose Fireworks because the process is quite simple and you can follow along using the free trial of Fireworks included on the CD accompanying this book. If you are using Photoshop (a free trial is also included on the CD), the steps are pretty much the same:

1. **Launch Fireworks and whip out your dictionary.**

   Graphic designers are notoriously bad spellers (myself included). I've got my Webster's in my top drawer. Fireworks appears, as shown in Figure 6-13. Note the location of the toolbar and menu.

2. **Choose File⇨New from the menu.**

   The New Document dialog box appears, as shown in Figure 6-14. You can also create a new file with the keyboard shortcut ⌘+N (Mac) or Ctrl+N (Windows). To give yourself enough room to work, enter 300 pixels for the width and 200 pixels for the height in the Canvas Size area and click OK. If you export without trimming it further, the graphic is 300 x 200 pixels in size. This size is too large for the header, but I like to start with a big canvas. Later in these steps, you will crop the canvas to match the size of the header. Cropping the canvas to the size of your graphics is always best. Smaller dimensions result in a smaller file size, which in turn speeds up download performance.

   Please note that while the screenshots shown in these steps show the Macintosh interface, Fireworks works the same on both Mac and Windows. Windows users should be able to follow the steps equally well.

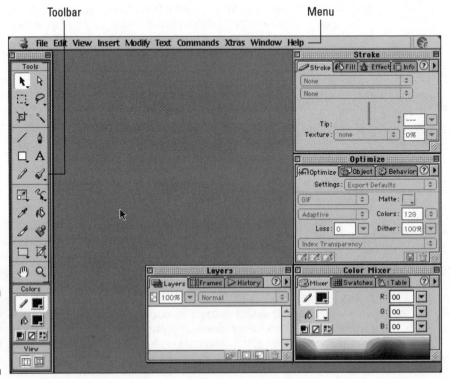

Figure 6-13:
The
Fireworks
interface.

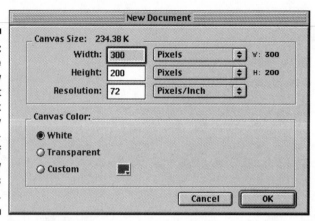

Figure 6-14:
Use the
New
Document
dialog box
to specify
the dimen-
sions of
your new
Fireworks
file.

For this document, I want to build a heading for a Web page with a white background (the color of a Web page is set in the HTML code for the page), so I leave the Canvas Color (or background color) white. When building graphics, you should always use a background color that matches the color of your Web page.

After you create a new document, your screen looks like Figure 6-15. When you build graphics in Fireworks, you work in Original mode (note the tabs at the top of the document). Later in these steps, you use the Preview mode to see how your palette and file format choices affect the quality of your design.

3. **Select the Text tool from the toolbar, and click anywhere in your document to begin typing.**

   The Text Editor window appears, as shown in Figure 6-16. Type the text for the heading and then apply various font, color, and size settings. You can use the Text Editor just like it's a miniature word processor. When you are finished, click OK.

4. **Select the Pointer tool in the toolbar (see Figure 6-15) to move your text around.**

   In Fireworks, you can tell if an object is selected for editing because it is surrounded by a blue outline. Selecting an object enables you to move it around, change its colors, and apply effects to it.

Pointer tool

Text tool

Original mode

Preview mode

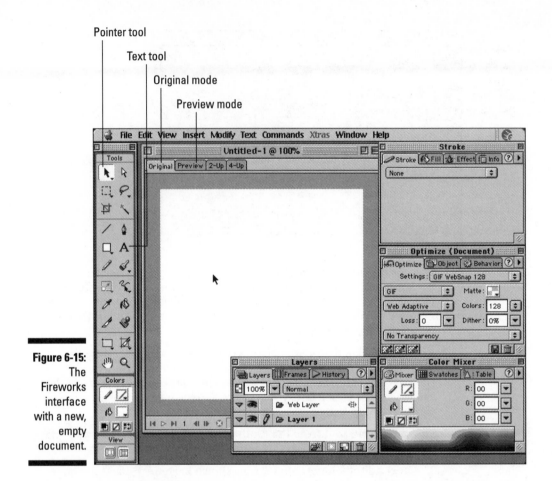

Figure 6-15:
The
Fireworks
interface
with a new,
empty
document.

5. Apply effects to your text.

Fireworks offers an array of live effects that you can apply to your text and graphics. By *live*, I mean that the effects are attributes that you can turn on and off at the click of the mouse. Choose Window⇨Effect from the menu to reveal the Effect palette, as shown in Figure 6-17. The Effect palette, like all other palettes, is marked by a tab called "Effects." The Effects palette may already be open in your workspace; look for its tab and click on it to access it.

For this document, apply a drop shadow effect to your text (make sure the text is selected — it will have the blue box around it). In the Effects palette, choose Shadow and Glow⇨Drop Shadow from the pull-down menu, as shown in Figure 6-17.

Choose a font size

Choose a font here   Pick a color for your text here

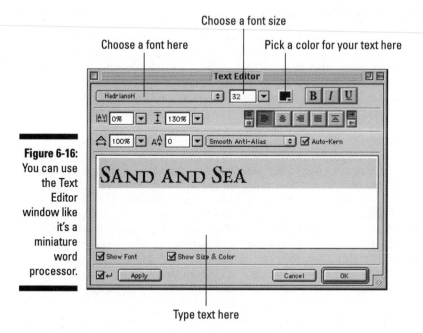

Figure 6-16:
You can use
the Text
Editor
window like
it's a
miniature
word
processor.

Type text here

Figure 6-17:
With the
text
selected,
choose
Drop
Shadow.

After you choose the drop shadow effect, a small *windoid* (what
Macromedia likes to call a small window) appears, allowing you to make
adjustments. Use the default settings, and click outside of the windoid to
close it and accept the settings.

At this point in the design, you can still change the text's color by selecting one from the Fill swatch in the toolbar. You can also change the font
or even the text itself by double-clicking on the text with the Pointer
tool. This action opens the Text Editor window.

6. **Trim the canvas down to just the text.**

When you are finished with the design, you can prepare it for Web export. If you don't trim the canvas, all the surrounding space gets included when you export the file, making the graphic a big white block with a piece of text swimming in the center. To trim the canvas size, choose Modify➪Trim Canvas from the menu.

7. **Choose a file format.**

Before exporting this heading, apply a file format setting. Choose Window➪Optimize from the menu to open the Optimize palette. In the Optimize palette, choose GIF WebSnap 128 from the Settings pull-down menu. This limits your heading to no more than 128 colors. To optimize the image further, enter **8** next to Colors, as shown in Figure 6-18. The fewer colors you use, the smaller the file size will be and thus, the faster it will download on the Web. Choosing too few colors, however, can degrade the quality of the image. In Fireworks, you can preview how your color palette and file type settings will look by clicking on the Preview tab at the top of the document window.

Choose GIF WebSnap 128 from the Settings option

Figure 6-18:
Choose the GIF WebSnap setting and limit the number of colors.

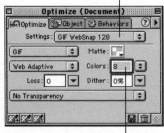

Limit the number of colors to 8

8. **Save the editable file and export the heading.**

That's it! Before exporting for the Web, save your work in the native Fireworks format by choosing File➪Save from the menu. In the Save window, enter a name but keep the ".png" extension after the name (such as "myfile.png"). Save it wherever you like on your hard drive. By saving the original .png file, you can always reopen it, make changes to the design, and then export it once again as a .gif or a .jpeg for the Web.

To export this heading to the Web, choose File➪Export. The Export window appears, as shown in Figure 6-19, where you can name and save your file. Select Images Only (next to Save As), enter a name for your file (keep the .gif at the end), select a folder on your hard drive, and click Save.

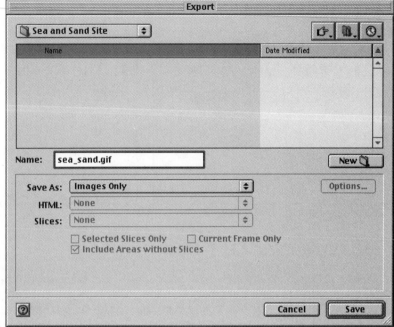

Figure 6-19:
Name and
save your
file in the
Export
dialog box.

Browser Fonts

Because most of your page is HTML-generated text, you should spend some time going over the lay of the browser font land. When you place text into a Web page, you have limited control over its formatting. You can use HTML tags to apply formatting, such as color, bold, italic, underline, and font size settings. To some degree, you can also specify a font.

When you specify a font in HTML, you are really requiring the user's computer to have that font and use it to display your page correctly. If the person's computer doesn't have the font that the page calls for, their browser substitutes a font. This can wreak havoc on your page layout, because as you may know, fonts vary a great deal in size and width — even when set to the same point size.

HTML pages load from top to bottom in a linear flow. For this reason, if the substituted font is larger than the one you specify, the layout shifts downward significantly. Moreover, different browsers interpret the text specs in their own way. On my computer, for example, Internet Explorer and Netscape display the same page very differently even though the font and font size are the same. Take a look at Figure 6-20. In this example, the top headings are set to Verdana size 6 and the body text is set to Georgia size 2 (Instead of point size, HTML uses its own font sizing scheme — arghh!).

Internet Explorer

Netscape

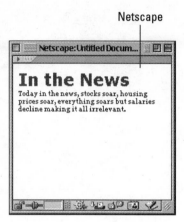

Figure 6-20:
Even on the same computer, different browsers display the same font settings differently.

The browser font flow

The best way to stay in control of your page layout is to go with the flow and use standard browser fonts instead of fonts that only you have on your system. Use fonts that practically everyone has on their computer, such as Helvetica, Arial, Times, Verdana, and so on. Take a look at Figure 6-21 for a listing of the standard browser fonts.

Another safeguard that you can take is to specify a *preference* list of fonts in your HTML tag. For example, when you write the font tag, list the preferred font first, and then follow it with an alternative list of fonts to use if the first font isn't available. When someone loads the page, the browser scans the font list until it finds a match — ideally finding the first font in your list. Here's what the HTML tag looks like:

```
<font face="Verdana, Arial, Helvetica, sans-serif"> Make a
            preference list of fonts </font>
```

In this case, Verdana is the first choice, followed by Arial and Helvetica. The last entry, sans-serif, tells the browser to insert any sans serif font on the system if it doesn't have Verdana, Arial, or Helvetica. (Incidentally, I've seen sans serif spelled with or without a hyphen, so it's really up to you.)

Relative and absolute font sizes

The propeller-heads who dreamed up font sizes for HTML-generated text had to have been in their own little world. HTML-generated text doesn't use the point system (10 point, 12 point, and so on) to specify font size. Instead, browsers use a scheme of *relative* and *absolute* font sizes. Relative sizes are just that: a list of choices that are all relatively larger or smaller than each another — not exactly rocket science. Absolute sizes are numbered sizes from 1 (the smallest) to 7 (the largest), as shown in Figure 6-22.

Font:	Example:	Size 2 Text Sample
Verdana	Sample Text	The quick brown fox tripped over the stump and slid into dog's den.
Arial	Sample Text	The quick brown fox tripped over the stump and slid into dog's den.
Arial Narrow	Sample Text	The quick brown fox tripped over the stump and slid into dog's den.
Helvetica	Sample Text	The quick brown fox tripped over the stump and slid into dog's den.
Georgia	Sample Text	The quick brown fox tripped over the stump and slid into dog's den.
Times New Roman	Sample Text	The quick brown fox tripped over the stump and slid into dog's den.
Times	Sample Text	The quick brown fox tripped over the stump and slid into dog's den.
Courier	Sample Text	The quick brown fox tripped over the stump and slid into dog's den.
Courier New	Sample Text	The quick brown fox tripped over the stump and slid into dog's den.

Figure 6-21:
Standard browser-safe fonts.

Relative sizes were created to address the non-standard means by which each computer and browser displays font settings. As you can see in Figure 6-20, different browsers and different computers have their own ideas about displaying text. (A lot of these browser discrepancies can be attributed to the user because they can change their browser's default display.) If you use relative sizes, at least you can be certain that the browsers will display all of your text in the appropriate proportions.

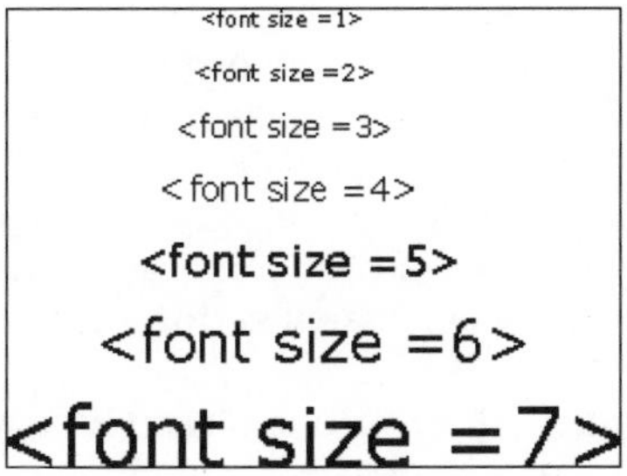

Figure 6-22:
This image shows you the various absolute font sizes you can choose from.

<font size =1>
<font size =2>
<font size =3>
< font size =4>
<font size =5>
<font size =6>
<font size =7>

The default browser base font size is 3. This is equivalent to about 12-point text. When you use relative font sizes, you use a plus and minus system to make the font larger or smaller than the default size 3. For example, the font size +1 is slightly larger than the default size 3, as shown in Figure 6-23.

Figure 6-23:
The first line shows the size of the default base font. The next lines are set in sizes relative to the base font.

Default base font (size 3)

Font set to +1

Font set to +2

Font set to +3

Font set to -1

Font set to -2

Font set to -3

Keep in mind that users can change their browsers to a different base font size. If they bump their base font to size 4, all your relative-sized text bumps up accordingly. Any time you use relative font sizes, their size is derived from the base font size setting. One way to get around this is to set the base font size in your HTML page. Doing this overrides the user's browser settings. To set the base font to the default size 3, use this tag just after the <head> section:

```
<basefont size="3">
```

CSS font control

Microsoft's Cascading Style Sheets (CSS) technology allows you to set up your own special set of font styles, which you can use consistently throughout your Web site. For example, imagine that you are designing a fairly large Web site and you want to ensure a consistent look across each page. All headings should be Arial Narrow Bold, 18-point (yes, you can use real point sizes in CSS!), and dark red. All captions should be Verdana Italic, 10-point, and steel blue. Note that it's still important to specify standard browser fonts like the ones listed in Table 6-3. The main advantage of CSS technology is that it saves you time by allowing you to quickly apply consistent settings to text elements.

Rather than applying all size, font, and color attributes each time, you can save them as a CSS style and give it a name, such as *Caption*. This way, the next time you type a caption, you can format it quickly by applying the Caption style.

Internal style sheets

Style sheets come in two flavors: *external* style sheets (which I discuss later in this chapter) and *internal* style sheets. Internal style sheets are styles that you define for only one page — not the whole Web site. The style information and the style name go in the top <head> section of the HTML code, as shown in this example:

```
<style type="text/css">
.heading {   font-family: "Arial Narrow Bold"; font-size:
      18pt; color: #990033}
.caption {   font-family: Verdana, Arial, Helvetica, sans-
      serif; font-size: 10pt; font-style: italic; color:
      #333366}
</style>
```

In this code syntax, you can see the <heading> style is Arial Narrow Bold in 18-point. The funny-looking number after color is a *hexadecimal* code that creates a dark red color. As you add headings to your Web page, you can quickly format them by applying the <heading> style that you defined for the page:

```
<span class="heading">Headings are a cinch to format</span>
```

Style sheets are cool because they make it remarkably easy to update the look of your page. For example, imagine that your client changes their branding and now wants a whole new set of font choices and colors. Yikes! This would normally require tedious hours of selecting and updating each individual text element on the page. If you used CSS, however, you simply need to update the style sheet definitions in the Head section and — voilà — the whole page updates automagically! (By the way, thanks to Joseph Lowery for that great term.)

External style sheets

External style sheets are even more powerful than internal ones. Internal style sheets define text styles for a single page, but external style sheets can control the text of an entire Web site. To quote an old TV commercial, "Now you're cooking with Crisco!" One file, the external file, contains all the style sheet information. All the Web pages that use the external file are equipped with a link to it. To update the entire site, all you need to do is update the master external style sheet file, and poof! The whole site has a new look. To find more about inner workings of CSS, look online at www.w3.org/Style/CSS, the World Wide Web Consortium's page devoted to CSS. At this site, you can find suggested books and tutorials on Cascading Style Sheets.

Chapter 7

Color My Web World

*T*he way that color works on the computer is one of those great mysteries that everyone appreciates on a daily basis — when it's handled well, that is. Most people figure, however, that it's just too complex to understand. And designers don't care about the inner workings — they just want their stuff to look good. But in the print world, designers must know how the color printing process works in order to get the most out of their designs. The same rule holds true in Web design — you simply can't get around the technical stuff. You have to know how color works on the Web in order to design effective Web pages.

Never fear — the technical mysteries aren't what they're cracked up to be. Whereas the printing process uses four colors (*c*yan, *m*agenta, *y*ellow, and blac*k*, or the CMYK system) to mix a wide range of colors, the computer uses only three colors (red, green, and blue) to generate its colors. What's amazing is that even though the computer uses one less color than its print counterpart in its mixing scheme, those three colors are capable of producing a mind-blowing range of hues — way beyond the possibilities of the CMYK system. There's a catch, of course: Web browsers can display only a limited subset of these colors with any reliability. This limited subset of colors is called the *Web-safe* palette. This means that you have to be selective in your color choices for Web graphics, or you may have unexpected results — arghh! The way you use color in your graphics also has a great impact on their download efficiency for the Web. For example, using fewer colors results in smaller file sizes, which speeds up delivery over the Internet.

If you read this chapter in its entirety, you'll understand more than you ever wanted to know about the mechanics of color on the computer and how to use color palettes properly in your Web graphics.

The Secret World of RGB

The secret to all the colors you see on your computer monitor is a system called *RGB color*. This system uses just three colors (red, green, and blue) combined together to create all colors (including black and white) on your monitor. Although this sounds like quite a feat, consider that the system works in a way similar to natural daylight. When the sun is up, you see white light. When the sun goes away, it's pitch black outside. Only if you use a prism to break up the spectrum can you see all the colors contained within white light. Like the sun, RGB color is an *additive* color process. The CMYK printing process, on the other hand, is a *subtractive* color process. I explain the difference in the following section.

Subtractive and additive colors

When you mix two or more colors together to create a new color in any medium — whether it's in print or on a computer screen — the method you use is either an *additive* or a *subtractive* process. These terms refer to the way you produce the color white.

In printing, you achieve the color white by mixing no colors at all. By removing (subtracting) all colors, you leave the color of the plain paper color — which is presumably white — shining through. Therefore, the print process is a subtractive color process. The only way to print white is by printing nothing at all — subtracting all colors from the page.

Combining cyan, magenta, and yellow inks in various proportions creates all the other colors. Black ink is added as necessary because it's more economical and reliable to produce black directly rather than from a CYMK mix. The color we perceive on the page is the result of the different spectral colors that the inks absorb (subtract).

At the other end of the spectrum (pardon the pun) is the computer's *additive* process. To create white on a computer screen, the display mixes all three colors — red, green, and blue — together at full strength. Just as if you switched on a light bulb, all colors of the spectrum come together to make "white light." And just as if you turned off a light switch, removing all the RGB colors leaves you with black.

Gazillions of colors

How do you mix all the colors of the rainbow using this *additive* system of just three colors? As with the CMYK process, the answer is to use different amounts of the three colors. The RGB color scheme contains 256 *levels* (variations numbered from 0 to 255) of red, 256 levels of green, and 256 levels of blue.

To generate (or mix) a color, you take one level of red and mix it with one level of green and one level of blue. For example, to make a nice turquoise color, you mix red number 51, green number 153, and blue number 153, as shown in Figure 7-1. (This book is in black and white, but work with me here.) In this scenario, red — set at just number 51 — is used at the weakest level. This makes sense because we're mixing turquoise, which is primarily a mix of green and blue shades.

Figure 7-1:
To make a turquoise color, mix red, green, and blue.

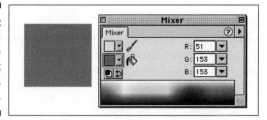

If each color (red, green, and blue) has 256 possible settings, how many colors can you mix with the RBG system? For those of you who are mathematically inclined, you know that the number of colors is 256 x 256 x 256, or 256^3, as shown in Figure 7-2. This number amounts to a whopping 16,777,216 different color combinations — many more than you or I can see with our eyes!

Figure 7-2:
You can create more than 16 million colors by mixing shades of red, green, and blue.

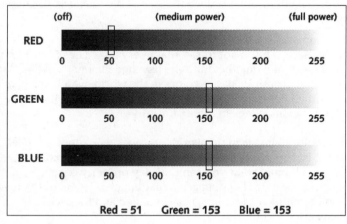

Color bit depth

Although the computer's RGB system is capable of mixing 16 million different colors, the monitor is not always capable of *displaying* all of these colors. To help you better understand this concept, I explain *bit depth* and how it relates to Web design in the following paragraphs.

A *bit* is a tiny segment of computer information — it's like the atom of computer data. Without getting too technical, a lot of bits are needed to make colors appear in an image. The more colors that an image contains, the more bits of data that it has, and thus the higher its *bit depth*. For example a 1-bit image has just two colors. An 8-bit image can have up to 256 colors.

The monitor has to work hard to display all these colors contained in an image. Some monitors simply don't have enough computer memory to display all the color data. Therefore, you may encounter a situation where the image has more colors than a monitor can actually show.

Terms like *24-bit color* refer to both images and computer monitors. A 24-bit monitor can display 24 bits of color information. A 24-bit image has a lot of colors — specifically, the millions that are possible with the RGB system. Here's more detail:

- **24-bit monitor.** Although the RGB system can make 16 million different colors, a computer needs a lot of power to show all these colors. More specifically, a computer uses 8 bits of data to display 256 colors. Therefore, in order to display the whole spectrum of just one of the red, green, or blue colors, your computer needs eight bits. To display the full spectrum of all three colors, you need a 24-bit monitor and a display card with sufficient video data storage to store and process the necessary colors. For a large 24-bit image that is 1024 x 768 pixels in size, you need about 4MB of video RAM. If you have less memory on the video card, you either must reduce the size of the image or the number of colors.

- **24-bit image.** A 24-bit image can show all 16 million colors of the RBG color space. This is not to say that every image *needs* all 16 million colors — that would be quite the psychedelic image. A 24-bit image has unlimited access to all the colors in the world, which can give the image a beautiful continuous tone. Color-wise, using a 24-bit image is like having a blank check in Monte Carlo.

The most colorful image in the world, however, won't look good if the monitor on which it is displayed can't support it. It is possible to have a nice, millions-of-colors, 24-bit image that you can't display properly because your monitor only supports 8-bit or 16-bit images. What happens, then, to the image? On an 8- or 16-bit monitor, a 24-bit image is simplified and then looks like a work of pointillism art.

Figure 7-3 shows the same 24-bit image as seen on two different monitors. On the left, the image is displayed on a 24-bit monitor, so it looks great even when you zoom in. The image on the right shows what the image looks like on an 8-bit monitor — very grainy. Because an 8-bit monitor is limited to a palette of 256 colors, it uses a pointillism-like approach called *dithering* to approximate the millions of colors in the image. Dithering places various colored dots near each other so that from a distance, they appear to create one color. For example, dithering places a yellow dot and a red dot close together so from far away, the eye sees orange.

Image viewed on a 24-bit monitor

Same image dithered on an 8-bit monitor

Figure 7-3:
The images in this example are both 24-bit.

But what does an 8-bit image look like when displayed on a 24-bit monitor? When the image is of low quality to begin with, viewing it on a high-quality monitor doesn't improve anything. If an image has been reduced to an 8-bit palette of just 256 colors, the monitor can do nothing to resurrect the lost millions of colors. The image looks dithered — regardless of the monitor's bit depth.

As I discuss earlier in this chapter, a computer uses 8 bits of data to show 256 colors. Each of the red, green, and blue primary colors has 256 levels. So does this mean that an 8-bit image is monotone, showing all 256 possible levels of red? The answer is no — an 8-bit image simply uses a select palette of 256 colors. These colors are a subset of all 16,777,216 possible colors. The decision that you as a designer must make is *what* subset of colors you want to use. To explain this concept further, I discuss palettes and how they work on the Web in the following paragraphs.

The Web-Safe Color Palette

The best reason to reduce the number of colors in an image — from millions down to just 256 — is to reduce the file's size. Small file size means faster transmission. You must sacrifice quality and detail for the sake of optimal delivery over the Internet. You can choose from among a few pre-fab palettes or you can make your own. The rule of thumb is that the fewer colors you choose for your palette, the smaller the file size.

To add to the complexity, only certain colors, those on the so-called *Web-safe* palette, are *standard browser colors* (meaning that the browser can display them properly). Before you create a custom palette of just four colors, then, you should first make sure that those four colors are Web-safe colors. Otherwise, the browser dithers the colors — using its standard set of colors in a pointillism style to approximate your custom color.

Reducing an image's bit depth

When you reduce an image's palette, you are reducing the bit depth of that image. A 24-bit image can use millions of colors if necessary, and an 8-bit image has only 256 colors. What happens if you choose fewer than 256 colors? What's the bit depth then? Table 7-1 is a handy chart that equates bit depth to the number of colors in the palette. For you techies, it's a simple binary formula of 1 bit equaling two possibilities — black (off) or white (on).

Table 7-1	Color Bit Depth	
Bit Depth	*The Math*	*Number of Colors in Palette*
1 bit	2^1	2: black (off) or white (on)
2 bit	2^2	4
3 bit	2^3	8
4 bit	2^4	16
5 bit	2^5	32
6 bit	2^6	64
7 bit	2^7	128
8-bit	2^8	256

The numbers in Table 7-1 illustrate the maximum number of colors that each bit depth allows. When you reduce the number of colors in your image to keep the file size small, you can choose any number of colors you like. For example, you can choose a palette of 200 colors. The image is still an 8-bit, but because it uses only 200 colors, the file is smaller than if you used all 256 colors.

Incidentally, I show this chart going only to 8-bit color depth because GIF images — the most common graphic format on the Web — must be 8 bits or less. The JPEG format, on the other hand, always compresses a 24-bit image.

If you are ever given the option to save your image as a 32-bit image, this means that you can save an *alpha channel* mask along with the 24-bit image. An alpha channel is a grayscale mask that controls an image's transparency. Where the mask is black, the image is completely masked and appears transparent. Where the mask is white, the image is completely opaque. Gray colors in the mask make the image appear at varying degrees of transparency.

The extra 8 bits for the alpha channel give you 256 levels of transparency control. So far, the only Web graphics format that supports alpha channel transparency is the PNG (Portable Network Graphics) file type, pronounced "ping." The problem, however, is that at the time of this writing, most Web browsers don't support this level of PNG functionality.

All of the most popular Web graphics tools, such as Photoshop and Fireworks, allow you to reduce an image's palette from millions of colors down to just a few colors. If you do this, however, you can't go back. After you remove colors from an image, the colors are gone forever — unless you use the Undo feature right away. You can't use Photoshop or Fireworks to convert the image back to 24-bit, and expect the millions of colors to magically reappear. The computer has no way of guessing where to insert the lost colors.

To prevent the disaster of losing all these colors, always work in the highest bit depth (24-bit) when building Web graphics and then save your original source files separately from your finished graphics. (When you work in Photoshop and Fireworks, the default color mode is 24-bit, so you don't have to do anything special to ensure that you're working at the highest bit depth.) Reducing the palette down to 256 or fewer colors is the last thing you should do before exporting finished art for the Web.

Color palettes

After you have a good understanding of color bit depth and how it relates to the number of colors in the palette, your next step is to look into the kind of palettes you can choose from for your design. In addition to some pre-fab palettes, you can also create your own custom palette. However, only 216 colors display the same on all Web browsers without dithering — these are the Web-safe colors. Whatever palette you choose, it's a good idea to include as many of these 216 colors as possible. Here's a list of some palette options:

✔ **System palettes.** Macintosh and Windows each have their own pre-fab palette of 256 colors. The palettes are pretty generic. They include reds, oranges, blues — and everything in between to do a fair job of dithering a 24-bit image. Take a look at the Macintosh's 256-color system palette in Figure 7-4. The palette of 256 colors actually contains all of the 216 Web-safe colors. The extra 40 colors (an assortment of blues, reds, greens, and grays) that appear dithered in the first two rows are not Web-safe. The problem with forcing an image into one of these system palettes, however, is that the image looks highly dithered, as shown in Figure 7-5, because not all the colors in the palette are appropriate for the image. For example, all the pinks, reds, and oranges in the palette are not useful for dithering a seascape image.

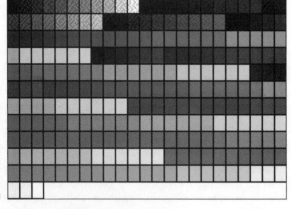

Figure 7-4:
The
Macintosh
system
palette of
256 colors.

Figure 7-5:
This image
is pixilated
because the
generic
Macintosh
system
palette is
being used.

✔ **Adaptive palettes.** An *adaptive* palette is a custom selection of colors that are best suited (adapted) for the image. For example, an adaptive palette for a seascape image uses a lot of blues and greens — not pinks and reds. An adaptive palette yields better results because more of the 256 color slots go to colors that the image actually needs. This is my favorite type of palette because you can reduce the file size and still retain nearly the quality of a 24-bit image. Compare the image qualities in Figure 7-6. The left image is the original 24-bit image. The right image uses an 8-bit adaptive palette but, in terms of quality, looks almost identical to the original. Keep in mind, however, that using an adaptive palette means that end users with 8-bit monitors will see a dithered image. Most users nowadays, however, have 16 and 24-bit monitor displays, so adaptive palettes look great.

Original 24-bit image   8-bit image with adaptive palette

Figure 7-6:
Even though the left image is 24-bit and the right image is 8-bit, the quality of the two images is nearly the same.

✔ **The Web-safe palette.** The 216-color Web safe palette is a generic palette, just like the system palettes. The problem with using one of the pre-fab system palettes or an adaptive palette is that you have no guarantee that the colors are *Web-safe*. Web-safe means that if someone's monitor supports only 8-bit color, the browser will dither the image into its palette. If the palette you choose is radically different from the Web-safe palette, your image will look different.

Export your image as a GIF with an adaptive palette. Then set your monitor to 256 colors and open the GIF in a Web browser to see what it looks like. If the quality is acceptable, go with it. If not, you can try a *Web-adaptive* palette instead (see the following paragraph for more info). Keep in mind that this display problem is only an issue if your intended audience is using an 8-bit monitor. Most computers are now equipped with 16- and 24-bit displays.

✔ **Web-Adaptive palette.** Although an adaptive palette provides the best quality, you run the risk of the image looking bad on an 8-bit monitor. To curb this effect, you can use a Web-adaptive palette. Like an adaptive palette, this palette finds colors that are best suited for the image. The difference is that wherever possible, the colors "snap" to the nearest Web-safe equivalent. This kind of palette gives you the quality of an adaptive palette with more predictable display results on 8-bit monitors. For these reasons, the Web-adaptive palette is my palette of choice for Web graphics. (If the graphic is mostly photographic, you shouldn't reduce its color palette, but leave it as a 24-bit image and save it as a JPEG. See Chapter 10 for more information on Web file formats.)

Deciphering the hexadecimal color code

When you specify colors in HTML code, you don't use their RGB numbers. Instead, you use something called a *hexadecimal code*. For example, plain old white is 255,255,255 in RGB but it is #FFFFFF in hexadecimal code. In hexadecimal code, FF = 255. The first two digits define the red color, the next two digits define the green, and the last two digits define the blue.

Imagine that you are designing a Web site for a company that has a handful of company colors that they want you to use throughout the site. Instead of using a super-duper decoder ring to translate RGB values into hexadecimal code and vice versa, you can retrieve the code by using a program like Fireworks. Otherwise, you really do need a special hexadecimal calculator (you can find numerous examples of them online).

Here's how to use Fireworks to find the hexadecimal number of a sample color:

1. **Launch Fireworks.**

2. **Choose File⇨New from the menu.**

   Because this is just an example, click OK to accept the default Canvas Size values.

3. **Choose Window⇨Color Mixer to open the Color Mixer palette.**

   If Color Mixer has a check next to it, the palette is already open. Make sure that the Color Mixer is in RGB mode (the three fields on the right should be labeled R, G, and B), as shown in Figure 7-7. If it isn't in RGB mode, you can quickly switch it by using the pull-down menu in the top right, as shown in Figure 7-7.

   I'm choosing RGB mode because I want to show you how to pick any color from the RGB spectrum (or enter RGB values directly) and then find the hexadecimal code for the selected color. In the following steps, I show you how to sample a color from an image and find its hexadecimal color.

Figure 7-7:
The Color
Mixer
palette in
Fireworks
allows you
to choose
any of the 16
million
possible
RGB colors.

Use the pull-down options menu to select the RGB color mode.

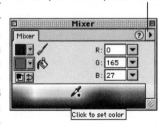

4. **Pick a color.**

   The Mixer palette allows you to either enter the RGB numbers of a color (if you happen to know what they are) or use the Eyedropper tool to select a color from the rainbow area. Before you select a color, click on the paint bucket icon in the Color Mixer palette to make sure you are selecting a fill color and not a stroke color. Then, click anywhere on the rainbow of colors to choose a color. When you click, the Fill Color swatch in the toolbar at the left of your screen updates to reflect your new color choice.

5. **Find the hexadecimal color.**

   After you select an RGB color, you can find its hexadecimal value in two ways. You can switch to Hexadecimal mode in the Color Mixer palette — the RGB values in the palette update with the hexadecimal equivalents of your selected color. Or, at the bottom of the toolbar, click on the Fill Color Swatch to open the pop-up palette of colors, as shown in Figure 7-8. At the top of the pop-up palette, you see the hexadecimal number of your color.

If you have an image that already contains colors, you can also use Fireworks to find the hexadecimal values of those colors. Open the image and use the Eyedropper tool in the toolbar to sample one of the colors. Then, click on the color swatch at the bottom of the toolbar to see its hexadecimal number in the pop-up palette.

If the image you are sampling is dithered, however, it may be difficult to sample a color accurately because of all the multi-colored pixels placed so close to each other. Before sampling a color, double-click the Eyedropper tool in the toolbar. A Tool Options palette appears where you can set it to sample an *area* of color rather than to a sample a single pixel's color.

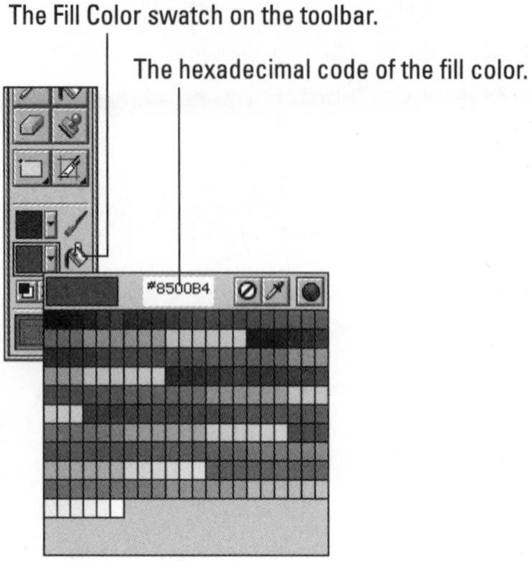

The Fill Color swatch on the toolbar.

The hexadecimal code of the fill color.

Figure 7-8:
Fireworks
tells you the
hexadecimal
code of the
selected Fill
or Stroke
color.

#8500B4

Smart Web Color Usage

As you work in a graphics program to develop Web graphics, you can perform a number of actions to ensure that you get the best image quality at the lowest file sizes — more bang for the buck. Your color choices for text and graphical elements, the way you draw gradient blends, and the number of colors that you choose all affect the final outcome. Here is a list of tips and techniques to help you create great-looking Web graphics (on all browsers and computers) while keeping the file sizes down for speedier delivery:

- ✔ **Use the Web-safe color palette for flat-colored graphics.** For example, your Web page layout probably includes more flat-colored graphics than photographs. All of the flat-colored graphics, such as text, graphical shapes and illustrations, cartoon characters, and backgrounds that are filled with one solid color should use Web-safe colors. This way, if the page is viewed on an 8-bit monitor, the flat-colored areas won't dither — they stay crisp and clean. Figure 7-9 illustrates flat-colored graphics: The left image uses Web-safe colors — so the flat colored areas don't dither — and the image on the right dithers because it doesn't use Web-safe colors.

- ✔ **Use as few colors as possible.** The fewer colors you use when reducing an image's palette, the smaller its file size will be. Therefore, your design should use a limited color palette. If your design uses a ton of colors from all over the rainbow, you have a hard time defining a small palette — you simply need more colors to draw the design.

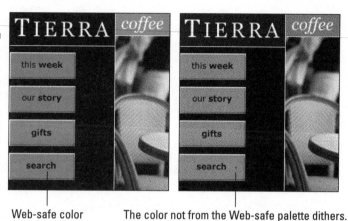

Figure 7-9:
When an image uses flat areas of color, make sure you fill the areas with Web-safe colors.

Web-safe color   The color not from the Web-safe palette dithers.

The design in Figure 7-10 uses a lot of different colors, not to mention the colored text and graphical areas. When I reduce the image down to just four colors, making the file size just 10K, the whole design is ruined. To make this design work, I have to use at least 100 colors. This makes the file 40K! In this case, I'd be better off slicing the image into two pieces — a top photo area and a bottom photo area. This way, I can save the top photo area as a four color GIF and the bottom photo area as a JPEG. For more information on choosing the right file format for a particular image, see Chapter 10.

Figure 7-10:
This design uses so many colors that it's impossible to reduce the palette to less than 100 colors.

The image with a palette of 100 colors

The image with a palette of four colors

✔ **Beware of the gradient blend.** A *gradient* is a gradual transition from one color to another. For example, on one end, the image is red and on the other end it's blue. Gradients have the potential to really bloat the size of your file. If you're going to save the file as a GIF, make sure that the gradient blend goes from top to bottom rather than from left to right, as shown in Figure 7-11.

Figure 7-11:
A top-to-bottom gradient blend compresses better than a left-to-right blend.

The top-to-bottom gradient is 2.3K.

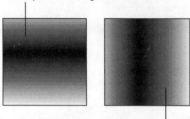

The same gradient left-to-right is 2.88K.

The type of gradient makes a difference because of the way the GIF format compresses an image. The GIF format reads each horizontal row of pixels in your image and records the color changes. In a top-to-bottom gradient, each horizontal row has the same color of pixels. In a left-to-right gradient, each pixel's color changes as you go across the horizontal row. For more information on image compression, see the sidebar in Chapter 10.

✔ **Use the Web adaptive palette when you have both photos and flat colors in the image.** When your Web graphics have a mix of flat-colored art and photographs, it's best to save the graphic as a GIF. To get the best quality for both the photographic areas and the flat colored areas, use the Web-adaptive palette. (Remember, if you use the GIF format, your image must use a palette of 256 colors or less.)

The Web adaptive palette ensures that the flat-colored areas remain solid (not dithered) and that the photograph looks as close to 24-bit quality as possible.

Chapter 8

Building Web Graphics from the Ground Up

*J*ust when you thought you could get away with a completely bland, text-only Web site, reality and peer pressure set in. Today's Web sites are chock-full of eye-popping graphical coolness. To keep up with the Joneses, your Web site has to sparkle with the best of them.

After you come to terms with this basic fact of Web life, how do the artistically-challenged proceed? A good place to start: Become proficient in the rules, tools, and techniques that surround the creation of Web graphics. Mastering the skills is half the battle. The other half is tapping your own creativity.

In this chapter, I discuss some basic issues surrounding Web graphics, I take a look at the leading software tools, and I walk you through techniques for churning out professional-quality graphics. Whether you're a seasoned designer from the print world or completely new to design, with a little practice you'll be cooking up Web graphics juicy — or cheesy — enough to eat.

Bitmap versus Vector Graphics

Before you can even think about making Web design your career, you must master the difference between bitmap and vector graphics. All graphics that you encounter on the Web will be in one of these two formats. The basic difference between the two is how they are drawn on your screen. This simple detail affects everything from image resolution to file size and format.

Bitmaps: A fabric of pixels

When explaining bitmap images, I can't help but think of my old childhood toy, the Lite Brite. Those of you who were pampered enough as children to play with this toy remember that you plugged little colored pegs into a grid and then flipped the switch to light them up.

Bitmaps work pretty much the same way. In simplistic terms, a bitmap graphic is a grid filled with tiny colored pixels, as shown in Figure 8-1. To draw a bitmap graphic on the screen, the computer lays out a grid, say 100 by 100 pixels, and then *maps* a color to each individual pixel. That's 10,000 pixels to draw!

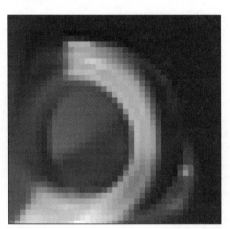

Figure 8-1: Zooming in on a bitmap reveals hundreds of colored pixels all working together to create an image.

Vectors: For the mathematically inclined

If you don't remember the Lite Brite, then surely you remember "Connect the Dots." Vector graphics employ a similar strategy. A mathematical formula places *points* on the screen and then connects them with *paths*. For example, to draw a triangle-shaped vector graphic on the screen, the computer simply lays down three points, connects them, and then fills them with a color. In Figure 8-2, you can see a handful of points — some with handles coming off of them. These handles control the curve of the path in between two points.

If you're thinking that vectors can draw graphics on the screen far more efficiently than bitmaps, you're right. Vector graphics have extremely small file sizes, making them ideal for online delivery. Both vector and bitmap graphics, however, have their pros and cons.

Figure 8-2:
Mooove over bitmaps: Vector images are defined by a series of points connected by curves.

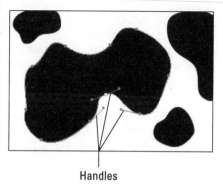

Handles

The vector-bitmap showdown

As a rising Web graphics star, you should know a few things about the ups and downs of vectors and bitmaps before you push your first pixel:

✓ **Bitmaps are highly prevalent on the Web.** All JPEG, GIF, and PNG graphics that you encounter on the Web are bitmaps. Ironically, many of these graphics began life as vectors before they were converted into bitmaps, as shown in Figure 8-3. Why? Because drawing graphics and interesting effects with vectors is often faster and easier than creating the same effect with bitmap graphics. It's much easier to make changes to vectors because you just move a point and the line follows. To make changes to bitmaps, you often need to redraw them. To become GIFs and JPEGs, vector graphics must be converted to bitmaps.

By the way, GIF (depending on whom you talk to) is pronounced either as it sounds — "giff" (my personal favorite), or "jiff" (as in Jiffy Pop popcorn), and stands for *Graphics Interchange Format*. JPEG, pronounced "jay-peg," stands for *Joint Photographers Experts Group*. PNG, pronounced "ping," stands for *Portable Network Graphics*.

Figure 8-3:
It's easy to change the shape of this vector-drawn button by moving its points.

✔ **Bitmaps are supported by more formats.** To date, the only standard Web format that supports vector graphics is the Flash SWF format (pronounced "swif"). Generally, the SWF format is used for making interactive animated movies that you can plug into your Web page. The format isn't used for saving static graphics (although you certainly can if you want). To view this format, however, your browser must have the Flash plug-in installed.

✔ **Bitmaps can't maintain quality if they are resized.** Bitmap graphics have fixed resolutions (see the section "Image Resolution" later in this chapter for more information on resolutions). As I state earlier in this chapter, bitmap graphics are laid out in a grid of pixels. Like ½-inch grade chicken wire, this grid is a fixed size. And like chicken wire, if you stretch the image, you end up with a contorted mess. So, as a general rule, don't use the HTML height and width tags to squash and stretch bitmap images to fit your Web page. Make your images the correct size in the first place.

✔ **Vector graphics can easily be resized.** Vector graphics, on the other hand, are resolution-independent. Because they're drawn according to a mathematical formula of placing points on the screen, the *grid size* (resolution) doesn't matter. This means that you can infinitely squish and stretch vector graphics up, down, and side to side without losing quality: They are the Play-Doh of the Web. Take a look at the contorted, albeit high-quality, icon that I made by stretching a vector illustration in Figure 8-4.

Figure 8-4:
You can have hours of fun stretching and squishing vector graphics.

For a quick reference chart of all the bitmap and vector Web graphic formats that you'll deal with, take a look at Table 8-1.

Table 8-1	The Scoop on Graphic Formats		
Format	**Full Name**	**Bitmap or Vector**	**Best Uses**
GIF	Graphics Interchange Format	Bitmap	Graphics like cartoons with a lot of solid-colored areas, or those with a lot of text elements.
JPEG	Joint Photographers Expert Group	Bitmap	Photographic images or images with a lot of blending colors (a rainbow, for example).
PNG	Portable Network Graphic	Bitmap	Images that have both photographic-like areas and solid-colored areas.
SWF	Shockwave Flash	Vector	Illustrated images (not photographic). Smooth motion animation.

Monitor resolution

If you've ever used a computer, you probably realize how clear the monitor is compared to your TV. Really, who can read all the legalese fine print that scrolls by in that fancy "0% down payment" car commercial? That same fine print is a cinch to read on your computer screen — and not just because you're sitting so darn close to the screen. You can see clearly because your computer monitor has a finer resolution than your household tube.

Resolution refers to the number of pixels squeezed into a linear inch. Standard computer screen resolutions vary from 72–96 ppi (pixels per inch) — that's a lot of detail. Your TV, on the other hand, is nearly half of that, and because broadcast TV is analog — not digital like your computer — the image is all blurred together.

Image resolution

Why should you give a hoot about monitor resolution? Because the monitor is your Web design canvas. Although the monitor is a fixed resolution (after all, it is a piece of hardware), graphics come in varying resolutions. In Web design, your graphics must match the screen's resolution.

Although monitors vary from 72–96 ppi, the Web graphics standard is 72 ppi. The professional lingo is *72 dpi,* which stands for "dots per inch," a carry-over from the print production days.

Here's a frequently asked question: Won't a higher resolution image look better on my Web page? The answer is no, because even though a 300 dpi image looks great in a printed piece, the fixed 72–96 dpi monitor isn't capable of showing all this detail. Regardless of the image's resolution, the browser simply scales it up to fit the monitor's resolution.

Both images in Figure 8-5 are 247 x 167 pixels. Because the left image is 150 dpi, each dot is smaller, so more dots can be squeezed into an inch. That's why the whole image shrinks when you print it. The computer monitor, however, isn't capable of displaying such tiny dots, so it blows each one up to 72 dpi size, as the example on the right shows. So, you're back where you started — higher resolution images don't improve the quality, so it's best to just stick with the default 72 dpi resolution in the first place.

150 dpi   72 dpi

Figure 8-5:
High-
resolution
images
have tiny
dot sizes —
much
smaller than
the pixel.

The Usual Software Suspects

Before you start making Web graphics, perhaps you should spend a little time building your tool arsenal. Whether you're the weekend warrior type or the sun-tanned professional, someone's got the Web design tool for you. Keep in mind that several tools are available on the market for pushing pixels around, so I'll just list the usual suspects:

✔ Adobe Photoshop

`www.adobe.com/products/photoshop`

For creating, editing, and manipulating bitmaps, no other tool on the market holds a candle to Photoshop. The problem with Photoshop, however, is that learning to use it to its fullest is akin to learning to fly a jumbo jet! In addition to the years it may take to fully master Photoshop's power, it also comes with a steep price tag.

✔ Macromedia Fireworks

`www.macromedia.com/software/fireworks`

Fireworks empowers us non-techies to design Web graphics and make them interactive — complete with whiz-bang rollover buttons and drop-down menus. Fireworks is also much less expensive than Photoshop. The one downside to Fireworks is that its bitmap creation and manipulation abilities are not as robust as Photoshop's. Fortunately, however, you can import Photoshop files, add to them, and export Web-enabled graphics and code.

✔ Paint Shop Pro

`http://www.jasc.com/product.asp?pf_id=001`

Paint Shop Pro is a slightly cheaper alternative than Fireworks for creating bitmap and vector graphics and then optimizing them for Web delivery. Paint Shop Pro also enables you to add links and rollover buttons to your designs. The downside is that it works only on Windows. Because many professional Web graphic production teams use a mix of Mac and Windows platforms, Paint Shop Pro files are not easily passed from one team member to the next.

✔ Adobe Illustrator and Macromedia Freehand

`www.adobe.com/products/illustrator`

`www.macromedia.com/software/freehand`

These two programs create vector graphics that you can import into other programs like Photoshop, Fireworks, Flash, and LiveMotion to prepare them for the Web (export them as GIF and JPEG files, and then add interactivity like links and rollover buttons). In other words, although these programs are great for building complex vector graphics, they aren't used for preparing graphics for the Web.

✔ Macromedia Flash

`www.macromedia.com/software/flash`

Flash allows you to program interactive Web applications with its robust scripting language ActionScript, and design animations that leverage the tight file sizes and scalability of vector graphics. Flash files are output as .SWF files like the one shown in Figure 8-6, an animated Flash Christmas card from `www.juxtinteractive.com`. The downside to Flash, however, is that it requires an end user to have the proper Flash plug-in installed on their browser to view.

✔ Adobe LiveMotion

`www.adobe.com/products/livemotion`

LiveMotion enables you to create interactive, vector-based animations and output them in the standard Flash SWF format. Although LiveMotion allows you to create interactive Web graphics and animation, it doesn't have the tremendous scripting power that Flash has.

Figure 8-6:
This animation has a lot going on, but downloads quickly even over a 56K modem.

www.juxtinteractive.com

ON THE CD Free trials of Flash, Fireworks, Photoshop are included on the CD that accompanies this book.

Pixel-Pushing 101

After you know just enough to be dangerous, it's time to roll up your sleeves and design a common Web page element — a banner for the top of the page. Not only does this exercise allow you to get some practice with creating actual Web graphics — you also get to put on your visual and user interface design thinking cap.

Designing a Web page banner

Just as your company letterhead has a logo and address at the top, many Web sites also have a graphical banner located at the top of each page. Usually, this banner is placed only on the *subpages* (Web design lingo for every page except the home page). The home page usually gets a similar, yet special, design treatment. Such a banner does three useful things for your Web site:

- **Consistency.** The same banner at the top of every page mentally anchors visitors to your Web site. Because people surf quickly from one site to the next, it's your job to make sure your Web site doesn't blend into the next site. A banner placed consistently at the top of each page can be just the thing to visually differentiate your site from all the rest.

- **Branding.** A banner at the top of each page is the perfect place to put your company's name and logo — just in case people forget who's providing them with such a great Web site. A banner is also a great opportunity to visually express your company's *brand* — the catch-all term for your company's colors, attitude, style, and message.

- **Navigation.** To help users get around your Web site, a banner can provide a consistent set of links to the main sections — or at least to the home page.

Many Web sites use the company's logo on the top banner as a hidden link that "advanced users" can use to return to the home page. The truth is that most users don't think of the logo as a link. In my humble opinion, if you provide a link to the home page, don't be shy about it — design a real link called *Home*. Figure 8-7 shows how National Geographic's Web site provides a banner of links at the top of each page — including a separate link to the home page.

Creating a banner in Fireworks

Now it's your turn to create a banner. Don't expect a design masterpiece from yourself. Just think of this exercise as a good way to get your feet wet with Web design software. In the following steps, I walk you through the process of creating a Web banner using Fireworks. Photoshop and ImageReady offer similar capabilities, but the process is pretty simple in Fireworks.

1. **Launch Fireworks and choose File⇨New from the menu.**

2. **Set the dimensions.**

   In the New Document window that appears, set the file's dimensions to 600 pixels wide x 60 pixels high. The general rule for setting the dimensions of your Web banner: Think long and skinny. Leave the screen resolution at 72 dpi — the standard Web image resolution.

Link to home page   Link to site index

Figure 8-7:
The banner
at the top of
each page
contains a
pop-up
menu with
navigation
links to all
pages in
the site.

3. **Set the Canvas color.**

   For Canvas Color, click on the Custom option as shown in Figure 8-8. Then, click on the color swatch to the right to pick a new color.

4. **Click OK.**

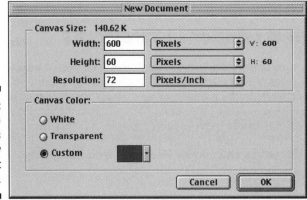

Figure 8-8:
The
Fireworks
New
Document
window.

5. Add some text.

Select the Text tool as shown in Figure 8-9 and click once in the upper-left corner of the document to begin typing. The Text Editor window appears. This window works just like a mini word processor. Simply type in the name of your company and then select the text and apply various font and color settings. When you are finished, click the OK button.

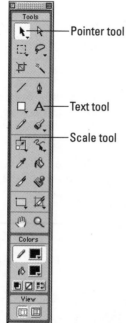

Pointer tool

Text tool

Scale tool

Figure 8-9:
The
Fireworks
toolbar.

6. Move the text.

After you click OK, your text appears in the document with a blue box around it, indicating that it is selected, as shown in Figure 8-10. To move it around, just click and drag with the Pointer tool.

Figure 8-10:
Selected
text can be
dragged
with the
Pointer tool.

7. **Add navigational elements.**

   Select the Text tool again and click in the middle of your document. In the Text Editor window, type three links, such as Home, Shop, and Services, and then apply font and color settings. Click the OK button.

8. **For extra credit, import your company logo.**

   If you're feeling really adventurous, you can import your company logo, or any other image, for that matter. Choose File⇨Import from the menu. In the Import window, locate your logo and click on the OK button. Your cursor now looks like a funny corner icon. To place your logo or image, click once on the document.

9. **Resize your logo to fit.**

   Select the Scale tool in the toolbar (refer to Figure 8-9). (When you slowly roll your mouse pointer over a tool in the toolbar, a pop-up label tells you which tool it is.) Handles appear around your image. Grab one of the corner handles, press and hold down Shift (to constrain proportions), and drag to scale up or down, as shown in Figure 8-11.

   After you've created the text object and the links, and after you've imported an image, Fireworks treats them as separate objects. To move them around on the page, choose the Pointer tool, and click on the object to move it, as shown in Figure 8-10.

Figure 8-11:
After you import images, you can resize them to fit using the Scale tool.

Just like in Illustrator or Freehand, you can change the *stacking* order of your objects. For example, if one object is behind another and you want it to be on top, select it with the Pointer tool and choose Modify⇨Arrange⇨Bring to Front from the menu.

Congratulations! You've just created your first official *programmer art* — the technical term for cheesy Web graphics. As you can see, you've only brushed the tip of the iceberg of what programs like Fireworks can do for you. Just imagine the level of cheese that you can achieve if you really put to your mind to it!

Why Fireworks?

Most of the banners that you see on the Web are interactive. They contain links, rollover buttons, or even drop-down menus like the National Geographic banner shown in Figure 8-7.

Fireworks is an ideal choice for creating Web banners because after you're finished building your graphics, it's easy to add links, rollover buttons, and even drop-down menus without needing to write any code. When you export your Fireworks file, you get not only the graphics, but also the HTML page that makes it all work.

Image Manipulation

Of course, not all Web graphics consist entirely of buttons, illustrations, and text. Invariably, your Web page will have a few photos sprinkled throughout the layout. So how do you get a photo from a camera into your computer? After you do that, how do you fix it up and resize it to fit your layout?

The first issue has been somewhat resolved by the recent proliferation of digital cameras. Now, even amateurs can take high-quality images and, with special software that comes with the camera, get the images into the computer. With regular cameras, the images must be scanned. Another route is to use *stock* photography and illustration: These are professional photos, already digitized, that you can purchase online with your credit card. Although nothing beats the convenience of stock images, you can't always get the image you want. For custom images, you need a good camera and a good photographer. Here's a list of a few good online sites for stock photography and imagery. They offer both royalty-free and licensed images (*royalty-free* means you pay one flat fee for the image and can use it for whatever purpose; *licensed* means you pay according to the extent of use you plan for the image):

- ✔ www.gettyone.com. This site is a good place to start because it's a compilation of multiple stock image companies.

- ✔ www.eyewire.com. This site offers a good mix of photography, photos of objects on plain backgrounds (like a tomato on a white background), illustrations, audio clips, and even video clips.

- ✔ www.tonystone.com. This site offers high-end — albeit expensive — images to give your project a little boost in style.

After you have an image in the computer, the next step is massaging it to suit your layout's needs. This entails everything from simple color adjustments and resizing to custom collage work when you need to combine imagery together. Bar none, the best software application for this type of image manipulation is Photoshop.

Direct from digital cameras

So many digital cameras are on the market that I don't even want to begin naming off my favorite brands; I could write a book on the subject of digital cameras alone. But I don't have to, because Julie Adair King already has — check out *Digital Photography For Dummies*, published by IDG Books. When shopping for a digital camera, however, here are a few things to keep in mind:

- ✔ **Image size and resolution**. When you buy a digital camera, make sure that the camera can take large photos. Most cameras offer a few different image size settings because the bigger the image size, the fewer photos you can fit into the camera's memory. Also, most cameras capture images at 72 dpi. That's okay if the camera is capturing a large image — say 1,000 x 1,000 pixels — because it can capture a lot of detail in that many pixels. This resolution is not okay if the image is small — say 500 x 500 pixels — because you won't get enough detail to work with. By capturing a larger image, you have more flexibility when you need to edit. Remember, it's always better to shrink bitmap images rather than blow them up. When you enlarge them, you distort and blur their quality.

- ✔ **Lighting**. Some of the less expensive digital cameras give you no control over lighting, whereas the more expensive cameras allow you to take pictures at night. Make sure that the camera you buy comes with a flash, or at least some other means to control lighting for indoor and outdoor situations.

- ✔ **Software**. After you take a digital photo, you need some sort of software to suck it out of the camera and get it onto your computer. Be sure that the software that comes with your digital camera works on your computer platform. Most software works on Windows, but if you're a Mac user, you need to double-check.

I should point out that software is becoming less of an issue. You can plug a lot of cameras directly into newer computers using a universal serial bus (USB) connection. This way, an icon representing your camera shows up on your desktop just like a floppy disk. You can double-click the camera icon to open a folder of images and copy them right to your computer.

Scanning images

If you are using a regular camera with good old-fashioned film, you must scan the prints, transparencies, or slides to get them into the computer. Because the Web is a relatively low-resolution environment (compared to the print world), you don't need to work with super high-resolution images. Remember that Web graphics should always be 72 dpi. The two primary options you have for scanning images for the Web are a *flatbed* scanner and a *drum* scanner.

A flatbed scanner, sometimes called a *desktop* scanner, is affordable enough to include in your home workstation. Flatbed scanners get their name from their big flat surfaces, which are sort of like a copier machine, where you place your photos to scan. A drum scanner, on the other hand, is a big fancy machine that — unless you did well with your Internet stocks — is something that only professional service joints own. Drum scanners yield extremely high quality that is ideal for print world, but overkill for scanning Web graphics. For Web graphics, all you need is an affordable desktop flatbed scanner.

For desktop scanners, always scan at roughly twice the resolution you need. For Web graphics that need to be 72 dpi, for example, scan the images at 150 dpi. This way you capture enough detail to make editing easier.

Using stock photography and illustration

You can find virtually any kind of photo or illustration that you need for a project at one of the many online stock photo companies. For instance, you can go to one of my favorites, www.gettyone.com, and search through thousands of images. If you are a registered user (it's free to register), you can download *comps* to work with and show clients. Comps are smaller editions of the real image that you can use in your designs. If the client likes the image, you can purchase it online.

Each stock image usually comes in a few different sizes and resolutions. The smaller the image, the less it costs. Fortunately in Web design, you only need the smallest image (and by *small* I mean 700 x 1000 pixels, which isn't that small). The price ranges according to the image. Generally, "royalty-free" images cost about $20.00 for a 72 dpi, 800 x 800 pixel image. Royalty-free images are cheaper than "licensed" images because you don't have to pay the photographer or the model each time you use the image. Licensed images are much more expensive, but they're generally more stylish.

The special sauce: Digital editing

More often than not, an image fresh out of the camera or off the Internet needs a little editing before it's ready for your Web page layout. For one reason, it's probably not the right size, and second, it may contain some imperfections or be in need of some embellishments.

The best tool on the market for editing bitmap images, as far as I'm concerned, is Adobe Photoshop. Photoshop offers extensive control over every aspect of your image. The problem, however, is that Photoshop is a very deep program. You may need a long time to figure out all of its power. In these next few steps, you scratch the surface of Photoshop's capabilities and learn some basic editing techniques, such as cropping, adjusting the exposure, resizing, and adding a soft, feathered edge.

1. **Launch Photoshop.**

   If you're using the trial version on this book's CD, see the instructions in the appendix on how to use the CD.

2. **Choose File➪Open.**

   Locate a photograph to work with. Choose a photo that needs cropping and a little work on the exposure.

3. **Crop the image.**

   Choose the Marquee tool in the toolbar and draw a box around the portion of the image that you want to keep, as shown in Figure 8-12. If you mess up, you can click once outside the selected area and start again. When you're satisfied with the selection, choose Image➪Crop from the menu.

Marquee tool

Figure 8-12:
Use the
Marquee
tool to draw
a selection
around the
part you
want to
keep.

4. **Adjust the contrast.**

   To enhance the contrast of this photo, choose Image➪Adjust➪Levels. The Levels interface, as shown in Figure 8-13, shows the balance of lights and darks in your image. To increase the dark areas, drag the left triangle toward the center. To increase the light areas, drag the right triangle toward the center. Your image updates as you drag the sliders, so you can see the effects of your actions.

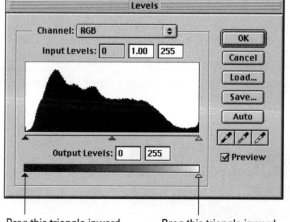

Figure 8-13:
The Levels interface allows you to adjust the contrast of your image.

Drag this triangle inward to increase dark areas.

Drag this triangle inward to increase light areas.

5. **Adjust the color.**

You can use one of several tools in Photoshop to adjust the color balance of an image. For this exercise, I use the Hue/Saturation tool to make the image monotone. Choose Image⇨Adjust⇨Hue/Saturation from the menu. The Hue/Saturation window appears, as shown in Figure 8-14. To make an image monotone, check the Colorize option in the lower right corner. The image becomes several shades of one color, such as purple, but you can change the color scheme by moving the Hue slider.

Hue slider

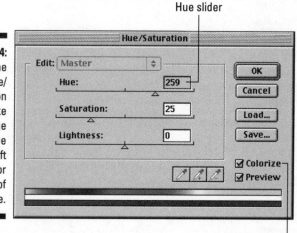

Figure 8-14:
Use the Hue/ Saturation tool to make an image monotone and to shift the color scheme of an image.

Colorize checkbox

6. **Resize the image.**

   To resize the image, first choose Select⇨All from the menu and then choose Edit⇨Free Transform. Handles appear at the corner of the image. Press and hold down Shift (to retain proportions) and drag one of the corner handles inward to shrink the image, as shown in Figure 8-15. When you reach the size you want, press Enter to shrink the image, and then exit the Free Transform tool.

Figure 8-15:
Use the Free
Transform
tool to scale
or rotate an
image.

   By the way, you can also use the Free Transform tool to rotate your image. If you place your cursor just outside the corner handle, you see a curved two-way arrow. Click and drag to rotate.

7. **Add a feathered edge.**

   To turn this image into an oval shape with a soft feathered edge, use the Elliptical Marquee tool. The Elliptical Marquee tool is hidden behind the square Marquee tool in the toolbar. To access it, click and hold on the square Marquee tool, and then select the Elliptical Marquee tool from the pop-up menu that appears.

   Start drawing an oval-shaped selection in the middle of the image. Hold down Alt or the Option key to make sure that the selection grows outward from the middle. After you draw the oval selection, you can reposition it to make sure that it encompasses the correct part of your image. Simply click anywhere inside the selection to move it.

   To soften the edges, choose Select⇨Feather from the menu. The Feather Selection dialog box appears, as shown in Figure 8-16. Enter a Feather radius of 10 pixels and click OK. When you click OK, you won't notice any change in your selection, but believe me, it's feathered.

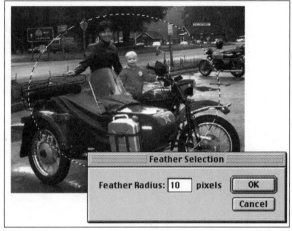

Figure 8-16:
Use the Elliptical Marquee tool to draw an oval-shaped selection over your image.

8. Lift the image onto its own layer.

To see the effects of your feathered edge, lift the image onto its own transparent layer. While the feathered selection is still active, press ⌘+J or Ctrl+J, or choose Layer⇨New⇨Layer Via Copy from the menu. In the Layers palette, you now have two layers (Layer 1 and Background), as shown in Figure 8-17. (If you don't see the Layers palette open, choose Show Layers from the Window menu.)

Hide your original background layer by clicking once on the Eye icon in the Layers palette. Now you can see the effects of your feathered edge.

Eyeball icon

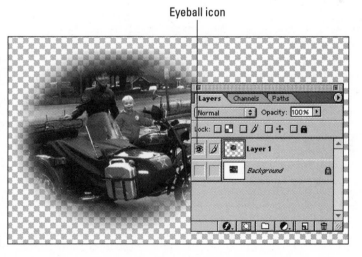

Figure 8-17:
After you lift your feathered image onto its own layer, turn off the background layer to see it.

9. Add the finishing touches.

To polish up this image, replace the image in the Background layer with a solid color and crop it one more time. In the Layers palette, click on the Background layer to make it active, as shown in Figure 8-18.

Figure 8-18:
To replace
the original
background
image with
a solid color,
you must
first select
the layer in
the Layers
palette.

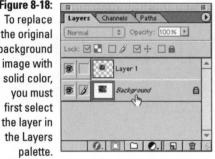

Choose a new foreground color by clicking once on the top-most color swatch in the toolbar (you see two swatches stacked on top of each other — the top one is for selecting the foreground color, and the bottom one is for selecting the background color). When the Color Picker window opens, choose a new color and click OK. To fill the Background layer with your new color, choose Edit⇨Fill from the menu. As shown in Figure 8-19, make sure that the Fill dialog box is set to use the Foreground color and click OK. Your background now fills with the new color.

Figure 8-19:
To fill the
Background
layer, use
the Fill
command in
the Edit
menu.

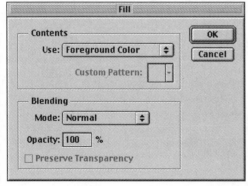

Finally, to crop your image, as you did in Step 3, select the square Marquee tool in the toolbar and draw a selection around the area that you want to keep. Then, choose Image⇨Crop from the menu. Voilà! You now have an image like Figure 8-20 ready to save for your Web site.

Figure 8-20: The final image — cropped and ready to save for the Web.

Chapter 9

Presenting Your Design Masterpiece

· ·

· ·

After a lot of planning, assembling a site map, and brushing up on a host of Web graphic design issues (everything from designing "above the fold line" to using type and color effectively), the next step is to put everything that you find out to good use. Before you can begin any graphic or HTML production on a Web site, you must first prepare a variety of design options and present them to the client for approval.

The designs should be mock-ups of a few finished Web pages so a client can get an idea of what the final site may look like. From these mock-ups, a client can choose the final direction of the site. In this chapter, I show you how to prepare an online presentation so clients can see how your designs look in a Web browser. I also show you how to print your designs and mount them on boards. Together, an online and a printed presentation helps clients to get a better understanding of your design ideas, which enables them to better choose a direction for their site. I also give you tips for pitching your work to the client and guiding them toward the design solution that you think is best.

Developing Design Directions

To help the clients visualize the final look and feel of the site, you should assemble a set of three to five different graphic design directions for them to choose from. A *design direction* is a complete digital graphical mock-up of a Web page — including all the HTML components, such as forms, text, and buttons. The idea is to visually show what the final page will look like without building the actual page in HTML. You should even go so far as to save the mock-up as one giant GIF file and show it in the browser window. As the mock-up for www.air.go.com in Figure 9-1 shows, this technique makes the page look even more real.

Each design direction that you present should include a set of two pages — the home page and one subpage. This way, the client can see how the proposed graphic treatment works throughout the site. The designs should also show how the navigation works in the site. After you round up a few different design directions that show a few pages each, you can organize them into a polished presentation.

Getting design ideas

The big question: Where do you start? Staring at a blank white screen can be quite intimidating. The knowledge that you've got to produce not just one but as many as three or more different designs is sure to conjure up the evil "creative block" that so often plagues writers. To ward off the block and start the creative juices flowing, I often find it helpful to not look inward but outward for ideas. Here's a list of three places to look:

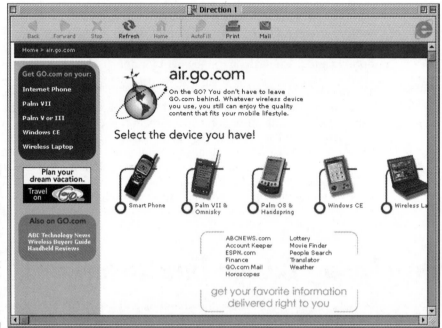

Figure 9-1:
If you make your design directions look real, the client can better choose a design.

✔ **Ask the client.** One of the simplest ways to find inspiration is to ask the client for ideas. To better understand the desires and expectations of your client, ask your clients to provide you with a list of Web sites that they like (and sites that they don't like) and why. This helps shape your creative thinking toward something that the client will ultimately appreciate.

✔ **Look online.** Another source of inspiration is to look online at various award-winning Web sites. In fact, always be on the lookout for interesting Web sites and bookmark them for future reference.

A few sites online hand out awards for various kinds of Web sites. These sites are one-stop idea shops that showcase different kinds of sites on a continual basis. As shown in Figure 9-2, one of my favorites is Communication Art's Web site at `www.commarts.com`. This site hosts an annual interactive design competition covering a number of categories from e-commerce to self-promotion. Plus, they maintain an archive of past year's winners for a truly expansive look at a variety of excellent Web site examples.

✔ **Look at the client's existing materials.** Finally, an obvious and crucial place to look for inspiration is the client's current set of creative material. Most companies probably have a number of things from which you can base your designs. Adding design elements, such as the company's products and packaging design, marketing brochures, office interiors, and logo, are great themes to incorporate into your design directions.

Figure 9-2:
Online design competitions are a great place to find a lot of ideas in one convenient location.

Ideally, you shouldn't be the only one developing all three or more of the design directions for a client. After you do the first design, regrouping and coming up with two more unique designs is very difficult. The best scenario is to delegate one set of design directions to a different designer. This way, you get a wide variety of solutions that don't just look like variations of the same design.

If you are a one-man show and can't afford to have multiple designers each working on a different design, you have to flex some creative muscle to come up with all the designs yourself, but you can do it. One idea is to think of different themes to explore. For instance, you can explore a colorful geometric theme in one design and a modern, monotone photographic theme in another. By planning a few different themes, you can stay focused and find unique solutions for each design.

Integrating the venerable "brand"

When designing your mock-ups, you must pay careful attention to how you integrate the client's branding. For those of you new to design, the *brand* is not just a company's logo and colors. It's also a company's image — the way they want a customer to perceive them. For instance, Starbucks is not just a place to buy coffee — it's an experience. It's a place for yuppity types to commingle and enjoy one another's company while sipping the world's best — or supposed best — coffee.

The designs you produce must exude the company's image and attitude through the colors, fonts, and imagery that you choose. The easiest way to guide your design choices while you work is to always keep the company's target customer in mind. For example, if you were to design a site for Starbucks, think about what kind of design would appeal to the kind of folks who call coffee "lattes" and "frappacinos."

Another way to approach your designs is to look at the client's other visual incarnations. In most cases, the Web site should look and feel like an extension of the current product designs, storefronts, packaging, brochures, and annual reports so that all visual communications work together.

In some ways, looking at the company's other creative materials makes your job a bit easier, but it can also limit your range of creativity. A good strategy is to make just one of your design directions feel very similar to the current creative line-up. Take a little more creative license with the remaining design directions. This way, you set the client at ease by showing them something that feels familiar, and then you excite them with more possibilities in the more dramatic examples.

Designing treatments for the home and subpage

As I stated earlier in this section, each design direction should contain two pages: the home page and one subpage. The home page is important to show because it is the first page visitors see. The subpage is important to include because it shows how the design themes on the home page carry through to the lower level pages. The subpage also shows how users will navigate throughout the site — an important detail for enabling the client to make an informed decision.

To build each mock-up, I like to start in a Web graphics program, such as Fireworks or Photoshop, and create a new file that is the size of the final Web page. A good dimension to choose is 750 x 500 pixels — the viewable area of most browsers. Also, set the background color to the color that you expect to use in the final Web page. Keep in mind that each design direction may have a different background color. This simple change can make a big difference in the overall feel of the direction.

Your mock-up should look as real as possible — even showing graphical renditions of the HTML components. You're better off mocking up the design in a graphics program rather than building it as a true HTML page because it's much faster to lay out the design graphically. At this point, your focus is on generating as many design ideas as possible — not spending time implementing a Web page that the client may not choose.

To graphically create HTML parts that look real, I like to use Web authoring software, such as Dreamweaver or GoLive, to quickly make buttons and fields with the right labels and sizes. Because I'm just making button elements and not laying out an entire page, the process is fast. After I build the HTML parts I need, I take a screen capture of them. Then, it's a simple matter of pasting the screenshots into my mock-up. Here's how you do it:

1. **Launch Dreamweaver.**

   Dreamweaver automatically opens with a new, blank document ready to go. If it doesn't, for whatever reason, choose File⇨New from the menu to start a new Web page document. (The CD included with this book contains a free trial of Macromedia Dreamweaver.)

2. **Set the background color.**

   If your Web page mock-up uses a background color other than white, you should set Dreamweaver's background to match. To change the background color, choose Modify⇨Page Properties. In the dialog box that appears, click the color swatch next to Background and choose a new color from the pop-up palette, as shown in Figure 9-3. For this exercise, I keep it simple and use the default white background color.

Click this swatch to set background color.

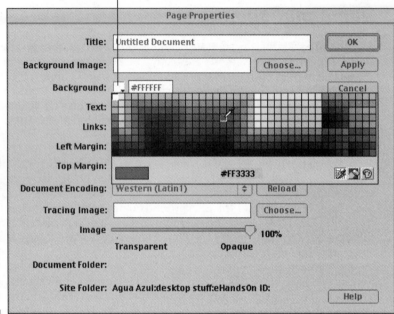

Figure 9-3:
You should
set Dream-
weaver's
background
color to
match your
layout's
color.

3. **Insert a text field.** On the main toolbar, change from the Common toolset to the Forms toolset by using the drop-down menu at the top of toolbar (you see a little arrow icon to access the menu), as shown in Figure 9-4. From the Forms toolbar, click once on the Text Field icon to insert a field in your page. In the document, you see a new field appear.

Insert Button icon

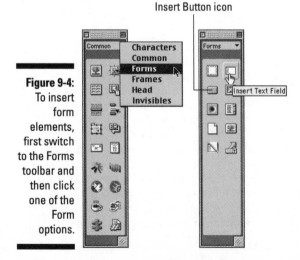

Figure 9-4:
To insert
form
elements,
first switch
to the Forms
toolbar and
then click
one of the
Form
options.

4. **Insert a new form element.** Building a Web page in Dreamweaver is a lot like using a word processing tool. In the main document window, click once after the text field. You now see a blinking cursor. Press Enter to start a new line where you can add a new form element.

Back in the Forms toolbar, click the Insert Button icon. In your document, a new button appears with the default Submit text, as shown in Figure 9-5.

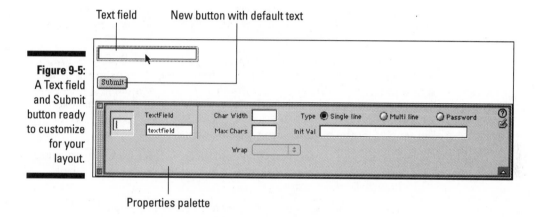

Figure 9-5:
A Text field and Submit button ready to customize for your layout.

5. **Customize the form graphics.** By default, the Properties palette should be open. This is the long skinny palette shown in Figure 9-5 that allows you to adjust each of the elements in your document. If you do not see it, you can access it by choosing Window⇨Properties.

In the document, click on the text field to select it. In the Properties palette, type **10** next to Char Width and press Enter to shrink the size of the field to accommodate just ten letters and numbers. By the way, the Properties palette will also let you turn this text field into a longer scrolling multi-line field. To do so, choose the Multi line option.

Next, select the Submit button in your document. In the Properties palette, change the text in the Label box from Submit to Sign In or some other text appropriate for your layout, as shown in Figure 9-6.

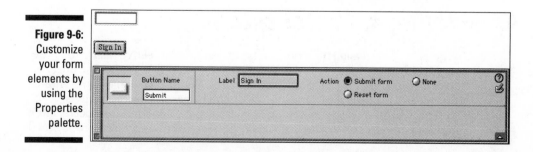

Figure 9-6:
Customize your form elements by using the Properties palette.

6. **Take a screenshot.** In your document, click once to the right of your new Sign In button and then press the Enter key. This will deselect the form elements so that they don't have any funny selection lines around them.

   To take a screenshot, Mac users can use the ⌘+Shift+4 keyboard combination. After you do, the cursor will turn into crosshairs. Click and drag a box around the form elements to take their picture. When you let go of the mouse button, you hear a camera shutter sound. The screenshot will be on your hard drive and named "Picture 1."

   Windows users can use the Alt+Print Scrn keyboard combination. This key combination takes a picture of the screen and stores it in the clipboard (in memory).

7. **Incorporate the screenshot in your Web page layout.** Open any graphics program, such as Fireworks, Paint Shop Pro, or Photoshop, and start a new file by choosing File⇨New from the menu. (In most graphics programs, a dialog box appears with the new file's options. For this exercise, create a file that is 600 x 400 pixels and 72 ppi.) To integrate the screenshot of the buttons into your new file:

   • **Mac users** choose File⇨Open and look for "Picture 1" on your hard drive (screenshots are always named sequentially as Picture 1, Picture 2, and so on).

   • **Windows users** have the screenshot stored in the clipboard. Simply choose Edit⇨Paste to place the screenshot in your layout. The Windows clipboard stores only one image at a time, so you must switch back and forth between the Web authoring software and the Web graphics software, capturing a screenshot and then pasting it.

After you open or paste the form graphic into your mock-up, sometimes you need to get rid of the white or colored background around the form. Both Fireworks and Photoshop have a Magic Wand tool that you can use to select and delete the background color. To use it in either program, first double-click it in the toolbar to open the Tool Options palette (Windows users can find the Options Window on the top right of the screen). In the Tool Options palette, set its Tolerance to 0 and turn off anti-aliasing. Then, simply click the unwanted background color around the form to select it and press the Delete or Backspace key to erase it.

Assembling a Presentation

With all of your design directions in hand, your next creative task is to figure out the best way to present them to the client. I find that the best strategy is to develop both an online and an offline presentation. The online presentation gives the client the chance to see, in the browser, how the various designs will look on the computer. Plus, if the page contains any special interactive features, such as Flash movies or rollover buttons, you can create a somewhat functional prototype or storyboard to demonstrate the functionality. The offline presentation is a series of printed pages, mounted on nice boards for a polished effect. The printed portion of your presentation allows the client to quickly compare different designs side by side. Overall, the online/offline combination is a powerful one-two punch presentation.

Presenting your designs online

The best way to showcase all of the design directions online is to build a special project Web site just for the client. Ideally, this Web site is password-protected so no one but you and the client can enter, but if you're limited on resources, a *hidden Web address* should suffice. A hidden Web address is one so arcane that only you and the client could ever find it without knowing the direct path. An address like `www.yourcompany.com/workinprogress/client/round1` should do the trick.

The project Web site is a design repository for everything from the approved site map to the design directions. As you go, you'll find that you want to present more than one round of design directions, so the project site is also a good place to store past rounds so that a client can see the design's evolution.

Organize a project index page that provides links to the pages of each design direction. Figure 9-7 shows one such page created by David Solhaug of `www.sgrafik.com`. In addition, I find it useful to give a descriptive name to each design direction, such as "Direction 1: colorful, geometric," just to make it easier to refer to them. I also like to provide a short paragraph that explains the logic and the benefits of each direction. Because this is the client's project site, they will refer back to it on their own and share the address with co-workers. Without any guidance from you, they may not understand what they are looking at.

The online presentation not only allows you to efficiently organize all of the design directions in one convenient location, making it easy for a client to see all the directions, but also allows you a chance to include your own branding for that extra professional touch.

Constructing working and non-working prototypes

For the most part, you don't need to provide working HTML prototypes. Simple GIF images should suffice to give a client a good idea of how the site will function. You don't want to invest too much time making a working prototype at this point because it's more important to spend energy on developing different ideas rather than implementing just one idea. If you need to show how a complex interaction will work, you may consider showing it in a simple storyboard rather than spending the extra time to make it really work.

In some cases, it may be worthwhile to make a small portion of the page work. In such cases, you can fake it by using HTML and various technologies that are easier to implement than the real deal. For example, you may find that in the bidding stage of a project, you may have to invest time in a semi-working, animated presentation simply for the "wow" factor, to help win the project in the first place.

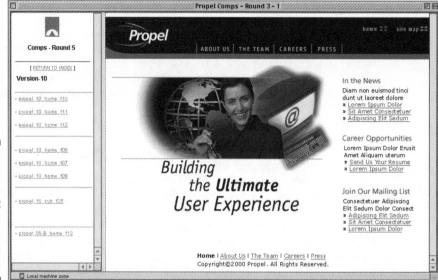

Figure 9-7:
This site offers the client access to all current and past design directions.

Creating Sizzling Printed Presentations

In addition to an online presentation, you should definitely have a color printed presentation — if only for backup purposes. Just imagine not having access to the Internet during your client meeting. Aside from having a good backup, it's always a good idea to surround the customer with visuals. For one thing, unless you have access to an oversized monitor or projection system, it's hard to have the same impact with a wimpy little monitor when presenting to even a small group of people. Besides, on the computer screen, the client can see only one screen at a time. Comparing two design options side by side is impossible unless you have printed copies.

Creating black and white copies of the designs for each client present at the meeting is also a good idea. This way, they can take notes on each design during the presentation. Along with the black and white prints, include a copy of the site map so clients can refer to it in the meeting.

In living color: Printing your mock-ups

These days, printing beautiful photographic-quality prints of your mock-ups is a simple and affordable process. The price of desktop color printers has come down remarkably in the last few years while the quality has increased ten-fold. For about $300, you can buy a great desktop color inkjet printer that will give you more than enough quality.

When printing your mock-ups for a presentation, always print at the actual size and keep the resolution at 72 dpi. If you alter the resolution, shrink, or enlarge your mock-ups, you run the risk of making them appear blurred in the printout or too small for presentation purposes. In addition, always print on standard 8½-x-11-inch paper in the landscape orientation, as shown in Figure 9-8. Most Web page designs are wider than they are tall due to the fold line. Thus, they look better in the wider orientation.

Figure 9-8: Most Web pages look better when printed in the landscape orientation.

Always use the more expensive photo grade glossy paper for your prints. If the paper isn't glossy, the ink soaks into the paper too much. When this happens, you can see the row lines of the ink dots — cheapening the effect of your presentation. Also, matte paper has a tendency to warp and curl when saturated with a lot of ink — an effect sure to raise your client's eyebrows.

Mounting your work on boards

Like a flimsy handshake or a wilting business card, your nicely colored prints just won't have maximum impact unless you mount them on sturdy boards. The standard in the Web design industry is to use black boards that are black all the way through. Don't use black-colored boards that have white interiors shining through along the cut edges. These have a tendency to fade even before you get to the presentation.

I like to use either black foam core or black Letramax brand boards. These two types of board, available at any art store, have ultra black finishes that don't detract from your designs. As for the thickness of the boards, the only thing that really matters is that the boards don't sag when you prop them up for display. Again, you must avoid the wilt factor! In the next section, I give you a few tips for mounting your prints on boards.

Adhesive schmesive

You may think that I'm being a bit retentive, but the sticky stuff that you choose to mount your boards makes a big difference, not only in the final look but also in the flexibility you have for remounting. Rule number one: Never use glue! After you use glue, the boards and the print are ruined — you can never separate them from one another. In addition, the drops of glue leave discernible lumps under your print.

The best adhesives to use are either Spray Mount or a lightly adhesive, ultra-thin, double-sided tape. These allow you to remove your prints for remounting (in case you mess up) or to reuse the boards later. Spray Mount comes in an aerosol spray can and is pretty easy to use. Always use it in a well-ventilated area and use it *sparingly*.

If you use Spray Mount, don't spray the board! The spray goes everywhere and makes everything sticky. Instead, spray your print face-down on an over-sized sheet of paper. Hold the can one to two feet away and make *one* pass. Let it dry for a minute or two and then mount the print to your board. If you use double-sided tape, place one strip at the top and one at the bottom of your print and then mount it to the board.

Consistency

One of the most important details in your presentation is to make sure everything is consistent. Use the same boards, use the same glossy paper, and make sure everything is cut to the same size! You don't want one board to be 11 x 14 while the rest are 14 x 17. Consistency ensures that the focus is on the designs and not the irregularities in the presentation. Here are two more tips to follow when preparing your printed presentation:

  ✔ **Leave breathing space around each image.** When you print your mock-ups on 8½-x-11-inch glossy paper, you may be tempted to trim away the white borders, leaving just the printed design. I find, however, that trimming your designs so tightly is like cutting your fingernails too close. I recommend leaving a little breathing room around your images. Either leave the prints centered on the 8½ x 11 page, or trim them all to the same size with at least a one-inch border all around.

✔ **Cut the boards to a manageable size.** Aside from cutting all the boards to the same size, make sure they are neither too big nor too small for the prints. If your prints are 8½ x 11, a good size for the boards is 11 x 14. The largest you should go is about 14 x 17. Any larger than that might require a fork lift to get the presentation in and out of the client's office and dwarf the people in the room — making it the "land of the little clients."

Presenting to Clients

This is the big moment: You worked long and hard developing a suite of design directions and assembled them into a stellar online and printed presentation. Now, all that's left is to sell the client on your ideas and remain professional, confident, and composed during the feedback. There's no special sauce to successfully pitching a client (other than a good cup of coffee), but there are certain behavioral guidelines that I can offer:

✔ **Dress the part.** On presentation day, make a point to dress appropriately. Even if you are presenting to a bunch of engineers in jeans and tennis shoes, you look more professional if you have some style (in other words, brush your hair and take a shower).

✔ **Be the discussion moderator.** Lead the show by presenting each design direction objectively as if you weren't the designer. Openly discuss your own professional opinions about what works and what doesn't about each direction and why. Ask for the client's opinion and be genuinely open to their suggestions and concerns.

✔ **Don't be "married" to your work.** Although you may have a favorite design, don't be defensive about any one design. You must be the client's champion and help them pick a design that works for them. The best way to sway clients toward your favorite design is talk objectively about the design's benefits. If the client expresses objections about the design, don't take it personally. Either concede and acknowledge their point, or find a logical counterpoint for them to consider.

✔ **Be confident; never berate your own work.** Always remember that design is a subjective topic, and no one will ever like the same things. But don't anticipate rejection by undermining your own work. If it's good enough to show, it's good enough to stand by.

Clients are suckers for the "ugly duckling"

You can count on at least one thing during a presentation: The client will pick the ugliest design in the group. A word to the wise, therefore, is to be careful about which design directions you decide to include in the presentation. Make sure that you can live with any of the ideas a client may pick.

Another thing to remember is that some clients have a knack for taking things too literally. If they see something they don't like or that doesn't make sense on a design, they reject the entire design. For example, if they see an ugly photograph that's just a stand-in for a future photo, they may dismiss the entire design. The same holds true for headlines and dummy text. If the headline doesn't make sense, they may think it's the design's fault. Go figure! The solution is to make everything look and read as real as possible.

Here we go again

More often than not, your designs won't hit the nail on the head the first time around. Be prepared for the client to like certain aspects of each design and ask you to do another round that combines the various elements into one new design. I call this the "Frankenstein" design round.

This is actually a healthy process, believe it or not, because you're still the designer and can control how the various aspects are combined into one. Plus, at the end of this round, you should be that much closer to something the client loves.

The worst scenario, however, is to let the client try their hand at assembling the Frankenstein round themselves. This can truly result in a monster of unbridled proportions. When the client gets their hands on it, their heart and their ego get involved too. The resulting design is likely to be a horrific mess that needs a lot of help. Unlike you, with your professional distance, a client might not take kindly to honest criticism, and there you are, stuck with their mess.

Chapter 10

Polishing Pixels to Perfection: Graphic Production

In This Chapter

▶ Knowing when to use the GIFs and JPEGs

▶ Keeping your page lean

▶ Using background tiles in your Web page

▶ Streamlining the graphic production process

*A*fter the client approves the initial design direction, the bulk of your Web design time is spent sitting glued to the monitor pushing pixels around with the mouse, which sometimes feels like you're drawing with a bar of soap. Needless to say, graphic production takes up the lion's share of time spent in Web design and is an art form — and a tedium — in and of itself.

The object of Web graphic production is to maximize the quality of the graphic while minimizing its download time — two goals that are diametric opposites. The higher the quality, the larger the file size, and thus, the slower the download. In this chapter, you learn to get the most out of your graphics by knowing which file formats to choose, and how to maximize download performance by reusing the same graphics on every page. You also learn how to slice images into sections that you can save with different file formats to maximize quality, how to prepare images to match the background color or tile of a Web page, the significance of "aliased" and "anti-aliased" graphics, and how to prepare transparent graphics.

To streamline the production process, you should design templates for each different kind of graphical element — from navigation banners and headings to buttons and images. This way, you can delegate the production work to a whole team while ensuring a consistent look and feel throughout the site. In this chapter, you learn the ins and outs of Web graphic production so you can be polishing pixels to perfection in no time.

GIF and JPEG Image Compression

The two most common graphic file formats on the Web, GIF and JPEG, were designed to compress an image's file size as much as possible. (By file size, I mean the number of kilobytes it occupies after you save it.) These two file formats use algorithms (mathematical formulas) to figure out the best way to save the image using the least amount of disk space — a process called "compression."

GIF uses an *RLE (Run Length Encoding)* compression scheme that looks across each horizontal row of pixels and records changes in pixel color by replacing areas of same-colored pixels with a short code, thereby reducing file size. If your image has large areas of solid color (like a cartoon, for example), it will compress better than a photograph with subtle tones. For

this reason, use GIF for solid-colored images, but not photos. GIF does not alter the actual pixels in an image — when uncompressed, the pixels can be restored exactly as they were before compression. For this reason, it's considered a *lossless* format.

The JPEG compression algorithm, on the other hand, works by modifying and averaging the color data of small blocks within the image. This method degrades the quality of an image and introduces noise called *artifacts*. JPEG, therefore, is considered a *lossy* format. The artifacts aren't as noticable in photographs as they are in flat-colored graphics such as graphic text and illustrations. For this reason, JPEG works great for photos, but not so well for flat-colored graphics.

Fun with File Formats

Although you can choose from a few different kinds of Web graphic formats, for the most part, you'll be using the GIF or JPEG format for your images. Which one you choose depends entirely upon the type of image that you're dealing with. There's no big secret to knowing when to use each format — you just need to know what to look for in your image. By choosing the right format for the job, you can preserve an image's quality and drastically cut down on file size, thereby improving its download time.

When to use GIF

The *Graphics Interchange Format* (GIF) is one of the older file formats on the Web. GIF has evolved over the years to include a number of features that make it a handy file format for a lot of different types of graphics — including animation.

GIF is best suited for graphics that have non-photographic elements in them, such as text and flat-colored graphical areas. This is because GIF is a *lossless* compression format (see sidebar). Unlike the *Joint Photographers Experts Group* format (JPEG), GIF doesn't corrode the quality of your images.

Figure 10-1 shows what text looks like when it's saved in GIF versus JPEG format. Zoomed in, the image is crisp and lossless — no detail has been lost, even though I reduced the palette to only six colors, making the image 2K. The example on the right has been saved in JPEG format at 50% quality, making it 4K — double the size and half the quality. Notice the severe amount of degradation in and around the text. This sort of degradation is less noticeable in photographs, which is why the JPEG format works so well for photographic images.

Figure 10-1:
The quality
of an image
saved in GIF
compared
to a JPEG.

The GIF format leaves crisp edges.

What's up with the cheese on this JPEG image?

The original file

Some images are fairly cut and dry. The original image in Figure 10-1 contains only flat-colored areas and text; it's a no-brainer to choose GIF. A problem arises, however, when a graphic contains text, flat-colored areas, *and* photographs. Which should you choose: GIF or JPEG? You can answer that question in two ways:

✔ If a graphic contains a mix of photographical and flat-colored art, use GIF with an *adaptive palette*. The adaptive palette chooses the best colors for an image. (See Chapter 7 for more infomation on the adaptive palette.) This way, you can retain the quality and readability of the text and graphics areas while still getting the best color fidelity for the photograph. The caveat, of course, is that in order to get the best quality, you need to use a lot of colors in the palette, which increases the file size.

WEB SPEAK

✔ The other solution is to chop, or *slice* as the industry likes to say, the graphic into pieces, as shown in Figure 10-2. This way, you can save the text and graphics portion as a GIF with few colors in the palette, and save the image portion as a JPEG.

Text

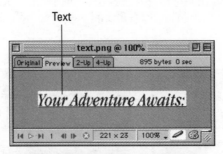

Figure 10-2:
By slicing a
graphic in
two, you
can save
each portion
individually.

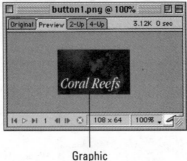

Graphic

GIF transparency

Another feature of GIF that makes it an interesting choice is its ability to make a color transparent. This feature comes in handy when you want to place an image on top of a wild pattern, such as a background tile. By making the background color around your image transparent, the image appears to float on top of the background pattern. If you don't make the background color transparent, you end up with a big block sitting on top of the pattern in your Web page.

REMEMBER

When you create a graphic, it *always* has rectangular dimensions. During the creative process, you can choose a background color upon which to build your graphic. When you export the graphic as a GIF, the background color that you chose goes with it. If you don't choose a background color or work on a transparent layer in Photoshop or Fireworks, the background defaults to white when you export. Either way, you end up with a file that has rectangular dimensions — the image sitting on a white or colored rectangular background, as shown in Figure 10-3.

Photoshop's transparency works only in Photoshop.

Figure 10-3:
The trans-
parency in
this case
is native
only to
Photoshop.

After you export, the background defaults to white.

The only way to get rid of this background is to make it transparent. When
you export a graphic as a GIF, you have the option to choose a single color as
the transparent color. If you choose the background color surrounding your
image as the transparent color, your image remains visible and appears to
float on top of the patterned background tile of the Web page, as shown in
Figure 10-4.

Figure 10-4:
If you
make the
background
transparent,
the image
floats on a
patterned
page.

Before you get too excited about the transparency feature, however, you need to be aware of a few "gotchas":

WARNING!

✔ When you designate a color as transparent, make sure the color isn't part of your image. Otherwise, your image can end up looking like Swiss cheese. For example, if you build your graphic on top of a white background and choose white as the transparent color, *all* white areas become transparent. Imagine the whites of people's eyes becoming transparent! Take a look at the ghostly image in Figure 10-5.

Figure 10-5: Parts of this image vanish because they are the same color as the background.

✔ If you want to use a patterned background tile in your Web page, you must use transparent GIFs in order to achieve the floating effect. Don't think you can simply build your graphic on top of a copy of the pattern and hope that it matches up with the pattern on your page — it won't. Each browser begins the tiled pattern in a different spot, so you never know where the pattern will fall on the page. You end up with an obvious misalignment of patterns, as illustrated in Figure 10-6.

Figure 10-6: Matching up a background tile with the pattern in an image is nearly impossible.

✔ The transparency feature comes in handy — even if you aren't using a background pattern in your Web page. If you are using a solid background color in your Web page, always build your graphics on a matching background color. Then, when you export, *make that color transparent!*

Although this technique sounds silly, it actually prevents a very common problem. Remember that different monitors have different bit depths and display even Web-safe colors a little differently. Even if the block of color surrounding your graphic matches the background color of the Web page, you can see a slight difference on some monitors, as shown in Figure 10-7. Without using transparency, some people can see the subtle outline of the square shape of your image.

Background of graphic

Figure 10-7:
Some monitors display background colors and Web page colors differently.

Background of Web page

GIF animation

Not only is GIF a great all-around format for saving Web graphics with transparency, it's also great for building simple flip book animations.

To create an animated GIF, create a series of individual GIF files that are all the same size and then string them together. The easiest way to do this is to use a Web graphics program such as Fireworks or ImageReady. The individual graphics are all saved together in one animated GIF file. You even have control over the timing (how long each GIF appears before flipping to the next one). You can make the animation play continuously in a loop, or you can specify a certain number of loops — from just one time through, to five or so repeats.

Another drawback to GIF animations is that you can't use a lot of frames. Because each frame is a separate GIF image, a lot of frames add up to a beefy file that takes forever to download. With fewer frames, the animation downloads and plays faster, but the action looks choppy. GIF animations work best for cycling messages, but not for complicated creations like animated characters, which must have a lot of frames to play smoothly. For that kind of animation, a program like Macromedia Flash or Adobe LiveMotion yields better results.

Take a look at the animated GIF banner in Figure 10-8. The animation has only four frames that cycle through a few different messages. The whole thing is just 10K — an ideal file size for a banner ad. Also notice that the graphics use solid-colored areas and text, making it possible to use just six colors for the whole enchilada.

Figure 10-8:
This
animated
GIF banner
has just four
frames that
cycle
through
different
messages.

Dithering: Pixel pointillism

You can't save an image as a GIF until you reduce its palette of millions of colors down to 256 or fewer colors. (The 256-color limit is a limitation of the GIF format. For more information, see Chapter 7.) When you do this, the image becomes *dithered*.

Dithering is the process of placing two or more colors in close proximity to visually create a missing color. For example, if you want to draw a picture of an orange, but you have only red and yellow markers, you have to do some creative pointillism to simulate the missing orange color. The same thing happens when you remove millions of colors from your image. The limited palette of 256 colors must work in concert to simulate the missing millions of colors.

Although dithering does degrade the quality of your images, you can compensate somewhat by using an adaptive palette when you convert your image. An adaptive palette chooses the best colors for the image. This helps to keep the dithering to a minimum. When the image is reduced to 256 or fewer colors, you are free to export the image as a GIF.

When to use JPEGs

The JPEG format was specifically designed to compress photographs for Web delivery. Although GIF is limited to images with 256 or fewer colors, the JPEG format works only for 24-bit images that can contain millions of colors — ideal for the gradients and subtle blends common in photographs.

Images that are saved as JPEGs don't dither because the image is free to use a ton of colors. When you save an image as a JPEG, however, the format introduces some *noise* (also called *artifacts*) in the image — especially as you increase the amount of JPEG compression. (Most programs like Photoshop and Fireworks allow you to adjust the quality of a JPEG image. The lesser the quality, the smaller the file size, but the greater the noise.)

In a photograph, you really don't notice the noise, but if you save an image with flat-colored graphics and text, the artifacts really stand out and make the image look terrible, as shown in Figure 10-9. As a result, the JPEG format is considered a *lossy* format because it corrodes the integrity of your original image.

Text in a JPEG shows lots of artifacts.

Figure 10-9:
The photo
on the left
looks great,
but the
image on
the right
shows a lot
of artifacts.

Use JPEGs only on purely photographic images. Use GIF for all other types of images — including those that have a mix of flat-colored areas, text, and photos. Unlike GIF, with all its added features of transparency and animation, the JPEG format does only one thing and does it well — compress 24-bit photographs for the Web.

Lean, Mean Page Design

When it all comes down to basics, your goal as a Web designer is to create a nice-looking, user-friendly page that downloads in seconds. After all, a big part of the user experience is waiting for a page to download. The longer it takes, the worse the user's experience — no matter how nicely you design the page.

The best way to speed up the download time for a Web page is to use graphics efficiently throughout your Web site. Take advantage of design features, such as transparency, background tiles, and the browser's ability to store graphics in its memory to maximize each page's performance. In addition, by chopping graphics into individual pieces, you can apply the most efficient file format and palette settings to each one. Not only does this give you more control over the quality of each individual graphic, it also helps you to shave precious kilobytes off your Web page, making for a speedier delivery.

Minimizing download times

In addition to choosing the right file format for an image, whether it's a GIF or a JPEG, you can use other techniques to reduce the file size of your graphics and speed up a page's download time. Here are a few techniques to add to your arsenal to get the most bang for your graphics buck:

- **Transparency.** By simply choosing a transparent color for a graphic, you can reduce its file size. The transparent color becomes one less color for the browser to worry about. For example, take a look at Figure 10-10. The example on the left uses no transparency and is 8.42K. The example on the right gets rid of the creamy colored background and weighs in at 7.97K. This may not seem like a huge difference, but if you use this strategy for an entire Web site full of graphics, you can shave megabytes off your site.

Shaving file sizes not only makes each Web page load faster, but it also can cut expenses for your company or client. Remember, hosting and serving up megabytes costs money.

Figure 10-10: Using transparency often reduces the file size of an image.

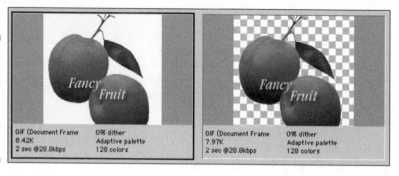

GIF (Document Frame   0% dither
8.42K   Adaptive palette
2 sec @28.8kbps   128 colors

GIF (Document Frame   0% dither
7.97K   Adaptive palette
2 sec @28.8kbps   128 colors

✔ **Background tiles.** Rather than including huge graphics on your Web page to add visual interest, get creative with repeating background tiles. Figure 10-11 shows a rather complex Web page designed by Juxt Interactive as a demonstration for Macromedia. The page looks graphically intense as a result of a clever and fast-loading background tile, shown in Figure 10-12, that's reused on every page. Although the tile is large, the file size is only 15K because the image uses so few colors. In addition, because it is reused on each page, the browser does not have to download it again on subsequent pages — it simply redraws it from memory.

By the way, this tile is much larger than the Web page because of the repeating nature of tiles. In this case, the designers don't want the tile to repeat until well beyond the visual bounds of the browser window. Users would have to scroll to see this pattern repeat again.

✔ **Caching graphics.** Whenever you can reuse graphics on a Web page, do so: It speeds performance. When a graphic downloads in a Web page, the browser *caches* it — stores it in its memory. The next time you use the graphic on the same page or on another page, the browser redraws it from memory. This process is a lot faster than downloading another, different image.

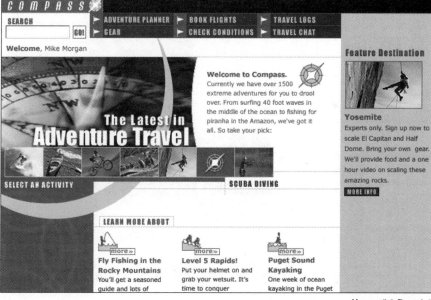

Figure 10-11: Much of the rich graphical nature of this page is due to a creative background tile.

Macromedia® Fireworks®

Macromedia® Fireworks®

Figure 10-12:
This
background
tile provides
visual
interest at a
relatively
low file size.

When you design a Web site, try to use the same graphics on as many
pages as possible. For example, the same navigation bar in Figure 10-13 —
complete with rollover buttons — can appear at the top of every subpage
in the site. When the user clicks to go to a new page, the navigation bar
loads quickly because all of its graphics are cached.

Figure 10-13:
After this
navigation
bar
downloads,
the browser
caches it.

Slicing and dicing Web graphics

Another way to optimize your page design is to chop, or *slice*, graphics into
individual pieces. This technique accomplishes three things:

✔ If graphics are sliced into pieces, the user doesn't have to wait for large blocks of graphics to download before they see anything on the page. The little individual pieces load in relatively quickly, so the user sees at least part of the page design almost immediately.

Don't get carried away with your image-slicing. Loading hundreds of tiny graphics can actually slow the page down.

✔ When you chop up graphics, you can save them individually. This means that you can apply different file format and palette settings to each one to get the best results. For example, as shown in Figure 10-2, the title area uses just one color, whereas the buttons are almost photographic. If you save the title separately, you can save it as a four-color GIF. If you keep it grouped with the buttons, however, you must choose a palette of at least 100 colors to accommodate both the text and the graphics.

✔ Graphics become free to act as independent moving parts in your Web page. For example, you can turn an individual graphic into a *rollover button* — which changes its appearance as the user's mouse pointer rolls over it. Because the button is sliced as a separate graphic, none of the other graphics on the page are affected when the user's mouse pointer rolls over it, as shown in Figure 10-14.

Figure 10-14: Each button in this navigation bar is a separate graphic.

Most graphics programs such as Fireworks and ImageReady (an application included with Photoshop that handles the interactive stuff) allow you to quickly and easily slice your Web graphics into independent parts. After you slice the graphics, these programs also enable you to add interactive links and rollovers to your graphics, assign links to them, and apply different file format and palette settings.

You get a lot of great benefits when you slice up a graphic, but you may be wondering how in the heck to piece them all together again. The answer is to use an HTML table structure. Fortunately, both Fireworks and ImageReady can output the necessary HTML to make all your sliced and diced graphics work correctly in the Web browser. Whew! And you thought you were going to have to do it yourself.

Backgrounds for Graphics

Before I turn you loose to churn out Web graphics, I want to equip your brain with one more production note. Above all else, the most common mistake you can make in producing Web graphics is to not properly prepare the edges of graphics so that they match the background.

If you don't proactively address the edges of your graphics, you can end up with a file that looks like it's sporting a halo, as shown in Figure 10-15. This image was built on a white background. Although the designer chose white as the transparent color, the semi-white edges around the image remain. Placed on a dark background, the white rim really stands out.

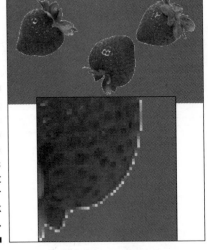

Figure 10-15: This image has a halo because its edges were not prepared for the dark background.

Understanding anti-aliased and aliased graphics

This white halo is the result of *anti-aliased* edges around the image. Because images are made out of pixels, and because pixels are square, an image with a curved edge looks jagged. To alleviate this problem and make the curved edges appear smooth, graphics programs include an outer rim of semi-transparent pixels around images and text — a process called *anti-aliasing*. The semi-transparent pixels blend the stair-stepped edge into the surrounding background color, as shown in Figure 10-15.

When you export graphics from a graphics program, you always end up with a solid background color (even if you were working on a transparent layer in Photoshop or Fireworks). In the exported graphic, the semi-transparent edges become solid-colored pixels. The color of these pixels is halfway between the background color and the image color.

This means that when you choose the background color as your *one* transparent color, the transparency stops just short of the blended in-between colors, leaving a rim around your image. You won't see the rim if the graphic is placed on the same background color it was anti-aliased to. You do see it, however, if the image is placed on any other background color.

The best way to avoid the halo is to always build your graphics on the same background color that you use on your Web page. This way, when you set the background color to be transparent, the anti-aliased pixels are pre-blended to match your Web page.

The one caveat to this method, however, is that by pre-blending the edges of your graphic, you lock yourself into using the graphic only on pages with the correct background color. For example, you can't reuse the graphic on a page with a different background color or the halo appears again. (So much for caching the graphic!)

The other way to avoid this is to use graphics with *aliased* edges — ones with no intermediate pixels between the image and the background. Just keep in mind that graphics with aliased edges appear jagged. For example, HTML text is aliased text: That's why it appears so chunky. Aliased edges, however, are also the reason why HTML text looks fine on all background colors and patterns. Without a rim of blended pixels to worry about, aliased graphics can go anywhere.

Preparing graphics with drop shadows

The halo problem is even more pronounced when your image has a *drop shadow*. After all, a drop shadow is really just anti-aliasing on steroids. Take a look at Figure 10-16. Because I built this image on a transparent layer in Fireworks, it's easy to assume that I can export the image and have it retain the transparent effect — especially because I chose the transparency option when I exported the image. The problem, however, is that this transparency is native only to Fireworks for the purposes of building graphics. When you export, the image defaults to a white background and the transparency only affects the one solid white color, leaving behind a big blob for the drop shadow.

Images on transparent layers have white backgrounds when exported.

 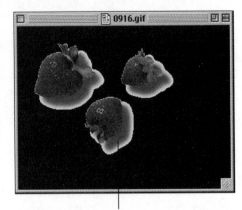

Figure 10-16:
The halo problem becomes an eyesore when an image has a drop shadow.

The drop shadow was blended to match the default white background, not black

To get some hands-on practice, in the next few steps I show you how to use Fireworks to prepare and export an image with a drop shadow ready for the Web.

1. **Launch Fireworks and start a new file.**

   Choose File⇨New from the menu. In the dialog box that appears, enter the dimensions 200 x 200 so you have enough space to work. Next, choose the Custom color option and click on the color swatch to choose a color that matches your HTML page (this way, your graphics will be anti-aliased to the proper color). For this exercise, just choose any old color and click OK.

2. **Create a circular shape.**

   In the toolbar, select the Ellipse shape tool (click and hold on the Rectangle tool to reveal the Ellipse tool option). Draw a simple circle in your document. When you let go, the circle should still be selected. With the circle selected, you can choose a new fill color for it by clicking on the color swatch at the bottom of the toolbar, as shown in Figure 10-17.

For this lesson, you are drawing a circle to achieve curved edges that will be anti-aliased to the background color. Shapes with straight edges, like a square, will not be anti-aliased because there are no rounded corners to smooth out.

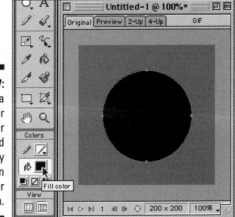

Figure 10-17:
Choose a
new color
for your
selected
circle by
clicking on
the Fill Color
swatch.

3. Add a drop shadow.

To add a soft drop shadow to the circle, open the Effect palette by choosing Window⇨Effect. (The palette may already be open in your workspace, so first look around for a tab marked Effect.) In the Effect palette, choose Shadow and Glow⇨Drop Shadow from the drop-down menu (click on the bar just under the Effect tab). After you select the effect, a mini window as shown in Figure 10-18 appears with setting options. Click anywhere outside this window to accept the default settings and close the window.

Choose an effect from the drop-down menu.

Figure 10-18:
The Effect
palette
enables you
to apply
drop
shadows
and bevels
to any
graphic or
text object.

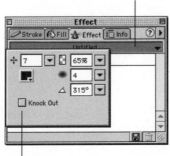

Adjust the effect's settings in the pop-up window.

4. Optimize the graphic as a transparent GIF.

If it isn't open already, open the Optimize palette from the Windows menu. In the Settings pull-down menu, choose GIF WebSnap 128 from the list of choices. Then, choose Index Transparency to make the background color transparent, as shown in Figure 10-19.

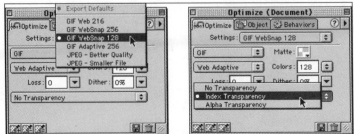

Figure 10-19: Choose GIF WebSnap 128 and then choose the Index Transparency option.

5. **Preview and export your image.**

At the top of your document, you see a Preview tab. Click on the tab to see how your image will look after you export it. As Figure 10-20 shows, if you zoom in (View⇨Zoom In), you can see how the edges have been anti-aliased to the original background color that you chose. The checkerboard pattern indicates the transparent portion of your image.

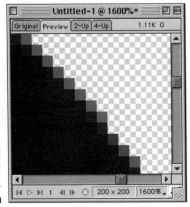

Figure 10-20: Edges have been blended to match the original background color.

To export this image for the Web, choose File⇨Export. In the Export dialog box, name your new image and then save it.

Matching a background tile

After you know how to prepare an image to match a solid background color, what if you want to match a graphic to a background pattern? The production process for both procedures is nearly identical. The only difference is that you must pick a median-valued color from the pattern and use that as your background color. When you set up the median color as the transparent color, the anti-aliased pixels that remain match the overall color of the pattern.

Using alpha channels

All digital images are comprised of three *channels* — red, green, and blue (the RGB system) — that create the image you see. Each image can have an additional invisible channel called an *alpha channel* whose sole purpose on earth is to control the transparency of the RGB image.

To control transparency, an alpha channel uses a grayscale image (an image colored shades of gray, white, and black). Like a digital stencil, completely black areas make the image transparent in those spots, whereas completely white areas let the image shine through in all its glory. Gray colors in the alpha channel equate to varying degrees of transparency — the darker the gray, the more transparent the image will be.

GIF allows you to use an alpha channel to set up multiple transparent colors, but it doesn't do a great job. An alpha channel is supposed to control the *degree* of an image's transparency. The way GIF uses alpha channels, however, turns all semi-transparent pixels completely transparent. The net effect is that using alpha channels with GIFs lets you make a handful of colors in an image transparent. GIF on its own can make only one color transparent.

The PNG format does support true semi-transparent alpha channel masking. At the time of this writing, however, I have yet to see a semi-transparent PNG in action on a Web page. This is truly the panacea to creating anti-aliased graphics with drop shadows that can work on any background color, such as the one shown in Figure 10-21. The benefit of true alpha channel transparency is that you can create a graphic once and reuse it throughout a Web site regardless of a page's background color or texture. This is in stark contrast to today's practice of creating multiple editions of the same graphic — one for each background color it uses.

Figure 10-21:
An alpha channel enables you to make the edges of an image semi-transparent.

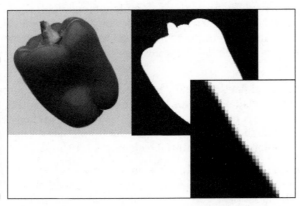

Graphic Production

Pumping out all the graphics that you need for a Web site is a daunting task. You must prepare hundreds of individual graphics. The best way to tackle this effort is to make templates that you and your production team can use for every different kind of graphic and layout. For graphics that you can't make templates for, create a style guide that covers issues on font choices, color choices, and so on. With the help of templates and style guides, you can delegate a lot of the production so that no one person is the "keeper of the kingdom."

When only one person knows how to design the site, you not only create a production bottleneck, but the client can never update their site without your help. This sounds like a brilliant plot to retain a client's business, but I think this is bad form. The client came to you in the first place for your design help, so providing them with the tools, templates, and style guides is not going to get them anywhere!

When you make templates for the team, you should adopt one graphics program such as Fireworks or Photoshop that the team can use. (If you need to, use one program for certain templates only — for example, Photoshop templates for all your images.) Provide templates in the native format of one of these programs. This way, the team members can open a template, edit a design piece, optimize it, and export it ready for the Web site.

You can make graphical templates for almost everything on the Web site — including entire page layouts. If you recall, most Web sites have just a few basic layouts — the home page, a subpage, and perhaps a few different variations of the subpage's interior to keep it interesting. Here are some of the different kinds of templates that you can prepare for a Web site:

- **Home page layout.** By providing a complete mock-up of the home page, you give the HTML people who assemble the actual page a visual guide to go by. In addition, a complete mock-up is your chance to show how all the different components — headings, buttons, and bullets — work together on the page.

- **Subpage layout.** Like the home page mock-up, a complete subpage design acts as a visual guide for both the HTML people and the graphic production folks. A complete mock-up gives context to the design elements, and, if push comes to shove, production folks can use graphics from this template to build interface elements for the site.

- **Variations on the subpage.** Because most pages of a Web site use the subpage template, it's a good idea to provide a few different layout variations. For the most part, the variations should focus on the interior of the page — always leaving the main navigation system in place.

✓ **Navigation bars.** Although the navigation system is probably included on the home and subpage templates, it's a good idea to save it as a separate template. As a separate template, it's easy to update.

✓ **Graphical buttons.** A Web site often contains a lot of graphical buttons, such as Submit, Next, Previous, and so on. Provide a template that has the basic button design — its color, shape, shadow, and bevel. Then, a production team member can open the template, make changes to the text only, and export buttons that have a consistent look.

✓ **Graphical headings and subheadings.** As you did for the button template, provide a template for all graphical headings and subheadings set in the right font, size, and color. This way, a production team member can open the template and simply change the content of the text without worrying about its formatting.

✓ **Graphical bullets.** Again, to ensure consistency throughout the site, provide a set of graphical bullets, arrows, and other widgets. For example, a team member can open the template, change the color of a bullet, and export it.

✓ **Image treatments.** If you have designed a special treatment for images on particular pages, you should provide a template with the proper sizing, masks, and coloration. For example, if all home page images are steel-gray monotone with a soft feathered edge on one side, you can set up a series of layer treatments in Photoshop that can do this automatically to any new image. This way, you can easily produce a series of images that all have the same graphical treatment.

✓ **Background tiles.** If your Web site uses background tiles, always keep the original art on hand in a template in case the team needs to make changes.

If the site that you are designing is a large one, you probably need a whole team of HTML people to create it. They must all use the same font, size, and color treatment for the headings, subheadings, links and other elements of a page. You can either provide the style guide as a printed document or as an HTML page. As an HTML page, the programmers can copy and paste the formatting. Either way, provide a style guide that covers the following:

✓ **Headings and subheadings.** Provide font, color, and size guidelines.

✓ **Body text.** Again, provide font, color, and size guidelines.

✓ **Captions.** If different kinds of captions are needed for different kinds of elements, the style guides should address how and when to use each caption type.

✓ **Pull quotes.** If a Web page ever needs a quote or other statement to stand out from the main body text, the style guide should address what font and size to use.

✓ **Links.** In addition to font and size guidelines, choose a color for the link in all its states. (Links often display in one color before they have been clicked and another afterwards.)

✓ **Table treatments.** If you use tables in a Web site, decide whether the tables should have border colors or background colors in each cell. Also, you may specify different font, color, and size treatments for the text within tables.

✓ **Background colors and tiles.** Finally, if certain areas of the Web site use different background colors, provide a list of the colors to use. For example, the Products section of the Web site may use a different background color from the About the Company section. The same holds true for tiles. Some pages or sections may use tiles, and others may not. The style guides should provide a roadmap for the use of background colors and tiles throughout the site.

Part III
Creating a User-Friendly Face

The 5th Wave   By Rich Tennant

Well, there's your Web page, Crypto. Designed like you asked. But personally, I think it has too many spinning spirals and blinking lights. It makes...hard reading. Make...tired...look...at...lose...all...con...cen...tra...tion...

Perfect!

CRYPTO THE HYPNOTIST

In this part . . .

One of your biggest responsibilities as a Web designer is to create graphical user interfaces that people understand and can use to successfully navigate the site. After organizing a site into logical categories and subcategories, the designer must design a consistent scheme of navigational buttons, icons, and text links that give people the tools to get around and not feel lost in the process.

In Chapter 11, you learn different techniques for designing effective Web user interfaces. Chapter 12 shows you how to test your designs with real people to make sure you get the interface right before you get too far along in the production cycle.

Chapter 11

Web User Interface Design

- -

In This Chapter

▶ Getting users around the site

▶ Designing buttons that look clickable

▶ Using interface elements consistently

▶ Adding animation, audio, and media to enhance interactivity

- -

*H*ave you ever gotten lost in a Web site and chalked it up to your own lameness? You're not alone, and you're probably not as lame as you think. More likely, the designer who put the site together is the guilty party. When you see icons that look like page decorations instead of buttons, and dodging buttons that disappear the moment you click them, it's no wonder you think you're visiting www.houseofschizophrenia.com.

Not to give you a power trip, but, as a designer, you have ultimate control over a Web site's so-called ease of use. Be careful, however, because with such control comes a big spotlight. When you get to the user-testing phase, be prepared to sweat. If the users can't figure out how to get around in the site, all furrow-browed eyes will be on you!

Designing an interface that people can actually use is part mental gymnastics and part good visual design. After all, the graphic design that you put together is intrinsically tied to the usability of the site. Users can tell a lot about what a graphic or icon does or doesn't do when they click it simply by the way it looks. Also, where and how you place interface elements on the page can affect a user's orientation in the site.

You may be thinking, "Great, yet another level of minutia to master." Don't sweat just yet: Designing a usable interface is a lot easier than you think. In this chapter, I show you how.

Navigation Design

Believe it or not, if you're at the stage of designing the user interface for a project, a lot of these design issues have already been worked out. When you create the outline and then whittle it down into a working site map, you organize the site into a system of logical categories and subcategories to help people navigate through the site. (For more about site maps, see Chapter 4.)

Because you already have directions in the form of a site map, all you need to do is follow some basic user interface design rules to make sure your navigation system is user-friendly:

✔ The navigation system should give the user some idea of how big the site is and where they are in the scheme of things.

✔ The interface should be idiot-proof. By that, I mean your buttons and icons should be fairly prominent on the screen and labeled by function.

✔ Your navigation system should look and function consistently throughout the site.

Just following these three simple rules of thumb can go a long way to boost the usability of a site.

"You are here" feedback

When you pick up a textbook, you can immediately get a sense of how in-depth it is. Just by the thickness of the book, the size of the print, and the table of contents, you know what you're in for. You can mentally prepare for the size and scope of everything inside. Most Web sites, however, offer no such immediate clues as to what you're getting into. You have no way to tell by just looking at the home page how big the site is, or if you'll find what you need. That is, of course, unless the designer tells you.

Unlike a book, a Web site offers no substantive clues about its identity. To give users a sense of place, size, and scope, you have to rely on visuals. This means that you need to dedicate a good chunk of the precious page real estate to a set of graphics that, in essence, says "you are here" and "this is how you get over there." This sounds like a no-brainer, but many sites don't provide such vital feedback.

Of course, your site won't be one of them. Here are a few techniques that you can use to orient people in your site and quickly get them around to all the main sections and subsections:

✔ **Cross-navigation.** As I discussed in Chapter 3, a cross-navigation system (usually shortened to *cross-nav* system) provides links to all the main sections of the Web site in one convenient place. This system appears on every page of a Web site as a handy tool to get users around. A cross-nav system is sort of like having a short table of contents on each page of a site.

Not only does it make it easy to jump around, but a cross-nav system also gives people a sense of how big the site is and where they are in the site. Just by looking at the cross-navigation graphic, people can quickly see how many sections they can visit. And, if you always highlight the area that they are currently in, as in Figure 11-1, they won't feel lost.

✔ **Color-coding.** After a person uses the cross-navigation system to get to a section of your Web site, they may spend a lot of time there. If the section is large and has a lot of pages to sift through, a person may begin to feel lost — regardless of the highlighted "you are here" button.

One way to reinforce a user's sense of place is to use a color-coding system. In this system, each section of the site uses a unique color scheme for its background color and buttons. Like the Yellow Pages versus the White Pages, the overall background color of the pages can help remind people of the section that they are in.

If you use a color-coded system, you should introduce it in the cross-navigation system. Each button in the cross-nav bar should be colorized accordingly. If you decide to use a color-coding system, however, don't get too carried away. Color-coding works best when you have just five to seven sections, because you can easily choose five to seven colors that work well together. Any more colors make your site look like a groovy tribute to the '60s. In addition, you should choose a complementary set of colors that all have the same light and dark value. For example, don't use three light colors and one dark color for the page background.

✔ **Tab system.** One of the most popular ways to represent a cross-navigation system is to make it look like tabs on a manila folder, as shown in Figure 11-2. This simple visual metaphor helps people instantly recognize how to use your cross-nav system.

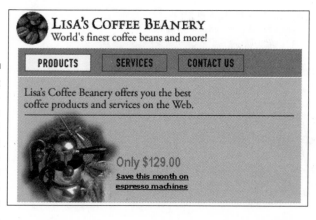

Figure 11-1: A cross-navigation graphic shows users where they are in your site.

To take the tab system even further, you can include a cross-nav system within each tab. For example, when a user clicks on a tab, a new row appears with a set of cross-navigable choices, as shown in Figure 11-3. Many sites, such as Amazon.com, have used this tactic successfully for years.

🗸 **Breadcrumb trail.** Another way to orient folks in your site is to keep track of their progress as they click through the various pages of your site. By leaving a "breadcrumb trail" of links, you give users a lifeline to retrace their steps back up the hierarchy, as shown in Figure 11-4. Generally, the trail doesn't record each click; instead, it shows each step of the site's hierarchy that they followed to get to the current page. Visually, a breadcrumb trail is a great way to show users how deep they are in the site, and how they can climb back out.

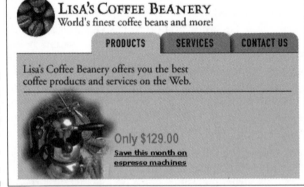

Figure 11-2:
Tabs are a great visual metaphor for a cross-nav system.

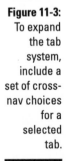
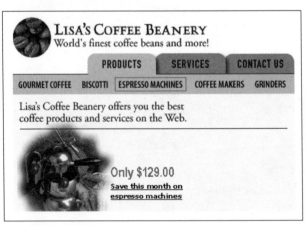

Figure 11-3:
To expand the tab system, include a set of cross-nav choices for a selected tab.

Figure 11-4:
A breadcrumb trail tracks a user's progress as they drill down into your site.

<u>Home</u> >   <u>Main Section</u> >   <u>Sub Section</u> >   **Current Page**

The proper use of icons

Rather than creating generic-looking buttons with text, a lot of designers like to spice up their pages with *icons* — little illustrations that, like pictograms, convey meaning. The problem with icons, however, is that no two people interpret the same meaning from them, so you can't rely exclusively on icons as the main interface buttons. You must attach descriptive labels to them. For a case in point, take a look at Figure 11-5 and see if you can figure out where each icon will take you in the Web site.

Figure 11-5:
Can you figure out where each of these icons will take you in the site?

Compare your guesses to where these icons really take you, as illustrated in Figure 11-6. Would you ever have guessed that the clipboard icon is intended to recruit people to join the company? The company in this example should be advertising for a user interface designer! As this little exercise points out, icons can rarely stand alone without some sort of text label to help users know what they do. Except for common functions like printing and saving, designing icons to represent areas of your site is a tricky process.

Figure 11-6:
Unless
properly
labeled,
icons can
be difficult
to interpret
correctly.

New Products   Our Catalog   FAQs   Join our Team!

Consistency is everything

When users first come to your site, they look around to get oriented. Hopefully, they quickly absorb the basic page layout and find the navigation system, so they know how to get around and can focus on the content. After people initially figure out the interface, they don't want to waste their time futzing with it again — the interface should become almost transparent.

The best way to make an interface familiar and transparent to the user is to be consistent. Don't change the design or placement of buttons from one page to the next. Not only does this kind of switch make users do a double-take on the page to find the button again, it also may lead them to believe that the button's function has changed. Either way, you've got to retrain the user how to use the page — and from what I've seen, users don't take kindly to that sort of treatment.

For example, if you design a fancy About the Company button on one page, but then shrink it down to a plain text link on the next page, as in Figure 11-7, the user may not even it recognize it as the same button — even if it has the same text.

First it's a button...   ...now it's a text link!

Figure 11-7:
If you
change the
design of a
button, the
user may
think it's a
new button.

Buttons That Look Clickable

As I discuss in the previous section, the visual design of your navigation elements can have a big impact on the usability of the site. For example, just by creating a cross-navigation system to look like familiar folder tabs, you make it instantly user-friendly. People immediately recognize the tabs as interactive buttons rather than static page décor.

In general, you can make your interface elements look more "clickable" in one of three ways:

- ✔ Make them look like everyday objects, such as the tabs on manila envelopes.
- ✔ Make the elements physically stand out on the page by giving them a three-dimensional appearance.
- ✔ Make them imply a navigation system, which can be as easy as grouping a bunch of similar-looking navigation elements together in one graphical block.

Taking clues from everyday life

Objects that you interact with on a daily basis, such as buttons on a phone, drawers, and dials, are great inspirations for the design of interactive elements on your Web page. People are already well-trained to use these everyday objects — everybody knows how to push buttons, pull drawer handles, and turn dials.

The visual design and shape of these objects provide clues as to how people must interact with them. For example, drawer handles usually have a little grip or carved niche to give your hand some traction. In user interface design circles, these clues are called *affordances*. Therefore, if your interface graphics somewhat resemble these everyday objects (or, have the same affordances), users have a good idea about how to use them.

Take a look at both the dial interface and the drawer scheme on Apple's QuickTime player in Figure 11-8. Figuring out how to use these little widgets to control the volume and access a menu of options is easy. For the volume, you click and drag the dial to turn the audio up or down. For the drawer of options, you grab the handle-like area and drag downward.

Volume dial   Drawer handle

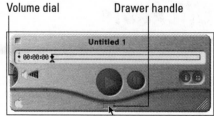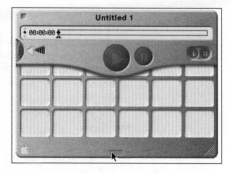

Making things leap off the page

Copying the design of real-life objects is not always technically possible or practical. Unless you're building a graphically rich interactive application in Flash, programming dial-like sliders like those in Apple's QuickTime player isn't worth the effort using standard Web technologies. Besides, it's more important for users to *know* that a graphic is interactive. You don't have to go the extra mile and make the graphic function as a dial-like slider.

 Users must know when something is interactive in order to consistently differentiate between clickable and non-clickable elements. Always make clickable elements leap off the page by giving them a little extra dimension with features like drop shadows, glows, and beveled edges, as shown in Figure 11-9. In this example, the tactile treatment of the four lower buttons invites people to click on them. On the flip side, make sure you give non-clickable elements a flat appearance to discourage interaction.

 When you break the consistency rule, users get confused. If you give non-clickable elements a three-dimensional appearance, such as the photograph in Figure 11-10, you confuse the user. Expecting it to be a button, they click on it, don't get anywhere, and then mistrust everything else in the site with the same treatment.

If you think that making your graphics three-dimensional is a lot of extra design work, think again. Adding drop shadows and bevels to your buttons is a cinch in both Photoshop and Fireworks. You just select the graphic, apply the effects of your choice using the Effect palette (in Fireworks) or the Layer menu (in Photoshop), and poof! — you instantly have a clickable-looking graphic.

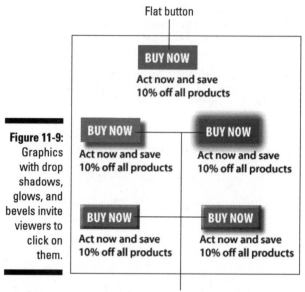

Flat button

Buttons with glows, bevels, and drop shadows.

Figure 11-9:
Graphics
with drop
shadows,
glows, and
bevels invite
viewers to
click on
them.

Figure 11-10:
This non-
interactive
photo with a
drop
shadow
looks too
much like
the buttons.

Grouping buttons into a navigation bar

Sometimes just grouping a series of similar-looking interface elements together in one graphical unit can give them a clickable appearance — even if the individual graphics don't look clickable. For example, if you string together a row of plain text labels with the same font treatment, you create a stronger graphical element that stands out from the other things on the page. (Sort of like the theory that there's safety in numbers.) As shown in Figure 11-11, seeing simple text in a group accomplishes two things:

✔ **A group implies interactivity.** A set of text or graphical elements grouped together creates one large visual unit that draws people's attention. The very fact that they are grouped implies something fishy and that the group is probably interactive.

✔ **A group implies a similar function.** By visually associating a set of links, you imply that they all perform similar functions. For example, all of the main navigation buttons should look like each other and, rather than being spread out all over the page, they should be contained in one area. If you have a set of less important links, you should still provide their own similar visual treatment, but group them elsewhere on the page.

Figure 11-11:
A set of
simple text
buttons
grouped
together
stands out
and looks
clickable.

"It's a Dessert Topping AND a Floor Wax": Inconsistent Visuals

Have you ever clicked on a button or icon on one page, but when you got to the next page, the same button or icon was a non-clickable decoration? In Figure 11-12, the same graphic that is a button on one page changes to a static graphical headline on the next. This is a big no-no. Remember the old skit on *Saturday Night Live* that featured Chevy Chase hawking a magical product: "It's a dessert topping *and* a floor wax!" In this case, the button is sometimes a "dessert topping" and at other times a "floor wax." Yummy — sounds delicious!

Reusing graphics from page to page to save on download time is smart, but not when it affects usability. The key to a good interface is to visually differentiate the interactive stuff from the content stuff.

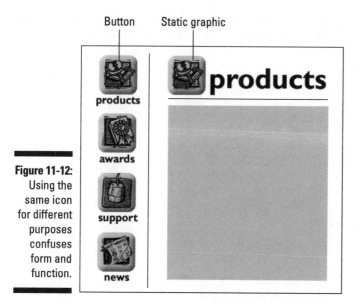

Button   Static graphic

Figure 11-12:
Using the
same icon
for different
purposes
confuses
form and
function.

Here's one of my favorite examples. Suppose you're reading through the text on a page and some of the words are bold, as shown in Figure 11-13. Your first assumption is that the designer wants to emphasize those words, but as you discover by accident, the words are, in fact, clickable. When you roll over the words with the mouse, the cursor changes to a pointing hand; from experience, you know that this means you've found a link. Normally, text is a link only if it's underlined, so visually, the non-underlined bold text looks like it's just part of the content.

Figure 11-13:
Because
the bold text
is not
underlined,
users
assume that
it is not a
link.

Mission Wars Wants You!

If you are interested in being a contestant on the **next Mission Wars episode**, please send us your completed **application** by January 31st. You must be in excellent physical and mental **condition** to apply.

When you are designing interactive buttons and static headlines, come up with a consistent visual scheme for each type so that users know what's clickable and what's not. In Figure 11-14, after you click on the Products icon to go to the Products page, you can retain the visual theme in the headline, but you need to give it a slightly altered design to differentiate its function. In this set, the headline doesn't have the same three-dimensional quality as the button, but it does retain the icon.

Figure 11-14:
The button and headline have different treatments to differentiate their functions.

There's Something Funny About That Graphic: Using Rollovers

All of the strategies that I discuss in previous sections of this chapter to make an object look interactive have one thing in common: They all provide some kind of *visual* feedback to the user that screams "click me please." Other kinds of feedback, however, can be used to give people clues that an object is interactive. You can also use sound, animation, and media to enhance the usability of your interface components.

The following is a list of some tried-and-true techniques that make people stop and think, "Hey, there's something funny about that graphic":

✔ **Rollovers.** A *rollover* is a graphic, usually a button, that changes its appearance when the mouse pointer rolls over it. This way, when a user peruses a page with their mouse pointer, the interactive stuff lights up, inviting them to click. Not only does the button light up when the user rolls over it, it also changes appearance again when the user clicks. Take a look at Figure 11-15. Here you can see the normal, rollover, and click-able state of a single button.

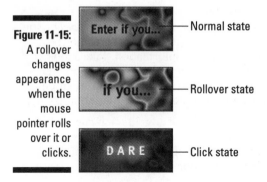

Figure 11-15: A rollover changes appearance when the mouse pointer rolls over it or clicks.

— Normal state

— Rollover state

— Click state

✔ **Audio.** Another way to make an interface element stand out is to use audio. Like a rollover button, you can play an audio clip when the user rolls over the button and a different audio clip when the user clicks.

✔ **Animation.** Nothing grabs a user's attention like movement on a Web page. Until recently, most Web pages were fairly static and silent, so any movement on the page stuck out like a sore thumb. These days, animation is more common than it used to be, but it can still command attention when used correctly.

The key is to use animation sparingly and to concentrate it on one area of the page. If the whole page is twinkling and twirling, forget it. Use animation only for important interactive elements. For example, make the lead story or featured product an animated GIF or Flash movie. You can also make your main interface buttons animated, or animated only when the user's mouse pointer rolls over them.

Maximizing Space

Because space is at such a premium on a Web page, the smaller your interface elements are, the better: You can fit lots of small elements on a page. However, the smaller you make interface elements, the less usable they become: Your visitors will need a spyglass to get through your site. It's the ol' double-edged sword conundrum.

So how do you get the best of both worlds and maximize your Web page space? With some clever use of Web technologies, you can design small interface elements that expand when the user rolls over them to present more options. Here's a catalog of different techniques:

✔ **Swap rollovers.** Similar to a rollover button, a *swap* changes the appearance of a graphic on mouse rollover, but the change occurs elsewhere on the page. For example, if the mouse pointer rolls over a small button, a larger adjacent area changes to reveal more information. Take a look at the swap rollover in Figure 11-16. When a user rolls his mouse pointer over the button, a large area appears next to it with more information. The additional information can help a user decide whether they should click.

✔ You can really use swap rollovers to their full advantage by using them not just as extra info for the button, but to display page content. Take a look at Figure 11-17. As you roll over each of the tiny thumbnails, the whole screen updates with new information.

✔ **Pop-up menus.** Another way to maximize your space is to use *pop-up menus*. These are a list of additional navigation choices that appear when the mouse rolls over a button. The concept is similar to a swap rollover; however, swap rollovers are not interactive. Pop-up menus are designed to give the user a more refined set of choices so they can jump quickly to the area that they need. You can also use pop-up menus to consolidate a lot of your navigation choices so you have less stuff on the screen, as shown in Figure 11-18.

When the button is rolled over...   ...more information appears.

Figure 11-16: When a pointer rolls over a button, a larger area appears with more information.

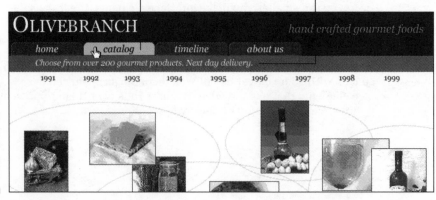

Figure 11-17:
You can
even use
swap
rollovers to
display
additional
information.

Figure 11-18:
Pop-up
menus
reveal more
navigation
choices
when the
mouse rolls
over a
button.

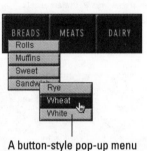

A button-style pop-up menu

An elegant, graphical style pop-up menu

✔ **Jump menus.** Like a pop-up menu, a *jump menu* contains a list of navigation choices, but the user has to click on it to reveal them. As shown in Figure 11-19, after a user clicks, they can choose from the list and jump quickly to the new page.

✔ **Shrink and expand.** This is probably one of the coolest styles of interfaces around, and it usually requires the help of Flash or Adobe's LiveMotion to make it work. On the page, all you see is a small interface area. As shown in Figure 11-20, when the mouse rolls over the area, it expands outward in an animation to reveal a full range of navigation choices. This example is the excellent mummies feature at www.discovery.com. This is an elegant way to conserve space and give users full-service functionality and an immersive experience all at the same time.

Figure 11-19:
A jump
menu
contains a
list of
choices, but
the user
must click to
reveal them.

Figure 11-20:
This
interface
starts out
small and
then
expands
when the
pointer rolls
over it.

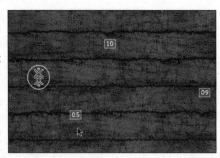

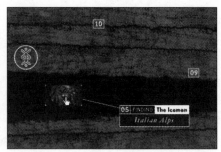

Photo courtesy Second Story.

Chapter 12

Usability Testing: Lab Coats Required

● ●

● ●

"The proof is in the pudding," or so the saying goes. I'm not exactly sure what pudding has to do with ferreting out the truth, but the phrase is just as applicable to Web design as it is to anything else in life. At some point in the design process, you have to put your work in front of a group of perfect strangers for the ultimate litmus test: Can they figure out how to use it?

Ideally, you give in to this test sooner rather than later in order to stave off any unforeseen usability problems before you're knee-deep in production (which is too late). By putting together a workable prototype early in the design phase, you can organize a bona fide user test, complete with a standard list of questions to ask and a plan for recording and evaluating the feedback.

Although a user test sounds academic and may conjure up visions of white lab coats, it's actually a fun and truly enlightening experience. You'll be surprised at the things a user test reveals about your design. In this chapter, I discuss how to make a testable prototype that you can put in front of users and how to get the most out of your testing efforts. In the end, you'll be glad you took this extra step. You'll end up with a Web site that is not only beautiful, but works too!

Developing a Testable Prototype

Before you can gather any useful feedback, you have to assemble a prototype that you can test. Working with a sketch on paper isn't good enough; people need to see the real deal — HTML pages in a browser. The graphic design of each page must also look real, the way it will appear in the actual Web page. As I discuss in Chapter 11, the visual design has a big impact on how users view the page and identify interactive elements.

In fact, you should test prototypes with the actual designs you are proposing. I remember testing page designs for a new area of an online auction company's Web site. The first graphical treatment didn't work — the test users didn't recognize the buttons on the page. Based on the feedback from the first round of testing, I changed the buttons slightly. In the next round of testing — with a new set of people — not a single user had a problem with the buttons and the pages were cleared for take-off.

This, and many similar experiences, has helped me to figure out that people — including clients — are extremely literal when it comes to reading Web pages. For testing purposes, don't design only half the page (leaving the rest of it blank), or use placeholder artwork. During the test, users often ask about these neglected areas. Even if you give them an explanation, they are forced to use their imagination to fill in the gaps. This can skew their reading of the page. Users need to see the page in its full context to give you the most accurate feedback.

Developing a workable prototype is not as much effort as it seems. You don't have to test each and every page of your site. Rather, you need to mock up just a few key pages that illustrate a user walking through a particular task, such as ordering a product. In fact, user testing is mostly about testing how people get through common tasks on your site.

Organize these few key pages into an HTML *click-through* — Web-speak for an online storyboard. As shown in Figure 12-1 and Figure 12-2, the click-through represents all the pages that a user sees if they step through the task successfully. Each of the pages can be a static mockup saved as a single GIF file, just like the design directions for the client that I discuss in Chapter 9. In fact, you can expand upon your initial design directions to make your first testing prototype.

For this stage in the process, the HTML coding for each click-through page should be just enough to place the GIF in the page. Remember, at this point, you just want to see if the interface works. After you determine that it does work, you can begin to spin your wheels putting actual HTML together (forms, text, and so on).

To prepare for testing day, it's a good idea to have a few different design options on hand for the users. As you begin to ask questions, you may present different ways of doing the same task and ask users to compare which way they prefer.

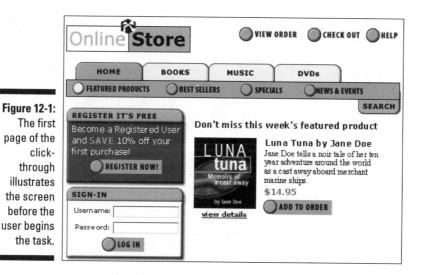

Figure 12-1:
The first page of the click-through illustrates the screen before the user begins the task.

Figure 12-2:
Using Search to find a product.

If your Web site relies heavily on technologies like JavaScript or Flash for the interface, you may have to create a quasi-functional prototype. Do what you can to fake it by building an interactive page in Fireworks or ImageReady in order to give users a sense of the interaction without spending too much time on a prototype users might not like. During the testing phase, users may offer suggestions on how the interface can be better or different. After all, the whole point of user testing is to open up to new ideas that better serve the end user. If you've already invested a lot of engineering time to make it work a certain way, you may be reluctant to change it.

Oooh, A Scavenger Hunt: Giving Users a Task

The most efficient way to conduct a user test is to send people on a kind of scavenger hunt to perform certain tasks. Prepare a list of two to five tasks that you want to test and then create a series of click-throughs that provide alternate ways to do each task. Keep in mind that the click-throughs are *your* ideas about how the tasks should be done. In a user test, it's always interesting to see how far a user actually gets in your click-through before suggesting an alternate route.

Along with your list of tasks, you should start thinking about what you want to find out from testing each task. Make a separate list of your own questions. This helps you to standardize a testing methodology that you can use on multiple people.

The more people you test, the more accurate the feedback. For example, if only one person out of five doesn't like the button design, you can probably chalk it up to their own subjective feelings. If that person was the only person you tested, you could end up redesigning something that was fine in the first place.

Creating a to-do list for users

In preparing a list of tasks for the user test, keep in mind the main goals of the Web site. For example, if the main objectives of the site are to get people to buy products and to become registered users, those goals should drive the to-do list of tasks to test. (Boy, that's a tongue twister!)

For testing day, create a to-do list document that you can give to each user. Create a separate edition for yourself that includes your standardized questions. In the following exercise, I assume that the marketing goals of the site are "Get users to buy products and sign up to be a registered user." Given these objectives, here's how to make a task list:

1. **Create a scenario that places the user in a role.** For example: "You're a customer looking to buy a book and sign up to be a registered user because you've heard you'll save 10% on your purchase." As you can see, this scenario exactly mirrors the marketing goals of the site, but is a little more focused on a typical task.

   Place this scenario statement at the top of the document that you give to users, as shown in Figure 12-3. You want the main goal of the test to be clear. With the overall scenario in mind, a user has the proper perspective for approaching each task — they have a point of reference. I've found that users become much smarter about the tasks if you include a scenario and then ask them to refer back to this scenario as the basis of their comments. For example, they may make comments such as, "Well, if I've heard that I can get 10% off by registering, I'd want to register first." This is a great nugget of information!

2. **Create three to four mini tasks that you want the user to try.** List these tasks below the scenario statement. The tasks can either be in the form of questions, such as "How would you buy a book called *Web Design For Dummies*?," or action requests, such as "Tell me how you would sign up to be a registered user." The questions should be fairly targeted toward a specific action and not too broad, such as "How would you buy any ol' book?"

User Scenario:
You're a customer looking to buy a book and register because you've heard you'll save 10% on your purchase.

Task 1:
How would you buy a book called
Web Design For Dummies?

Task 2:
How would you add a second product
to your order—say, a music CD?

Task 3:
How would you get to purchasing
area to check out?

Task 4:
How you would sign up to be a registered user?

Task 5:
Any additional comments and suggestions?

Figure 12-3:
Sample user
testing
sheet.

3. **Make your own cheat sheet.** Create a separate document for yourself that lists each task accompanied by a set of specific questions that you want answered about each one. At the top of your cheat sheet, list the main objectives of the site, followed by the user scenario. For example, the goal is to sell books and get registered users, as shown in Figure 12-4. The scenario is a user who comes to the site looking to buy a book and sign up in order to save on their purchase. These two statements become the measuring stick you use to evaluate the results of your tests.

Following these statements, list the three to four tasks — just as you did on the user's sheet. After each task, however, list your own questions about the task. This helps to focus your interrogation during testing.

Goals:
The main goal of the Web site is to sell products and get users to register.

User scenario:
You're a customer looking to buy a book and register because you've heard you'll save 10% on your purchase.

Task 1:
How would you buy a book called *Web Design For Dummies*?
- Can the user find the Books section of the online store?
- Are the navigation buttons clear?
- Can the user find and use the search function?
- Does the user understand how to add the book to their order?

Task 2:
How would you add a second product to your order—say, a music CD?
- After the user adds the book to their order, can they find the other product sections?
- Do they think their initial book order will be lost if they continue shopping?

Task 3:
How would you get to the purchasing area to check out?
- Does the user find the check out area?
- Does the user know they can continue to add products in the check out area?
- Is the credit card ordering process clear?
- What sort of order confirmation do they expect?

Task 4:
How you would sign up to be a registered user?
- Does the user find the registration button?
- When registered, can the user find the log in area?
- Does the user understand why it's important to register?

Any additional comments and suggestions?

Figure 12-4:
Your own testing cheat sheet.

Developing a Testing Methodology

After you develop a list of tasks for the user and your own cheat sheet, the next step is to come up with a standard testing methodology. By standardizing one testing methodology, you have a more accurate means of evaluating the test results. In addition, you can delegate the testing to a few people on the team. Here's a checklist to help you build your own testing methodology:

TIP

- ✔ **Target audience.** Before you recruit a bunch of poor saps to be your test subjects, you must know what kind of people to go after. A *target audience* is the kind of folks your site caters to. For example, a shopping site with books, music, and videos may target 20- to 35-year-old professionals with money, but not time, to burn.

- ✔ **Number of users.** The more users you test, the better your results. Testing more than one person is critical because you can minimize the effects of each individual's bias. For example, if only one person out of six complains about the look or placement of a certain button, you can probably disregard their comment. If five out of the six people have the same complaint, you know you've got a genuine problem. A good number of people to shoot for is four to seven people. Any more than that is probably overkill. You should also make sure that you have a good mix of men and women (unless the site focuses on one group).

- ✔ **Testing style.** Because you can test in more than one way, you should decide which style of testing you want to use. The serious labcoat style of testing involves setting people up in a room by themselves behind a one-way mirror (I kid you not) and videotaping their actions as they work through the task list. I've found that this method is way too intimidating for the user — they don't want to look stupid on camera, so they hold back.

  The other, more casual way, is to sit down with them side-by-side, asking questions and taking notes as they respond. This method is a lot more empowering, and users really seem to spill their guts and tell it like it is. You can still videotape the session. Videotaping enables you to see where their mouse goes on the screen as they work through the tasks, and record their feedback in case you can't keep up with notes.

The Gloves Come Off; The Truth Comes Out

The whole point of user testing is to catch the usability problems of your design before you go into production. Therefore, you must be mentally prepared for the feedback that comes out — it may not be pretty. In some cases, you may be faced with a substantial redesign if user after user can't figure out your interface.

Give yourself a good two weeks before testing day to line up enough people to make the test worthwhile. Recruiting people to donate their time for an hour or two can take some doing. To help recruit them, tell them exactly how long it will take — hopefully no more than one hour — and let them know what sort of compensation you can offer.

After you get people in the door, make sure you honor the time commitment that you promised and stick to your testing plan. Other than that, just sit back and take notes!

Finding willing guinea pigs

The real trick in user testing is to actually find and convince a bunch of people to be willing guinea pigs for your test. If your target audience is 25- to 40-year-old busy professionals, you may have a harder time recruiting people away from their jobs than if your audience doesn't work or is self-employed.

If your client has an established clientele, coming up with a list of people to call on is fairly easy. Simply cull their customer database for people in your local area. The best approach is to call these people directly. I've found that in this impersonal online world, people respond warmly to a personal phone call — especially when they are made to feel that their opinion counts.

For new Web sites that have no clientele, it's a little more difficult to find a good group of testers. In this case, the easiest path is to recruit friends, colleagues, and family members that fit the profile of the proposed target customer. Have the client provide you with a list of people that they know.

Friends and family may be more lenient in their feedback because they don't want to hurt your feelings. At the start of the testing, you must remind them that the only way they can help is to be honest and forthcoming with their feedback.

If the site's clientele is highly specialized, such as doctors and their staff, try calling their offices directly. Getting people to participate in early user tests is also a great way to cultivate future customers.

After you identify a list of testers, you have to sell them on the idea of taking time out of their day to come test. Here are a few tactics that I've found to be successful:

> ✓ **Set a time limit.** Put a time limit on the user test so people know what they're committing to, and schedule a time that's convenient for them. For example, tell a potential tester that the test portion only takes one hour, plus an extra half hour for setup and conclusion. If they come in at 1:30, they can be out by 3pm.

Make sure you follow through with the promised schedule. If you don't finish all the tasks in one hour, it's your loss. Conclude the test and thank them for their time. If you're almost finished, however, the user usually offers to stay.

✔ **Give out tchotchkes.** In appreciation of their participation, offer small gifts at the end of the test. Most companies have marketing T-shirts, hats, coffee mugs, and pens with the company's logo, which make great give-aways. In the industry, people commonly call these things *tchotchkes*. It's amazing how far these little gifts go — people can never seem to get enough of them.

In addition to tchotchkes, if your client makes a product such as software, for example, you're sitting on a goldmine of give-aways. There's nothing like giving away a shrink-wrapped product that retails for a few hundred dollars to lure potential testers — especially when you consider that it costs the company only a few dollars to make.

✔ **Pay people.** Depending on your client's "coolness" factor, you may or may not have to pay people. If the client is a new company that no one has heard of, you may have to offer testers a small cash stipend, such as $20 for an hour of their time. Money should be the last thing in your sales arsenal. Before you resort to giving away cold hard cash, see if people agree to come in simply by scheduling a convenient time and offering free gifts.

✔ **Send out thank-you cards.** After the test, send users a thank-you card in the mail. Although this isn't a sales tactic to sway people to come in, it's a great way to build good faith for the future. You may be able to call on this person again, or use them as a reference to find other testers.

Conducting a user test

When you sit testers down in front of computers, start by reviewing the scenario and the task list and describe how you plan to conduct the test. Tell them that you'll be asking a few questions about each task, taking notes, and videotaping the session (if that's true). Tell people that they should talk out loud about their thoughts and reactions as they work through a task. Tell them that it's okay to criticize the design or express doubts, such as "I'm not sure what that button does."

You should remind them not to feel stupid about completing any of the tasks. Tell them that if they can't do something, it's probably the design's fault. Also, remind them that they're looking at a semi-functional prototype, and that not all the buttons are hooked up yet.

Start on the first page of your click-through and ask the user to complete the first task. Then, sit back and start taking notes as they talk out loud about what they're thinking. You should hear things like "I'm looking for a Search field. I should be able to just type in what I want to find and click on a Find It button." Give them some time to think through the problem before you ask any questions about the task.

Avoid leading questions that give clues, such as "Do you think that that Search button looks clickable?" Not only are you pointing out a button that they should be able to find on their own, but you're also already expressing doubt about the button's design — thus skewing their perception of it.

Because your click-through storyboard is limited in its functionality and only illustrates one path through each task, you must moderate each click. As soon as the user tells you that they have clicked on one of the buttons, ask them what kind of page they expect to see next. If they choose the correct button, let them click and then gauge their reaction as they view the next page.

If they choose a path that's not illustrated in your click-through, they may have just given you a great alternative way of navigating. On the other hand, maybe your interface isn't clear. Show them the path that you are proposing and ask them what they think. They may yield and tell you "Oh, that makes more sense, I just didn't see the button," or they may say, "That makes no sense at all." If their response is the former, you just need to redesign the button or put it in a different place. If they say it makes no sense at all, ask them if they can think of a better way to perform the task.

After the user completes a task, or you notice that they are stuck, ask the bulk of your remaining questions and then ask for their opinions on best ways to do the task. After you wrap up the task and your questions, move on to the next task. Each task should take about 15 minutes to complete — any longer than that and you risk burning testers out.

"Houston, We Have a Problem. . ."

After spending an hour or so with four to six people — running each one through the same set of tasks and questions — you should have many pages of notes to evaluate. The best way to sift through and make sense of all of this data is to transcribe your notes into some sort of visual graph.

Consolidate all of the feedback for each task into one table, as shown in Figure 12-5. This table shows how you can organize the feedback from testing the click-through in Figure 12-1. The table system is a great way to compare all the notes for each task so you can better see where the problems lie. Make a grid that lists each user down one axis and each of your questions along the other axis. Also, leave one column for the users' suggestions and comments. At the top of the document, include the site's goals, the user scenario, and the testing methodology that you used so that you and the client have a better basis from which to analyze the feedback.

Figure 12-5:
User test
12.12.03 for
Online Store
Web site.

Goals:
The main goal of the Web site is to sell products and get users to register.

User Scenario:
You're a customer looking to buy a book and become a registered user because you've heard you'll save on your purchase.

Testing Method:
- Three subjects—aged 25 to 40—who are all working professionals with incomes over $60,000 per year.
- One-on-one testing, one-hour videotaped session
- On-screen click-through shown in Web browser

Task 1: How would you buy a book called *Web Design For Dummies?*

	User 1: Male aged 32	User 2: Female aged 25	User 2: Female aged 36
Can the user find the books section of the online store?	Yes, store sections are clearly marked.	Yes, likes button treatment.	Yes, easy to find.
Are the navigation buttons clear?	Yes, likes consistent mini tab for all buttons.	All the buttons except for the subnav buttons under main tabs. Not clear that you are in the Featured Products section.	Not sure about the subnav treatment under the main tabs. Didn't realize that they were in the Featured Products section.
Can the user find and use the search function?	Yes, though not sure why it's a different color or upside down.	Did not realize that it was clickable. It looks different than the rest of the buttons.	Found it ok, just does not like its treatment. When you click on the other tabs, you go to a page. When you click on the Search tab, a mini search window appears. Thinks everything should be consistent.
Does the user understand how to add the book to their order?	Yes, after he found the book, it was easy to use the mini tab button to add the book to his order.	Yes, very clear.	Yes, likes the way that all the mini buttons look the same.
Additional comments and suggestions?	Thinks the search function should always be present on the page.	Make the subnav buttons look like the other tabs or like the mini buttons. Try a different highlighting system.	Feels strongly that the Search button should not be an upside-down tab—maybe have the mini search function always visible on the page. Also, try a different way of highlighting the subnav—make them look more like the main tabs?

With this sort of visual arrangement, it's easy to see where the big problems lie and to evaluate what things really need fixing. By using the grid system, you'll notice that the comment column often fills up with the same suggestions for fixing the big problems. This makes your redesign process that much easier.

Armed with this data, you can create a new set of designs. You may even consider e-mailing the updated designs to the testing group for one last chance at feedback from them before you go into final production. This also gives your testers a chance to see that their feedback made a difference.

Part IV

Producing the Final Web Site

In this part . . .

At the end of the day, when all the designers go home for their well-deserved rest, the HTML and programmer folks come in — lattes in hand — and begin final assembly of the Web site. Although Web site design is a team activity, everyone on the team must know a little bit about everyone else's job in order to make the whole process go smoothly. As a Web designer, this means you must know enough about how HTML and programming languages work so you can maximize their strengths.

For example, if you design a graphically heavy interface with a weird, slanted layout, the HTML people have a hard time implementing the design and making it look the way you intend. By knowing how HTML works, you are in a better position to design practical Web pages that load fast, are easy to update, and look great.

You also need to know what can and can't be done with modern programming languages. Tons of languages out there, with names like *ASP, PHP, CGI,* and *ColdFusion,* are all designed to do one thing — extend the power of your Web page and turn Web sites into near software-like applications.

Chapter 13

Surveying the HTML Landscape

In This Chapter

▶ Understanding HTML tags

▶ Using tables and frames

▶ Designing visual effects with HTML alone

▶ Figuring out HTML's interactive capabilities and limitations

*E*very Web page has two sides — the nice-looking side that the site's visitors see, and the HTML side that holds everything together and makes it all work. As a Web designer, you must know how the less-glamorous flip side of your page works so you can be a more effective designer. I'm not saying that you must know how to program HTML with your eyes closed, but you do need to know how HTML is structured, how you can maximize it, and under what circumstances you can copy and paste it (my favorite form of HTML editing).

HTML is great because mastering it is really not that difficult. Also, the Web makes discovering HTML tricks, tips, and shortcuts from other Web pages easy because your browser enables you to take a sneak peek at the HTML coding behind any Web page. In addition, the many powerful HTML software tools available make assembling whole Web sites as easy as using a graphics program to build your graphics — in fact, many of these software programs' interfaces look similar. In this chapter, you learn how to use tables and frames effectively to control your layout, how to use background tiles in your Web page, and how to make your page interactive with links.

So, without further ado, put on your propeller cap and take a look under the hood and into the world of HTML coding. Before long, you'll be trading in your designer's leather jacket for a set of waist-high floodwaters and a pocket protector — or not.

Understanding HTML: The Glue that Brings the Page Together

Everything that you see on most Web pages is held in place by a page layout language called *HTML* (HyperText Markup Language). Since the time that HTML was first introduced around 1990, it has evolved through the years from a simple way to display and link documents on multiple types of computers to its current capabilities to support complex page layouts, embed streaming media (see Chapter 15), and support add-in languages such as JavaScript.

A browser, such as Netscape or Internet Explorer, interprets the HTML code and draws the nice-looking side of the page that we all know and love. (It's interesting to note, by the way, that the first real Web browser on the scene, introduced in 1993, was called Mosaic. This little program was an overnight success and, just one year later, evolved into Netscape.)

Within the browser window, HTML is sort of like the "man behind the curtain" in the *Wizard of Oz,* pulling off an amazing display of graphics, animation, and media, all without being seen — that is, of course, until you peek.

Upon first glance at a page's HTML code, you may think that you're looking at specs for a rocket launcher, but it's really not that complex. HTML uses a system of *tags,* bits of code that define every type of element (from links to images) on a Web page. Tags are available to place images, create tables, define the font used, and just about every other task in between. All these tags are marked by a set of opening (<) and closing (>) characters. For example, an <href> HTML tag used for buttons and links looks like this:

```
<a href="page2.htm">Page 2</a>
```

In this code example, the user would see only an underlined Page 2 link on the Web page. Clicking on the link would take the user to another page — specifically, one called page2.htm. The link's text does not have to mirror the name of the page you are linking to. For example, the same <a href="page2..htm"> code can work just as well for the text "Click here to see my collection of pocket protectors." In this example, the whole sentence would appear as an underlined link to page2.htm:

```
<a href="page2.htm">Click here to see my collection of pocket
            protectors.</a>
```

For the most part, tags come in pairs. Each pair has an opening tag, in this case <a href="page2.htm">, and a closing tag, such as </a>. Both the opening and the closing tags are contained within the < and > characters. The text in between the *tag set*, Page 2, is the text you actually see on the Web page. For example, on a Web page, this HTML code would appear like the simple text link shown in Figure 13-1.

History of HTML and the Web

Though HTML and the Web as we know them today seem like they've only been around for a few short years, their roots actually trace back to the 1950s. Take a look at these interesting sites for a catalog of the Web's history:

`www.webhistory.org`

The people behind `webhistory.org` are assembling a definitive history of the World Wide Web. As of this writing, the timeline was still under development, but take a look — you may find some interesting nuggets here.

`www.w3.org/MarkUp/#historical`

The World Wide Web Consortium is sort of the keeper of the World Wide Web kingdom — approving all new HTML standards and just about every technology that integrates with HTML. This area of their site tracks the history of the Web's development.

`www.isoc.org/guest/zakon/Internet/History/HIT.html`

This last site has a great timeline that traces the idea of networked information all the way back to 1957.

Figure 13-1:
All links use `<href>` HTML tags.

Page 2

Learning HTML is mainly about learning about all the various tags and where they go in the code structure. If you can remember this much, you can get pretty far in your copying and pasting career. You can literally build Web pages by copying and pasting tags from other pages and then modifying them slightly for your own purposes. In fact, learning HTML by copying, pasting, and modifying is encouraged in the Web industry.

Sneaking a peek at the HTML source

For those wanting to use HTML, Web browsers are cool because they enable you to view the HTML source code of a page. As shown in Figure 13-2, sneaking a peek at the HTML code of a Web page is a great way to see how it's built and to see how you can do something similar. To see the HTML code behind a Web page, follow these simple steps:

1. **Get online and open a Web browser, such as Netscape Navigator or Internet Explorer.**

2. **Go to any old Web site by typing in the URL of any Web page that you'd like to see the HTML source of.**

3. **Look at the HTML source of the page:**

- In Netscape, choose View⇨Page Source from the menu.

- In Internet Explorer, choose View⇨Source.

As shown in Figure 13-2, you see a new window with the HTML code for the current page you are viewing. If you glance through, you'll see the text content of the page and all the ‹href› tags for each link. You can select and copy any portion of the page.

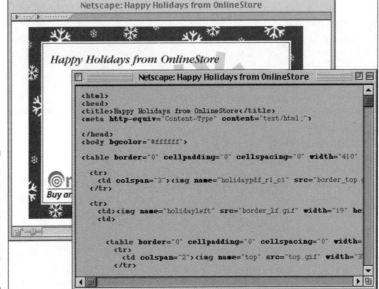

Figure 13-2: Browsers let you take a sneak peek at the HTML code of any Web page.

Learning (borrowing) from others

Now that you know that you can peek behind the HTML curtain, the next time you see an interesting Web page when surfing around the Internet, bookmark it for future reference. I've found that the best way to teach yourself HTML is to study the structure of pages you see every day. After looking at a number of these pages and picking them apart, you start to understand the basic structure of HTML code and the order in which tags should be laid out on a page. Understanding this before you start copying and pasting HTML code is crucial.

Like the wings of a butterfly, opening and closing HTML tags mirror each other in their position on the page. For example, the first line of an HTML-coded page opens with the ‹HTML› tag. The last line is the closing ‹/HTML› tag. This sort of mirrored hierarchy continues even down to the object level (like sentences, buttons, and so on). For instance, as Figure 13-3 illustrates, you can pile a few different tags onto a line of text. In Figure 13-3, notice how each closing tag follows in the reverse order of its opening tag. The first `<font face>` tag, for example, is paired with its closing `</font>` tag on the last line.

The HTML code

```
<font face="Verdana">
<b>
<font size="4">
Learn where to copy and paste code and you're golden!
</font>
</b>
</font>
```

Figure 13-3:
Three HTML
tags mirror
each other
in their
position on
either side
of the text.

Learn where to copy and paste code and you're golden!

What appears on screen

After you know the basic structure of an HTML page, you understand what parts to copy from other Web pages and where to paste them into your own page for further editing. If nothing else, copying and pasting HTML can save you a lot of typing and bugs due to accidentally leaving something out.

No two browsers interpret the same HTML code in the same way. Also, some HTML tags are unique to each browser. When a browser doesn't recognize a tag, it simply ignores it. Building a Web page that looks horrible in one browser and perfectly fine in another is entirely possible. Take a look at Figure 13-4 and Figure 13-5, for example. In Figure 13-4, this mini holiday greeting card is all screwed up when viewed in Internet Explorer. In Figure 13-5, this same card looks fine when viewed in Netscape Navigator. The reverse scenario is also true. You can build pages that look great in Internet Explorer, but look messed up in Netscape Navigator.

The main problem in Figure 13-4 is the size of the fonts. In this case, the fonts are much larger in Internet Explorer. The larger font size enlarges the size of the table cell, expanding the whole design. The other problem is that the cell is using a background tile. (Using a background tile is the only way to get the effect of writing HTML text on top of an image.) When the table cell expands with the larger text, you see the tile repeat.

One way to correct the repeating tile problem is to make the tile much larger than the table cell. This way, if the cell accidentally expands, you won't see the tile repeat. If you use large background tiles, just make sure you keep their designs simple and use fewer colors to keep the file size down. Otherwise, the page will take a long time to download. To fix the too-big font problem, use smaller absolute font sizes (see Chapter 6 for more information on that topic). In any case, it goes without saying that you must always test your HTML page on both browsers to make sure that your page works before you put it on the Internet for all to see.

Figure 13-4:
In Internet Explorer, this HTML page is stretched because the text is so large.

Figure 13-5:
In Netscape Navigator, the same page looks perfect because the text is the intended size.

Using Frames and Tables

By itself, HTML likes to arrange content from top to bottom and from left to right on the page. You can't get the effect of multiple columns or rows like a newspaper without using some sort of container system. Fortunately, two HTML container-like constructs are available to help you segment the page and to give you a lot more design flexibility: frames and tables.

A Web page that uses frames is similar to an old-fashioned window that contains several panes, each pane being in the shape of a square or a rectangle. Like a window, a Web page that uses frames is the "parent" that organizes multiple "child" Web pages within each of its "panes" (or frames). Inside each *frame* is a whole new Web page. This versatility enables you to design independently operating segments of your page. For example, as shown in Figure 13-6, one frame may contain a long scrolling list of content, whereas another frame with navigational choices does not scroll. This way, your navigation choices don't scroll away off screen along with the content!

The other way to segment content on the page is to use tables. Unlike frames, tables don't segment the page into multiple window panes. Instead, tables go *on* a Web page. A *table* is like a graph system that enables you to put different content into each cell of the table's grid. Tables give you tremendous control over the page layout because you can slice the table grid any way you like in order to create a number of cells. Each cell is like a mini Web page. As illustrated in Figure 13-7, each cell can have its own background color or tile, text, graphics, and form elements. In this example, I first show you a diagram of the table's structure and then show you how the table is filled with different form elements in each cell (text, text fields, a graphic, and a button) to create an interesting layout.

Why two pages are not always better than one

When you use frames, you chop the original Web page into multiple pages. You can use as many frames as you want to break the original Web page into multiple Web pages, but if you get too crazy, the Web page can become too difficult to manage.

When you click on a link in one frame to change the stuff in another frame, the link has to "target" that frame. If the link does not target another frame, the new page loads into the current frame. Before long, you've got a mess on your hands. Basically, when using frames, you must also pay special attention to the way you set up links and make sure to direct them to specific locations. Also, older browsers have difficulty bookmarking pages with frames. The browser doesn't know which Web page to bookmark!

Top frame with nav choices

Figure 13-6:
Because
this Web
page uses
frames, it's
actually
three pages
in one.

Side frame with photo   Content frame with scrolling list

Using frames also locks you in to a design structure. For instance, if the page
uses three frames, all a certain size, you've got to design three Web pages
that fit that size. If you ever want to update the site in the future, unless you
keep the same frame structure, you've got to redesign everything from the
ground up. Over time, this forced obedience to design structure makes rolling
out updates difficult.

Because of these kinds of problems, many designers have moved away from
using frames. Two pages are not always better than one for segmenting your
layout. Instead, many designers now rely more on tables.

How to keep it simple with tables

Tables are a lot more flexible than frames because tables make taking a modular approach to your page layout possible. You can have multiple tables of
all shapes and sizes on one Web page. I like to use one table for each major
area of the page — for example, one table for the navigation bar, one table
for the content area, and one table for the footer of the page. By using three

separate tables, each section is a modular unit that is easy to update. The navigation bar shown in Figure 13-8 is in its own table. Having the navigation bar in a separate table enables the company to dress the navigation up for the holidays without affecting the other content on the page. The folks at this Web site need to update only one table.

Plain image centered on page

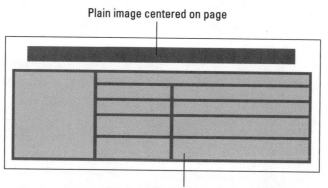

Diagram of table structure on next line of Web page

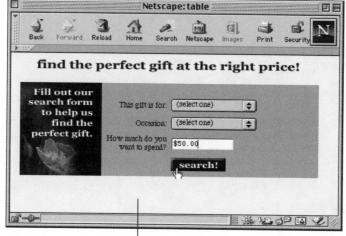

Figure 13-7:
A table structure is a grid system.

Page designed with help of table structure

When you do update tables, you can change their size and internal structure without affecting anything else on the page. Such flexibility is in stark contrast to the rigid structure of frames. To change the size and structure of a page with frames, you've got to redo all the frames making up the page. As the diagram in Figure 13-9 shows, tables are like blocks on the page. If you change the size of the top one, the one below just moves down the page a little to make room. Within each table, you have infinite control over the size, number, and placement of the cells.

Figure 13-8:
The navigation bar at this site is in its own table.

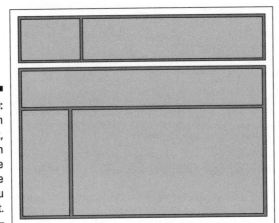

Figure 13-9:
Within each table block, you can structure the cells the way you want.

Within each table is a series of *cells,* smaller units that can each hold text, graphics, forms, and even their own background tiles. In a sense, each table cell is like a mini Web page layout. In fact, you can even place another whole table inside of a cell. Placing tables inside of table (called *nesting* tables in the biz) gives you an amazing amount of layout control. Take a look at how the table diagram in Figure 13-9 looks when it's filled with content, as shown in Figure 13-10.

Figure 13-10:
You can
place text,
graphics,
forms, and
even whole
other tables
inside each
table cell.

Letting HTML Do the Design Work

By using HTML features to their fullest, you can gain a lot of creative control over the layout of your Web page. In addition to enabling you to control the layout, HTML features (such as tables, background tiles, and background colors) can also contribute to the visual design of your page. By using colored tables, for instance, you can add visual effects while cutting down on the need for graphics.

 By using fewer graphics and more HTML, you can enhance the performance of a Web site. In addition, by relying less on graphics and more on HTML, you make the page easier to update, translate into other languages, and automate with database integration technologies.

Coloring your world with tables

 You can create a lot of visual effects just with tables alone. For example, each table cell can have its own background color that you set with HTML tags. In addition, each table can have a border that's any color you choose. Take a look at the banner graphic in Figure 13-11. This rich design actually uses no graphics at all. The whole thing is done with a fairly complex HTML table, as shown in Figure 13-12.

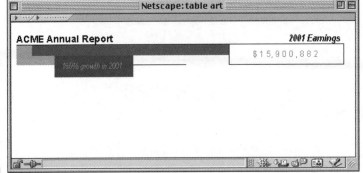

Figure 13-11:
This design
contains no
graphics,
just HTML
tags.

A colored table is placed within the cell of another table.

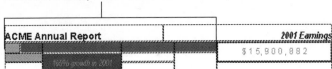

Figure 13-12:
The table
structure for
Figure 13-11.

To give you an idea of what the HTML code looks like for just one of these cells filled with color, I include it here:

```
<td width="57" height="46">
    <table width="57" border="0" cellspacing="0"
           cellpadding="0" height="46">
    <tr>
    <td width="23" height="15" bgcolor="#FF9900"> </td>
    <td width="34" height="15" bgcolor="#336666"> </td>
    </tr>
    <tr>
    <td colspan="2" height="13" bgcolor="#FF9900"> </td>
    </tr>
    <tr>
    <td colspan="2" height="18"> </td>
    </tr>
    </table>
</td>
```

The opening (`<td>`) and closing (`</td>`) tags define the table cell. Within the cell, I placed a separate table, marked by the opening and closing `<table>` tags. And just to confuse you further, within the table are more cells. This sort of arrangement of cells within a table within a cell — which somewhat resembles the arrangement of those wooden Russian dolls that stack inside each other — is called *nested tables*.

As you look through the code, you can see that I included a few attributes for each table cell, such as `height`, `width`, and `bgcolor`. The `bgcolor` attribute enables me to assign a unique background color to the cell. By simply coloring a bunch of cells with the `bgcolor` attribute, I was able to achieve the multicolor scheme shown in Figure 13-11, earlier in this chapter.

Designing with background colors and tiles

HTML also enables you to specify a background tile and a background color for an entire page. These additions provide two great ways to add texture to each page before you even put anything on it. It's like buying preprinted paper for your printer.

Plus, if you use the same background tile throughout a Web site, you can take advantage of the browser's caching ability. After the background tile loads in once, the browser stores it in memory. The next time it appears, the browser quickly redraws it from memory — a much faster process than downloading it again.

Adding a background tile and a background color to your HTML page is simple. You just need to add two tags in the `<Body>` section of the page like this:

```
<html>
<head>
<title>Using Background colors and tiles</title>
</head>

<body bgcolor="#FF9900" background="tilename.gif">
</body>

</html>
```

In the `<Body>` tag, the background color is defined with the `bgcolor` attribute. The number that follows, #FF9900, is the hexadecimal number for the color of the page. Following `bgcolor` is the `background` attribute that points to the filename of the art needed for the tile (in this case, tilename.gif.)

When you use background tiles, remember to take the word *tile* seriously. The nature of tiles is that they repeat and create a pattern. You can make your tile as big or as small as you'd like. In fact, a lot of designers like to make interesting designs that are much larger than the Web page. This way, you have a lot of control over the design because you have a larger canvas size to work with, and it won't repeat as a pattern until way off the screen — where the user is not likely to see it.

In Figure 13-13, look how much larger the tile is than the viewable space of the browser window. Because this design is fairly monotone, I can compress it down to just 25K. That's still a little on the large side; but if I use it on other pages throughout the site, its size becomes less of an issue because the browser simply redraws it from the cache.

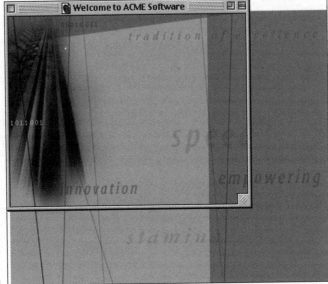

Figure 13-13:
A back-
ground tile
much larger
than the
Web page
will not
repeat until
off-screen.

Making Your Pages Interactive

Of course, the best part about HTML is the hypertext that the *HT* stands for. The capability of linking from one page to the next is what makes the Web so powerful. HTML, on its own, is capable of a few types of links that make a page interactive:

- ✔ **Regular links.** When you see an underlined text link or a single graphic, sometimes with a blue border around it, you're looking at a normal HTML link. The normal link uses the `<href>` tag:

  ```
  <a href="page1.htm">Page 1</a>
  ```

  In this case, the user sees an underlined text link "Page 1" on the page. Clicking it takes them to page1.htm.

- ✔ **Image maps.** Normally, one image can have only one regular link associated with it. If you want to assign multiple links to an image, you must use an image map. A few years back, this was a complicated task that required a separate file on the server with the link information. Yuck!

These days, the image can reference an image map that's located right on the page. The image map file contains all the active area data and links the image needs.

For example, the single GIF image shown in Figure 13-14 has four links. A rectangular *hotspot* defines the active area of each link. When a user rolls their mouse pointer inside the hotspot, the link becomes active.

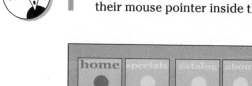

Figure 13-14:
This single
GIF image
has four
links
attached
to it.

Four hotspots define active link areas.

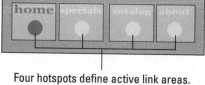

To make a hotspot work in HTML, you must have two things: an image map that is a set of coordinates defining each hotspot and its link and a `usemap` attribute tied to the image. Because a picture's worth a thousand words, take a look at Figure 13-15 to see how the two work together on an HTML page.

✔ **Anchor links.** Rather than jumping you to a different Web page, like a regular link or the links of an image map does, an *anchor link* jumps you to a specific point on the current page.

Anchor links are useful when you have long scrolling pages and you want the user to get to the right section quickly. For example, you can make a table of contents at the top of the page that has anchor links to the appropriate sections.

To make an anchor link work in HTML, you need two things: a link to the anchor and the anchor point itself. An anchor link looks pretty much the same as a normal link, but instead of typing the name of a Web page, such as **page1.htm**, you type # followed by the name of the anchor:

```
<a href="#part1">Part I</a>
```

The anchor point is basically the `<a name>` tag inserted at the spot in the Web page you want to jump to:

```
<a name="part1"></a>Part I: The quick brown fox jumped
        into a ditch.
```

✔ **E-mail links.** Finally, HTML can link to someone's e-mail address. E-mail links look just like any other links on the page, but usually when you click on them, the browser opens an e-mail composer with a message preaddressed to the intended recipient.

E-mail links use `mailto` in the normal `<href>` tag like this:

```
<a href="mailto:lisa@lopuck.com">Email me!</a>
```

The usemap attribute tells the image which map to use.

```
<html>
<head>
<title>Image Maps</title>
</head>
<body bgcolor="#ffff66">

<img name="content" src="content.gif"
width="279" height="69" border="0"
usemap="#lots_o_links">

<map name="lots_o_links">
<area shape="rect" coords="219,10,276,64" href="about.htm" >
<area shape="rect" coords="150,10,216,64" href="catalog.htm" >
<area shape="rect" coords="76,10,142,64" href="specials.htm" >
<area shape="rect" coords="6,10,72,64" href="home.htm" >
</map>

</body>
</html>
```

Figure 13-15:
In the HTML page, define a map of coordinates and links for each hotspot.

The lots o links image map is defined here with a set of coordinates and links.

Aside from these kinds of links, HTML can't do much more by itself to make a page interactive. You can define form elements, such as buttons and text fields, but to make them do anything worthwhile, such as process a credit card order, you've got to sprinkle in some programming written in other languages like ASP (Active Server Pages), Perl, or JavaScript. These kinds of languages weave right into the HTML code to supercharge the interactive experience. For more discussion on programming languages integrating with HTML, see Chapter 15.

Coding to Make You Feel Proud

Now that your head is spinning with all the things you can do with HTML coding, the good news is that you don't have to write a smidge of HTML by yourself if you don't want to. A number of WYSIWYG (What You See Is What You Get) software tools on the market can make you code like a true techie, and no one will ever have to know that you're just a lowly designer. (A WYSI-WYG editor is a software program like Dreamweaver or GoLive that enables you to build Web pages visually by clicking icons and making menu selections instead of typing code into a text editor.)

What's more, a lot of these HTML-writing tools have interfaces similar to those in graphics programs that you may already be familiar with, such as Fireworks and Photoshop. If pussyfooting around in a WYSIWYG editor is not your style, there are a few HTML text-only editors out there that'll put a few hairs on your chest — even if you're a woman!

You should know that there are two schools of thought on using WYSIWYG HTML editors. Some hard-liners think WYSIWYG editors are the "easy way out" and unnecessarily muddy up the code. Other folks think WYSIWYG editors are a great tool that can help you speed up the Web page production process and create Web pages without forcing you to know all the details of HTML coding.

Using WYSIWYG tools: HTML editing for Dummies

If you're like me, you want as much help as you can get when you're building a Web page. I have no pride when it comes to using a WYSIWYG HTML editor if it saves me from typing out tons of HTML code. I am more than happy to click on a cute little icon that inserts a whole table structure — and I gladly take full credit for that little maneuver.

A few different WYSIWYG tools are on the market for you to choose from. As shown in Figure 13-16, these tools enable you to click on buttons and icons to insert media into your page. In most cases, the interface of these tools looks like that of a graphics program, so if you're already comfortable using graphics software, you should take to these HTML editors like flies to sugar. In no particular order, my favorites are the following:

✔ **Adobe GoLive.** GoLive is a very visual environment that enables you to build a Web page by dragging elements such as text fields, images, and so on right onto the page. GoLive also helps you manage your whole site by automatically checking for bad links and making sure that the most current versions of your pages are the same on your computer as they are in your online site directory (where the Web site is hosted). You can download a free trial version of GoLive at the Adobe site:

```
www.adobe.com/products/golive/main.html
```

✔ **Macromedia Dreamweaver.** Like GoLive, Dreamweaver enables you to build Web pages and upload them to a remote server. In addition, Dreamweaver provides extensive tools for managing your whole Web site.

```
www.macromedia.com/software/dreamweaver
```

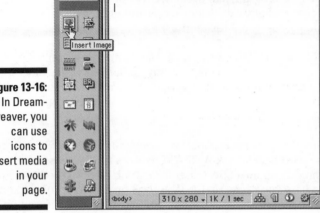

Figure 13-16:
In Dream-
weaver, you
can use
icons to
insert media
in your
page.

Both GoLive and Dreamweaver offer similar capabilities: Which you choose really comes down to which interface you prefer. Don't miss the free trial of Dreamweaver on the CD included with this book.

Using a text editor: Commando-style HTML

For you code warriors out there who want to type each line of HTML code yourself, you can use almost any text editor, including Microsoft Word. Some text tools, however, are specifically built for writing code. Some of these tools, such as BBEdit (a text editor that you can purchase online, designed specifically for Macs), number each line (so you can brag about how many or how few lines of code you've got in your Web page) and offer some nice features, such as Find and Replace.

In addition, these text editors enable you serious programmers to build forms and other common HTML elements quickly without feeling like you're cheating. Instead of clicking on an icon to insert such things, with BBEdit, you type code into "builder" windows that give you a little more control at the cost of being more complex to use.

Chapter 14

Controlling HTML Page Layout

*U*nless you take the bull by the horns, HTML has its own mind about laying out your page content. HTML starts at the top of the page, with a margin of just ten pixels from the top and left edges, and works its way downward, left to right, from there.

You can, however, take control of your HTML page. You can set your own margins for the page and design tables that shrink and expand with the size of the browser window while effectively organizing all your content. You can also use layout control technologies, such as CSS (Cascading Style Sheets) or DHTML (Dynamic HTML), to place graphics and text anywhere you want on the page. After you've finished laying out your pages, you can save them as HTML page templates that the production team can use throughout the site for a consistent presentation of the content. In this chapter, you find out how to use these techniques together so you can be the master of your own HTML page layout destiny — placing content exactly where you want it on the page.

Controlling Page Layout

HTML was designed by a bunch of technology folks who were thinking less about design and more about the cool factor of linking pages of text together. As a result, a lot of page design features were afterthoughts, like "Oh, maybe it would nice to let people set their own margins."

Since designers have become a part of the Web industry, HTML has evolved to include a few more page layout control features, such as Cascading Style Sheets, which allow you to place stuff wherever you want. For every other page layout need, designers have become fairly resourceful in pushing the capabilities of existing HTML features, such as table margins and transparent GIFs, to add a little extra space around page elements and control the presentation of content on the page.

Page margins

By default, an HTML page leaves about a ten-pixel margin from the top and left border of the page. You can, however, set the margin to whatever you'd like. You can make your page squished right to the edges of the browser window, or you can leave a large margin like the one shown in Figure 14-1. In this example, I used a decorative background tile with the company's logo and set the page margin so that all the content falls on the large colored block.

You can use two sets of margin attributes in the <Body> tag of your HTML page: one for the left margin of the page and one for the top margin of the page. You can't set a right or bottom margin because it's the nature of Web pages to scroll. Plus, you can never predict the width and size of a person's browser window — people have different-sized monitors.

Background tile

Figure 14-1:
The background tile and the page margin work together to create a layout.

Content spaced on tile with margins

If you want to get the effect of a right margin, use a table that spans only a certain percentage of the page. If you set the table's width to just 90 percent of the page, no matter how big or small the user's browser window, the table will stretch or compact to fit and leave a right margin.

The one drawback is that Netscape Navigator and Microsoft Internet Explorer honor different ways of writing the margin attribute. Take a look at what happens to the page in Netscape Navigator if you use only the Internet Explorer program's method of setting page margins. In Figure 14-2, the page content defaults to the ten-pixel margin and overlaps the background tile and logo.

Figure 14-2:
Netscape
Navigator
cannot
understand
the Internet
Explorer
program's
page margin
attribute.

To overcome this situation, include both ways of setting margins in your pages. The browsers read only what they can understand and skip the stuff they can't, so you're not going to confuse the browser by including two sets of margin instructions. Here's the HTML code needed to set the margins of your Web page:

```
<body bgcolor="#FFFFFF" background="bgtile.gif"
leftmargin="60"
topmargin="60"
marginwidth="60"
marginheight="60">
```

Internet Explorer understands the first two margin attributes, `leftmargin` and `topmargin`. Netscape Navigator understands the last two. Notice that they go inside the brackets, < and >, of the `<Body>` tag. This is an example of dual HTML coding as a way of dealing with different tag standards in the two browsers.

Even if you include both sets of margin attributes, I have found that sometimes the user has to reload the page in Internet Explorer for it to work correctly. If you continue to have problems with the margin attribute, you may want to look into alternative ways of getting the same effect, such as by using tables.

To use tables to create a margin, set up a table that has a blank first column and a blank top row. Set this column and row to a particular size and let them be your margins.

Ice, Jell-O, and liquid Web pages

Glenn Davis, founder of Project Cool (a company famous for the "Cool Site of the Day" awards), used the terms *ice*, *Jell-O*, and *liquid* as a way of describing and critiquing the design of Web pages. The terms refer to the way a Web page adjusts itself when the user resizes the browser window.

Like the term implies, an *ice page* remains frozen in place no matter what the user does to the size of his or her browser window. An ice page does not stretch or shrink to match the browser's window size; an ice page continues to cling to the left edge. *Jell-O pages* are little more flexible. When the user resizes the browser window, the page jiggles a little and centers itself on the page. A few elements adjust to the new window size. *Liquid pages* are, in Glenn's mind, the best kind of Web pages because they dynamically resize themselves to fit the size of the browser window. The content appears to pour into the window.

The fluidity of your Web page is important because it affects the user experience of your site. For example, if you have a small screen or an extremely large screen, an ice page looks funny. On a very small screen, the user can't see the whole page without scrolling. On a large screen, the Web page looks like a postage stamp stuck in the upper-left corner of the page.

So, how do you design a liquid page? You can start with tables. You can set the width of your tables to a percentage of the page; for example, make a table 90 percent of the browser's width. As shown in Figure 14-3, when the user resizes the browser window, the table and all its content resize, too, making the content look as if it was poured into the page.

Here's how to make a liquid table:

1. **Open any text or HTML editor, such as BBEdit, Dreamweaver, GoLive, or even Microsoft Word.**

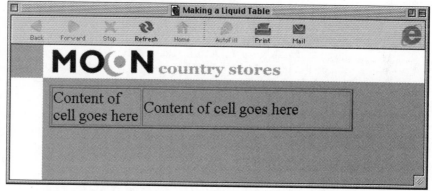

Figure 14-3:
Make tables
a percent-
age of the
browser's
width; they
will resize
with the
window.

2. **Insert the page basics.** Before you build any elements like a table on the page, you must first put the standard <HTML>, <Head>, and <Body> tags. Type the following into your page:

```
<html>
<head>
<title>Making a Liquid Table</title>
</head>
<body bgcolor="#FFFFFF">
```

3. **Build a liquid table.** For now, keep it simple and make a table that has just two columns. The key to making this table liquid is the percentages given to both the table itself and the individual columns within the table marked by the two <td> tags (a <td> tag creates a cell in a table). The table is 90 percent of the browser window's width. The cells defined by the <td> tags, however, make up 100 percent of the table's content, so their numbers must add up to 100. Type the following code next:

```
<table width="90%" border="2">
  <tr>
    <td width="30%">Content of cell goes here</td>
    <td width="70%">Content of cell goes here</td>
  </tr>
</table>
```

   4. **Finish up the page.** After the closing table tag, start a new line and type the following code:

```
</body>
</html>
```

   5. **Save the page as an HTML page (give it the .html extension after the filename), save it to your desktop where you can find it easily, and open it an a browser like Internet Explorer to view.**

   Except for the background tile and page margins added to the ⟨Body⟩ tag, your table and its cells should be the same size as the top image in Figure 14-3. Try resizing the browser window to make it small and then large and watch how the table resizes dynamically as in the bottom image in Figure 14-3. No matter what size you make your window, the table will always be 90 percent of its width.

Somewhat precise positioning with CSS layers

Although tables do afford you a lot of layout control, placing things exactly where you want them to go within the table (and thus on the page) is still difficult. To solve this problem, you can use CSS (Cascading Style Sheets) layers instead of (or in addition to) tables.

CSS is a standard Web layout technology that enables you to define and apply style sheets to HTML text. For example, you can create a CSS style to specify a particular font, font size, color, and paragraph alignment for any HTML text element, such as a header, a caption, and so on. CSS technology also allows you to layer HTML elements like text and graphics on top of one another and place each element anywhere you want on the Web page. This layering ability of CSS technology is called CSS layers. When you use a CSS layer, you basically create a mini-Web page that you can place anywhere on the page. Inside the CSS layer, you can place text elements, buttons, graphics, and any other HTML element.

CSS layers are difficult to create from scratch commando-style in a text editor. You must learn a whole different language of tags and code syntax to make CSS layers work. For this reason, my advice is to use a Web authoring tool like Dreamweaver to build them.

Within each CSS layer, you can place the normal lineup of tables, text, graphics, and forms. To position a CSS layer on a Web page, enter specific X and Y coordinates. For example, if X equals 25 and Y equals 25, the upper-left corner of the CSS layer starts 25 pixels down from the top and 25 pixels from the left edge of the page. If you are using Web authoring software, you can simply drag a visual representation of the CSS layer anywhere on the page and the software will automatically keep track of its X and Y position and update the CSS code in the HTML. If you are creating a CSS layer from scratch, the X and Y information is an attribute listed inside the CSS `<div>` tag as follows:

```
<div id="Layer1" style="position:absolute; left:73px;
        top:50px; width:139px; height:132px; z-
        index:1">Insert graphics, text, or whatever
        here</div>
```

In this example, the CSS layer named Layer1 is positioned 73 pixels from the left edge of the page and 50 pixels down from the top edge. I also want to call your attention to the `z-index` attribute. This attribute controls how the layer falls on top of or below other CSS layers. Layers with higher `z-index` numbers overlap those with lower `z-index` numbers.

CSS layers are cool because, as their name implies, you can place multiple layers on one Web page and overlap them. This capability enables you to achieve the unique effect of overlapping text and graphic elements, as shown in Figure 14-4.

CSS layers are not without their problems. I say that you can get "somewhat" precise positioning with them because older browsers, Netscape Navigator in particular, can have trouble interpreting them. If the user resizes the browser window after a page with CSS layers loads in, the layers may shift all over the page, and some of your text formatting may be lost. The user must reload the Web page (using the browser's Reload or Refresh button) to correct the layout.

CSS layers shown in a Web authoring tool.

Figure 14-4:
CSS layers
enable you
to overlap
elements
and place
them where
you want.

Overlapping CSS layers shown in the browser.

Finding Your Space

Whether you are using frames, tables, or CSS layers to position elements on the page, oftentimes you need a little extra space here and there in between graphics, or you may just want to nudge graphics in one direction or another. To get this micro level of page layout control, you can use a number of tricks that add breathing space around your elements.

Adding margins to tables

When you create a table, you have two options for adding a margin to the cells within: the Cellpadding and Cellspacing attributes. These two attributes are included in the opening `<table>` tag to define the table's margins. Each works a little differently, but the net effect is that each cell has a little space around it.

Cellspacing creates a gutter between the cells, as shown in Figure 14-5. Cellpadding adds a margin *within* each cell, so any content you add to the cell will be inset from the cell's edge, as shown in Figure 14-6. As the figure shows, the two methods have a dramatic impact when you assign a background color to the cells. Cellpadding creates no gaps between the cells themselves, however, so their background colors look like one solid color. If you want to get the effect of a continuous background color between cells but you want the content within the cells to have a margin, use Cellpadding but *no* Cellspacing.

You should always include both attributes in your opening table tag, even if you enter a value of zero for both. If you leave one or both of them out, the table will use its default settings: cell spacing of two pixels and cell padding of one pixel. Here's the HTML code for the effect shown in Figure 14-6:

```
<table width="53%" height="100" border="0"
cellspacing="0" cellpadding="5">
```

Figure 14-5:
Cell-
spacing
leaves a gap
between
cells, but
the content
is flush to
the cell's
edge.

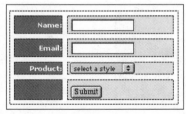

Figure 14-6:
Cell-
padding
adds a
margin with-
in each cell.

 Incidentally, if you use a table structure to piece a graphical image back, make sure that you set both cell spacing and padding to zero. As shown in Figure 14-7, this makes the image look like one seamless image. (You would cobble an image together rather than insert the image in its entirety so you can cut up the image and save each piece individually as a GIF or a JPEG. This practice, called *slicing*, allows you to get the best quality for each section of your image.) For more information on slicing graphics, see Chapter 10.

This image is broken into four cells

These two are GIFs.

These two are JPEGs.

Figure 14-7:
This table
uses no
spacing or
padding, so
each piece
butts up
perfectly to
one another.

Adding space around graphics

In the course of adding graphics to your HTML page or even within a table cell, you occasionally need to insert a little space here and there so that your images and text elements are not too close together. You may also want to nudge graphics a little to the left or to the right. In this section, I share various techniques that you can use to add that little extra space where you need it.

Soft and hard page breaks

When you type a line of text in HTML, the line, when it displays in a Web browser, goes all the way across to the end of the page or table cell and then automatically wraps to the next line. Left to its own devices, the text may look funny because, as in the case of the long headline in Figure 14-8, you could have one word left dangling on the next line.

Figure 14-8:
With no line breaks, the headline may wrap, leaving just one word on the next line.

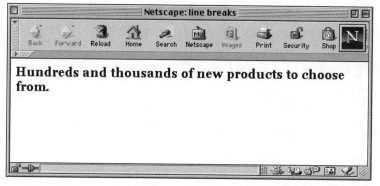

If you want to control where the text line breaks and wraps to the next line, as in Figure 14-9, you can insert a *soft line break* with a simple <br> tag. A soft line break creates less space than a hard line break, which is used to designate the space between paragraphs. Use the <br> tag like this:

```
Hundreds and thousands <br> of new products to choose from.
```

If you insert a soft line break, the page can look funny if the user shrinks the browser window. The line always breaks where you insert the <br> tag. Look what happens to the headline in Figure 14-10 when the user resizes the window. When you insert soft line breaks, you cause the page to become less "liquid" in its design.

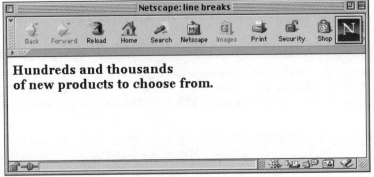

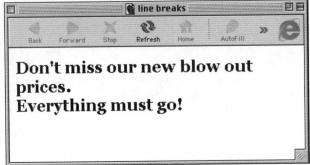

Entering a *hard line break* is like using the Enter key on the keyboard: Doing so leaves a big gap so you can start a new paragraph of text, as shown in Figure 14-11. Insert a hard break by entering the <p> tag:

```
Hundreds and thousands <br> of new products to choose from.
        <p>
Act now and you can save on all products in our new fall
        lineup.
```

Horizontal and vertical space around graphics

You can also assign a margin around each graphical element by using the vspace (vertical space) and hspace (horizontal space) attributes in the image tag (<img>). These attributes add a number of pixels on either side of the graphic. For example, if you assign a vspace of five pixels, you create a margin of five pixels above and below the graphic, as shown in Figure 14-12. The same principle applies for hspace. The code looks like this:

```
<img src="computer.jpg" width="168" height="140" hspace="0"
        vspace="10">
```

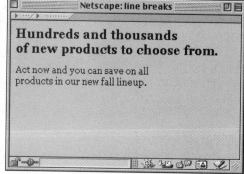

Figure 14-11:
By using
line breaks,
you can
control
the gap
between
lines and
line length.

Margins set by hspace and vspace

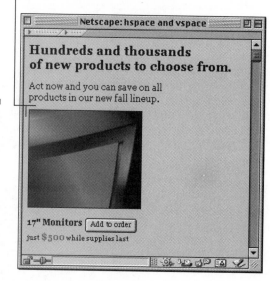

Figure 14-12:
The
vspace
and
hspace
attributes
add a
margin
around a
graphic.

The nonbreaking space trick

One way to add a little extra space wherever you need it is to insert a *non-breaking space*. Using this little gizmo is like using the space bar, only a little more effective. When you type text and enter a space between words by using the space bar, HTML honors only one space between words. You cannot press the space bar multiple times to get extra space.

To get a larger gap between words, graphics, and form elements, you can insert a nonbreaking space. The nonbreaking space is just a sequence of six characters like this:

```
 
```

To use it, simply type it where you want the extra space. To get a lot of space like at the beginning of the indented second line in Figure 14-13, repeat the nonbreaking space a few times like this:

```
Order online!<br>
   We guarantee fresh delivery every day.
```

Figure 14-13:
Use the
nonbreaking
space trick
to add an
indentation.

Order online!
We guarantee fresh delivery every day.

Nonbreaking spaces are also used to fill the contents of unused table cells. Some browsers do not render a table correctly if no content (for example, text or a graphic) appears between the opening and closing <td> tags of a cell. Therefore, if you have a table that has nothing in one of the cells (as is the case if you are using the cell to create a margin), make sure that you at least include a nonbreaking space in the empty cell. For example, in Figure 14-14, many of the table cells are just decorative — using the cell's background color as a design element only. In order for these empty cells to show up correctly, you must include the nonbreaking space, like this:

```
<tr>
     <td bgcolor="#CCCC33"> </td>
     <td bgcolor="#999900"> </td>
     <td bgcolor="#CCCC33"> </td>
     <td bgcolor="#999900"> </td>
     <td bgcolor="#CCCC33"> </td>
</tr>
```

Figure 14-14:
To ensure
that empty
table cells
show up
properly,
insert a
nonbreaking
space.

CATALOG

In this example, you can see the cell's background color attribute within the `<td>` tag. The content between the opening and closing `<td>` tags is just a nonbreaking space. If you do not include the nonbreaking space between the tags, the same design ends up looking like the one shown in Figure 14-15.

Figure 14-15:
If you
remove the
nonbreaking
space, the
browser
displays the
design
incorrectly.

Figure 14-15:
If you
remove the
nonbreaking
space, the
browser
displays the
design
incorrectly.

Keep in mind that using nonbreaking spaces is not a reliable means of maintaining the size and shape of a table cell. Nonbreaking spaces are best used to add extra space in between words and HTML elements like buttons and text fields (instead of, or in addition to, using the normal space achieved with the space bar). For the most reliable way of maintaining the size and shape of table cells, insert a small transparent GIF, called a *shim,* into them. What's a shim? Read on. . . .

Transparent shim images

If nonbreaking spaces are the only things in your table cells, different browsers may draw the cells differently. For example, if you set the table cell to be a particular size, some browsers ignore the dimension if the only content in the cell is a nonbreaking space. The best way to guard against this event occurring is to place a single 1 pixel x 1 pixel transparent GIF in it. As long as something is in the table cell, the browser will properly interpret the sizing. These transparent spacer graphics, often called *shims,* are a handy addition to your HTML design tool kit.

For example, take a look at Figures 14-16 and 14-17. In both designs, a table creates the effect of a rule line and a one-pixel border around the word *Catalog.* This table uses cells set to just one pixel high or wide with a black background to create the rule and border. If I use only nonbreaking spaces in the table cells, the cells expand, spoiling the effect, as shown in Figure 14-16. If I simply put a 1 pixel x 1 pixel shim in each cell, the browser draws the cells perfectly, as shown in Figure 14-17.

Figure 14-16:
A browser won't draw table cells correctly if they use only nonbreaking spaces.

Figure 14-17:
If you insert a transparent shim in each cell, the browser draws the table correctly.

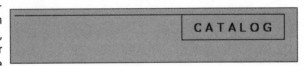

 Transparent shims come in handy not only as placeholders in empty table cells, but also as spacer graphics. You can resize shims any way you want with the HTML <image> tag. With the <image> tag, you can really control the amount of spacing between two page elements. For example, if you want to place a 20-pixel gap between two elements, such as the text field and the Find button in Figure 14-18, you can insert a transparent shim and resize it in the HTML code like this:

```
<input type="text" name="product">
<img src="shim.gif" width="20" height="8">
<input type="submit" name="find" value="Find!">
```

 Transparent shims do pretty much the same thing as nonbreaking spaces, but because shims are images, you can resize them to add space in the vertical direction, too. Besides, if you use the same 1 pixel x 1 pixel shim again and again for all your spacing needs, you don't increase your Web page's download time. The shim has a tiny file size to begin with, and after the browser downloads the file, it goes into the browser's cache, where it is quickly redrawn from memory whenever needed.

With no spacer, the form elements almost touch.

Figure 14-18:
Unless you insert space between form elements, they butt up against one another.

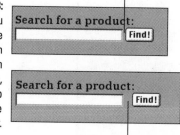

A 20-pixel wide shim creates space between the elements.

Because the shim is transparent, you can resize it as much as you want in the HTML <image> tag — you won't see any distortion. If you mess with the sizes of opaque graphics, however, you really do some damage. Take a look at Figure 14-19. Never use the HTML <image> tag to alter the size of an opaque image. If you want the distorted look, doing the distorting in a graphics program, where you can control the effect, is better.

Figure 14-19:
Resizing an opaque image with the HTML <image> tag can cause distortion.

When building Web pages, shims are great tools to keep on hand. You can create a shim in almost any graphics program. You simply create a 1-pixel-x-1-pixel image of any color and export it as a transparent GIF. You can even create such a pixel image by using the trial version of Fireworks on the CD accompanying this book. To make a shim in Fireworks, follow these simple steps:

1. **Launch Fireworks and start a new file.** In the New Document dialog box (shown in Figure 14-20), make the image 1 pixel wide and 1 pixel tall, choose the white background color option under Canvas Color, and click OK.

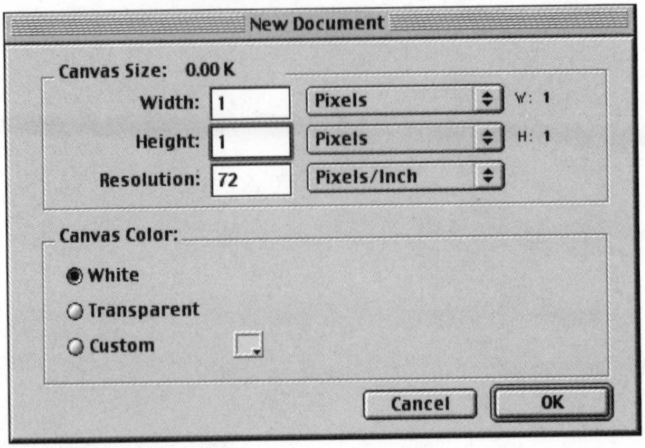

New Document

Canvas Size: 0.00 K

Width: 1   Pixels   W: 1
Height: 1   Pixels   H: 1
Resolution: 72   Pixels/Inch

Canvas Color:

● White
○ Transparent
○ Custom

Cancel   OK

Figure 14-20:
Create a
new file that
is 1 pixel x 1
pixel with
a white
background.

2. **Optimize as a transparent GIF.** To make this image a transparent GIF, use Window⇨Optimize to open the Optimize palette. (Check your screen first; the Optimize palette may already be open.) Choose the GIF format from the pop-up list as shown in Figure 14-21. Then choose Index Transparency from the bottom pop-up list.

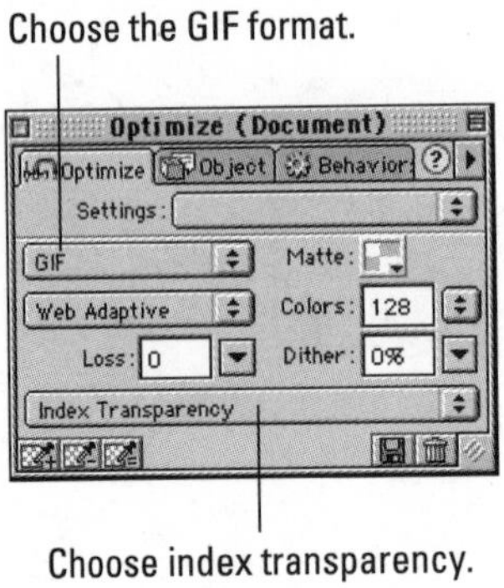

Choose the GIF format.

Figure 14-21:
In the
Optimize
palette,
choose the
GIF format
and then
choose
Index Trans-
parency.

Optimize (Document)

Optimize   Object   Behavior

Settings:

GIF   Matte:
Web Adaptive   Colors: 128
Loss: 0   Dither: 0%
Index Transparency

Choose index transparency.

3. **Export the transparent GIF.** To export this shim ready for use in your Web page layouts, choose File⇨Export. In the Export dialog box that appears, name your file as shown in Figure 14-22 and make sure that Images Only is chosen from the list of save options. Click Save.

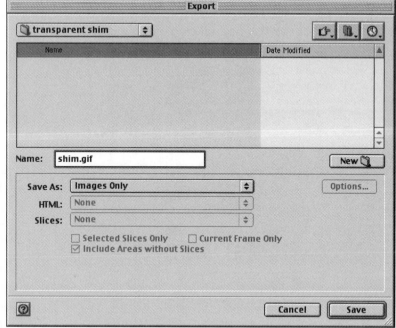

Figure 14-22:
Choose
File⇨Export
and then
name and
save your
transparent
GIF.

Building HTML Design Templates

After you've massaged your HTML page layouts to get them looking exactly as you'd like, you can save them as templates that the production team can use throughout the site. Many Web sites have hundreds of pages, but most of these pages are based on just a handful of templates. I like to distill my template pages down to the bare essentials with dummy stand-in images and text that are easily replaced with the real content.

In addition, if you design your pages with tables, you can architect the page so that certain components each use a different table layout. For example, as shown in Figure 14-23, you can design the main navigation bar in one table and the subnavigation in a different table. The main body of the page can go in yet another table, and the footer of the page can go in its own table. This modular approach makes assembling pages by stringing a few different tables together easy. It also makes updating your pages in the future easy. If you update just the navigation bar, replacing the navigation table on each of your pages by simply copying and pasting is easy.

Design the navigation system in independent tables.

Inside the main body table, you can paste a new table.

Figure 14-23:
By using
tables to
separate
sections,
you can
take a
modular
approach to
layout.

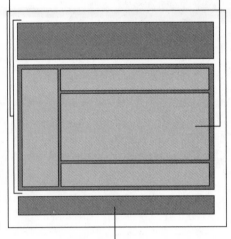

Design the footer section in its own table.

Chapter 15

Web Sites on Steroids

In This Chapter

▶ Boosting an HTML page's interactivity with programming languages and media

▶ Building automated, personalized Web pages

*F*inding a major commercial Web site these days that's not using some form of technological steroids to boost performance, enhance interactivity, and allow its Web masters to automate it is rare. HyperText Markup Language (HTML) by itself can do some basic linking and control the layout presentation of the page, but that's about all. In order to do the cool stuff, such as inserting a personalized greeting, you have to interweave code in languages such as JavaScript, ASP, and others into the HTML code.

I put this chapter last in this part because you don't have to know how to become a serious programmer in order to be a good Web designer (audible sigh of relief here); you just need to know what kind of technological options are available to you. You must know what is and what's not inside the realm of possibility in order to be an effective Web designer.

In this chapter, I take a survey-like approach to all the different technological options that you have available to you, what they do, and what sort of ramifications they have on your site. After you read this chapter, you'll be able to talk intelligently about Web technologies, or at least give people the impression that you know what you're doing.

Injecting Power into HTML Pages

HMTL is great because you can interweave other programming languages right in to it. Without knowing any better, you could look at an HTML page, like the one shown in Figure 15-1, and not know where the HTML code stops and the programming begins.

Figure 15-1:
HTML and programming code can interweave side by side in the document.

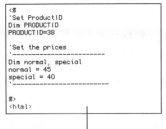

The ASP code opens a connection to an online database.

In the page layout, the ASP code grabs the correct data and the HTML formats it.

In the example shown in Figure 15-1, Active Server Pages (ASP) programming opens a connection to an online database. The ASP code goes at the top of the page before the opening `<html>` tag. Then, later in the page layout, the form elements reference the ASP programming to insert the correct data in the page. The coding language and the HTML work perfectly together, leveraging each other's strengths. The ASP code grabs the data, and the HTML formats it.

The one drawback to some programming languages is that if you're the tinkering designer type, you can't teach yourself by looking at the examples on other Web pages. Using the browser's View⇨Source menu option shows only the HTML code, not the programming code within. Only some languages that are included in the HTML page, such as JavaScript and DHTML, show up in the View⇨Source window. For a closer look at Web programming languages, check out books like *JavaScript For Dummies* by Emily A. Vander Veer and *Dynamic HTML For Dummies* by Michael Hyman (both published by Hungry Minds, Inc.).

JavaScript junkie

JavaScript is a fairly robust, object-oriented programming language you use to add all manner of interactive features to your Web page, such as the ever-popular rollover buttons and jump menus. Because you can see JavaScript code in the browser's view source window, you can easily see how the language is used and utilize the example for your own purposes.

To use JavaScript in your Web page, define a few functions and commands at the beginning of your HTML code (before the closing `</head>` tag). Then reference these commands in the media that you place on the page. For example, if you want to make a rollover button, you first define the rollover function up in the `<head>` section. In the following example, the JavaScript code creates three functions:

✔ MM_findOjb. This function is used by the swapImage function to help it
identify the correct image to use for the rollover.

✔ MM_swapImage (). This function exchanges the current graphic for
another that reflects the rollover state of the button when the user
moves their mouse over the button.

✔ MM_swapImgRestore. The purpose of this function is to restore the original graphic, representing the resting state of the button, when the user
moves their mouse off the button.

This code was generated automatically in Fireworks. After you build a rollover
button in Fireworks, the program will export not only the graphics, but the
HTML page with the JavaScript code needed to make the button work:

```
<script language="JavaScript">

function MM_findObj(n, d) { //v3.0
  var p,i,x;  if(!d) d=document;
              if((p=n.indexOf("?"))>0&&parent.frames.length) {
    d=parent.frames[n.substring(p+1)].document;
              n=n.substring(0,p);}
  if(!(x=d[n])&&d.all) x=d.all[n]; for
              (i=0;!x&&i<d.forms.length;i++) x=d.forms[i][n];
  for(i=0;!x&&d.layers&&i<d.layers.length;i++)
              x=MM_findObj(n,d.layers[i].document); return x;
}

function MM_swapImage() { //v3.0
  var i,j=0,x,a=MM_swapImage.arguments; document.MM_sr=new
              Array; for(i=0;i<(a.length-2);i+=3)
  if ((x=MM_findObj(a[i]))!=null){document.MM_sr[j++]=x;
              if(!x.oSrc) x.oSrc=x.src; x.src=a[i+2];}
}
function MM_swapImgRestore() { //v3.0
  var i,x,a=document.MM_sr;
              for(i=0;a&&i<a.length&&(x=a[i])&&x.oSrc;i++)
              x.src=x.oSrc;
}
</script>
```

After that mess is out of the way, you can then reference each function by
name (for example, mm_swapImgRestore) in the HTML code. In the following
example, button.gif is replaced with button2.gif (the highlighted state)
when the mouse pointer rolls over it. The SwapImage function takes care
of the rollover by making button.gif disappear and replacing it with
button2.gif. When the user's mouse pointer rolls off the graphic, the
SwapImageRestore restores it to its original state by displaying button.gif
again. Notice that the reference to the JavaScript code goes inside the <href>
link for the button.gif graphic:

```
<a href="#" onMouseOut="MM_swapImgRestore();"
          onMouseOver="MM_swapImage('button','','button2.gif
          ',1);" ><img name="button" src="button.gif"
width="60" height="60" border="0"></a>
```

JavaScript comes in two forms: client-side and server-side. In *client-side* Java-Script, like the example above, the Web page itself contains all the JavaScript functions needed to work properly. Pages with *server-side* JavaScript must reference code on a remote server in order to function properly. The Web page by itself does not work correctly. Although server-side JavaScript sounds like a pain, you can actually do cooler things with it, such as access an online database to personalize the page or automatically insert information. Because server-side coding is hidden from an end-user's view, server-side JavaScript (and any other server-side coding) prevents people from altering (also known as hacking) the code of important stuff like a login or credit card processing function.

Embedded media

If you can't create something with HTML or programming languages woven into the page, you can probably create it with whole self-contained applications, such as Flash and QuickTime movies embedded in the page. These movies have their own interactivity, and in the case of Flash games and applications, can be fairly complex on their own.

To place these kinds of media elements in the page, use the <object> and <embed> tags. The process of embedding a movie is similar to placing a still image in your page. You have to specify height and width and various other attributes like this:

```
<embed src="movie.swf" quality=high
          pluginspage="http://www.macromedia.com/shockwave/d
          ownload/index.cgi?P1_Prod_Version=ShockwaveFlash"
          type="application/x-shockwave-flash" width="500"
          height="350" loop="false">
</embed>
```

After you place a media element in the Web page, it has its own set of controls and acts independently of the other elements (text, links, buttons, and so on) on the page. Take a look at the full-screen video presentation in Figure 15-2. In this presentation, for example, users can watch a video and hear the instructor's voice teaching them how to use Fireworks. Users can control the volume, pause, play, and even skip around to different sections for review. Plus, the QuickTime compression makes the movie download quickly over a 56K modem.

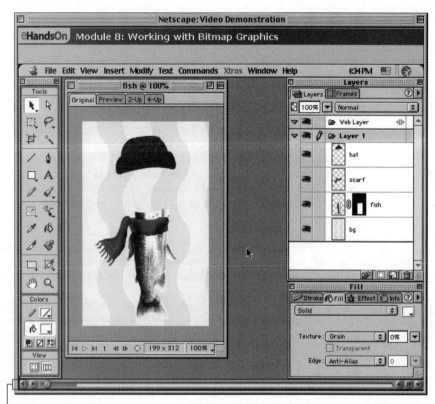

Figure 15-2:
A full-screen
training
video from an
instructional
Web site.

Playback controls

Users must have a special plug-in downloaded and installed in their browser in order to view embedded media properly. For example, users who don't have the QuickTime Player plug-in get an error when loading the page in Figure 15-2. You can plan for this possibility by adding a JavaScript function to the page that auto-detects the plug-in. If the plug-in is not found, the JavaScript code could automatically redirect users to another version of the Web page that does not require a plug-in. Another way to handle the plug-in problem is to include a link on the page that directs users to a URL where they can download and install the correct plug-in like this one for the Flash plug-in:

```
Pluginspage="http://www.macromedia.com/shockwave/download/ind
             ex.cgi?P1_Prod_Version=ShockwaveFlash"
```

Webcasts and streaming media

Although video, audio, and animated files add a lot of life to your Web site, they can be cumbersome for users to download. Most users today access the Internet via their phone lines and their computer's internal modem. The speed of these internal modems is usually 56,000 bits (56K) per second — meaning that they can download only 56K worth of data each second. If you consider that a Web page with a media like a QuickTime movie can add up to one megabyte (which translates to 1,000,000 bits), the page would take nearly 18 seconds to download. That's almost the same time it takes to sit through a TV commercial (commercials are 30 seconds long). Viewing the Web through a 56K modem connection is like drinking syrup through a straw — there's simply not enough bandwidth (a fat enough straw) to deliver Web content quickly.

Until fast broadband Internet connections like DSL (Digital Subscriber Line) and cable modems are mainstream, expecting users to wait for large files to download before they see anything cool is simply not practical.

To get around the problem of inadequate bandwidth, you can use media (such as movies and audio) that *stream* instead of download when a user visits your Web site. Streaming media downloads one chunk at a time so that people can start watching or listening almost immediately to the first chunk while the rest of the chunks download. Streaming media can come in two forms:

- ✔ Live *Webcasts*, which are events that are accessible only during the actual broadcast time
- ✔ On-demand media that's accessible at any time

Working with and preparing streaming media is a little different than preparing other media like graphics. You must encode the file for a number of Internet speeds; for example, prepare one for 56K connections and another for DSL connections. The server then delivers the correct file for the user's connection speed. For even better performance, you can upload the files to different servers. If a lot of people look at the same file simultaneously, then you don't put undue strain on one server or slow down the media's delivery time.

A number of different file formats support streaming, and each includes its own special server needs and production procedures. The following is a list of different file formats and links to purchase and download software for preparing streaming media files:

- ✔ **Apple's QuickTime**

    (www.apple.com/quicktime)

    Use QuickTime for streaming audio, animation, and video presentations.

✔ **Macromedia Flash**

(www.macromedia.com/software/flash)

Use Flash to build interactive, vector-based applications, movies, and games and to save them in a streaming format.

✔ **RealMedia**

(www.real.com)

RealMedia offers two streaming formats: RealVideo and RealAudio formats.

✔ **Windows Media files**

(www.microsoft.com/windows/windowsmedia)

Use for audio and video presentations.

✔ **MP3**

(www.mp3.com)

Use this format for streaming audio and music files.

Creating Dynamic, Database-Driven Web Pages

To be a true business machine, a Web site has to act as the bridge between the customer and the company's processes. The Web site must be able to funnel a customer's requests to the right company databases so that the company can serve them. For example, customer service inquiries must route to the customer service database, whereas ordering info must first be processed and then sent on to both the shipping and accounting departments.

In addition, business Web sites must be easy to scale in size (quickly add and subtract new pages) and update (change ads, change promotions, and so on). To make these two things happen, Web pages must have extra programming code added into them to make them dynamic. In the Web design world, a *dynamic* Web page is automated through the use of programming languages that interact with online server scripts and databases.

Client-side and server-side programming languages

You can add two kinds of scripting to your Web page to make it more dynamic: client-side scripts and server-side scripts. You embed these scripts, written in programming languages such as ASP, Java Server Pages (JSP), Common Gateway Interface (CGI), Hypertext Preprocessor (PHP), and Visual Basic Script (VBScript), right into the HTML page.

Client-side scripts are those that are self-contained and do not rely on an external script or database in order to function. Here's an example of a simple client-side VBScript that greets a user in a small window that is separate from the Web page:

```
<HTML>
<TITLE>Sample of VBScript</TITLE>
This page has a tiny VBScript program that greets the user.
<SCRIPT Language=VBScript>
Msgbox "Howdy partner"
</SCRIPT>
</HTML>
```

Server-side scripts are written with languages like ASP and PHP. The Web server processes these scripts before the Web page loads into your browser. Server-side scripts enable a Web page to open a connection to a database where certain information, such as product names, pictures, and prices, is stored. After the connection is established, the programming code can retrieve this data, and the HTML can format and place it on the page. The page can also add information, such as a customer's registration info, to the database.

For example, imagine an online store with hundreds of products. Building each product page by hand is simply not practical. Prices change on a daily basis, products change or are discontinued, and others are added to the mix. Building one Web page as a template to display each product is much more efficient. The HTML portion takes care of the page presentation, while the embedded programming retrieves the correct product image, description, and price from the online database.

Take the easy route: Change a product's price once in the database and have all the Web pages in the site that reference it automatically update. Then, when customer orders a product, the scripts in the page can update the online database with the customer's order.

Server-side includes

To take the dynamic Web page approach to the extreme, you can design a Web page as a layout template that is automatically filled with content from the server. This tactic is useful for frequently used content items that occur on multiple pages throughout your site, such as headers, navigation systems, and footers. To make this work, the Web page uses server-side includes.

Server-side includes (SSI) enable you to populate a Web page with content on the fly as users download it. To work correctly, the Web page using SSI must be named with the `.shtm` or `.shtml` file extension rather than the usual `.htm` or `.html` extension. This extension tells the server to look for the SSI commands on the page, find the appropriate content on the server, and deliver that to the page.

The best part about using SSI is that if you ever need to make a change to one of the dynamically inserted content pieces, such as the header, you just need to make the change once. By changing the one header file, all the pages in the Web site that include it automatically update faster than you can say, "Isn't that cool?!"

Although server-side includes sound like amazing time-savers from a site maintenance point of view, they do put a strain on the servers: Every time that a user comes to the site, each page has to access the server to retrieve some of its content. This can significantly slow down the site's performance and adversely affect the user experience.

Personalized Web pages with cookies

Did you ever visit a Web site and were shocked that the site greets you by name? The magic sauce that makes this sort of personalization possible comprises little bits of code called cookies.

In the Web design world, *cookies* are little pieces of data that a Web page leaves behind on your computer — sort of like a trail of data crumbs. As you use the site (for example, to order a product), the cookie stores information about your computer, your preferences, your name, and so on. The next time that you return to this Web site, it can seem personalized. The site reads the information on your cookie, and presto! — the page welcomes you by name.

Users can turn off the cookie feature in their browsers; so if you plan to use cookies, make sure that your Web pages can work without them. The user's experience shouldn't rely on cookies, just be enhanced by them.

Cookies can also pose a security risk for users. Because they store personal information like the user's name or Web site login information, cookies can be a target for other Web sites trying to get a user's personal information. Only the Web site that left the cookie on the computer is supposed to be able to retrieve data from it, but some folks have suspected that it's possible for other sites to hack into them. For more information on cookies, see `www.cookiecentral.com`.

E-commerce shopping carts

To facilitate online shopping, designers and programmers have come up with a shopping cart metaphor that enables people to pick out things to buy and add them to their virtual shopping basket. Shopping carts are not tangible — you don't buy a particular piece of software and plug it into your Web site to create a shopping cart. A shopping cart is more of a user interface design metaphor that enables people to pick out multiple things as they shop, review their items, make changes to their order, see how much everything costs, and then make purchases with their credit card.

To orchestrate all these features, a series of Web pages, online server scripts, and databases work together. The Web pages use programming languages such as ASP, JSP, CGI, or Perl to connect with online scripts and databases to process a customer's order and credit card information.

Part V

The Part of Tens

"Just how accurately should my Web site reflect my place of business?"

In this part . . .

No *For Dummies* book would be complete without the requisite lists of ten that you can use as a handy reference. In this part, I compile convenient lists of all the important stuff you need to know — from tips to running your own Web design business to user interface techniques and HTML tricks.

If you read nothing else in this book, read this part: It gives you the quick basics to get you designing effective Web sites in no time. Chapter 19 concludes with a Top Ten list of the things that can go wrong in the Web development process, so you can plan for them and know how to respond like a pro.

Chapter 16

Ten Tips for Managing Your Web Design Business

- -

In This Chapter

▶ Assembling an online and offline portfolio

▶ Taking screen shots of your work

▶ Talking about your work with clients and employers

▶ Assembling a proposal

▶ Determining your hourly consulting rate

▶ Understanding how Web design agencies charge for work

▶ Managing a client's expectations for a project

▶ Setting and enforcing a client's responsibilities

▶ Managing a Web project

▶ Hiring and managing subcontractors

- -

My favorite saying that sums up almost any professional's life is "You go to work for a company for the illusion of security, and you go to work for yourself for the illusion of freedom." (I give credit for this saying to inter-face designer Abbe Don.) Nothing could be truer. When you start your own Web design business, you spend more time than you realize doing nondesign-oriented stuff like assembling presentations, billing, collecting, and marketing your services. All your free time goes out the nearest open window.

On the flip side, when you work for a company — especially in the design services arena — you never know how the company will shrink and expand with the changing market forces and when you might be laid off. For these reasons, it's good to be proficient working in both settings: as an independent consultant working for yourself, and as a designer working with a team in a larger organization.

In this chapter, I offer tips on how to do the ten tasks that I've found most crucial for your Web design career, either when you're on your own or when working for a company.

Presenting Your Portfolio to Clients

Whether you are going on a job interview to work at a company or you are presenting your work to clients to help win their business, keep these techniques in mind when assembling and presenting your portfolio:

- ✔ **Assemble an offline and an online portfolio package.** Different clients and employers have their own ways of evaluating prospective designers. Some ask you to send them your *book* (a book with prints of your work), and others ask for a list of URLs of sites you've designed. To plan for these different scenarios, you should design a portfolio package that contains both an online and an offline component. Each should be self-contained so you can send either on a moment's notice and trust that they'll do the job.

- ✔ **Build an online portfolio Web site.** Often, a client asks for a list of URLs to Web sites you've designed. Rather than just e-mailing a list of URLs to the client, assemble samples of your work in one nicely designed online portfolio site and e-mail just the URL of your portfolio site.

  By making your own online portfolio site, you can also show work that's no longer live on the Web. Rather than providing a link to a nonexistent site, you can show images from the site and provide a little blurb about the project. In fact, I like to show images (scaled down to about one-quarter size) of the Web site and include a little paragraph that describes what I did, what design challenges I encountered, and how I solved those challenges. As shown in Figure 16-1, providing a little background on the project helps clients and employers better evaluate your designs.

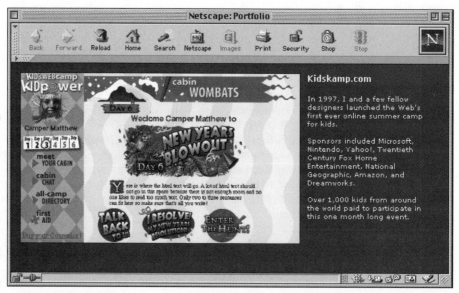

Figure 16-1: In your online portfolio, show screen shots of your work and include a blurb.

✔ **Build an offline portfolio book.** In addition to your online portfolio Web site, you should assemble a book full of printed editions of your work. You can buy any one of a number of cool-looking portfolio books at your local art (not craft) store for about $80. These usually have black paper in a binderlike book, so you can take the pages out and rearrange them as needed.

You may be surprised to find out that a lot of employers at design agencies ask you to send your portfolio to them, rather than asking you to bring it in personally. If you aren't present, your book is your only representation, so you've got to make sure that it is polished, consistent, and professional.

Take screen shots of your work and print them at full size in full color on glossy paper. Glossy paper gives you better color results than matte paper. You can decide whether to leave the browser interface in the screen shots, but whatever you do, do it consistently. Use a light spray adhesive, such as Spray Mount, to mount your prints onto the black paper of the book. Finally, make sure that your book is not too big and not too small: Fourteen by seventeen inches is a good size to shoot for.

✔ **Put together a biography.** If you are an independent consultant, a client does not want to look at your résumé to get a sense of your qualifications. A client looks mainly at your portfolio of work. Still, providing a short paragraph that outlines your professional experience and accomplishments is a good idea. Remember, after you sell a client on your services, the client has to turn around and sell you to the other people he or she works with. If the client can rattle off a few fun facts about you to grease the skids a little, her job is easier.

In addition, a bio is helpful to include at the top of your résumé when you are seeking a design job at a company. A bio is like an executive summary that sums up your experience and gives you a chance to sell yourself before the potential employer drills into the job-history listings. Listings can get a little monotonous because they all follow the same format: job, date held, title, and what you did.

✔ **Present your portfolio to clients and employers.** When the big day arrives and you meet with a client or employer in person, dress the part. Come armed with not only your portfolio, but also some sort of leave-behind material. As the name suggests, a *leave-behind* is a version of your portfolio with some added information, such as your bio and résumé, which you can leave with the client or employer. (I like to bind these together in a customized booklet. I think it lends an added touch of polish to your presentation.)

✔ **Be enthusiastic about your work.** The biggest mistake that new designers make is being too humble about their work (or even making excuses for — or berating — their work). As I always say, "If it's good enough to show, it's good enough to defend." Talk positively about your work. Discuss design challenges you may have faced, such as "This client wanted a way to organize a lot of products on the home page without making it look too cluttered," and talk about how you overcame them. This positive approach makes your presentation much more objective and informative than if you simply discuss the cool logo that you designed for the client.

Assembling a Proposal from an RFP

When clients want work to be done, they prepare an official *RFP* (Request For Proposal). An RFP is a document that outlines the goals and scope of the project so designers can better prepare a proposal. Often, however, the clients themselves are not sure what they want or what can be done, so the RFP is not as helpful as you may hope.

Taking screen shots

To take a screen shot of your online work, go to the Web site you would like to show. Size the browser window to show the page as you want it to appear in the screenshot (no gaping white spaces in the page or clipped images and text). To take a screen shot, use either the computer's built-in capabilities (as I describe in the next few paragraphs) or a special screen capture utility such as HyperSnap, Snapz Pro, or CameraMan.

Mac users can use ⌘+Shift+3 to take a picture of the whole screen or ⌘+Shift+4 to draw a box around just a portion of the screen (with this latter option, the cursor changes to crosshairs and you drag a marquee around the portion of the screen you want). The resulting screen shot is saved to your hard drive named as Picture 1. (After it's on your hard drive as Picture 1, you can rename it to better remember what the screenshot represents.)

Windows users can use the Alt+Print Scrn key combination to capture an image of the active window. This key combination instructs the computer to take a screen shot and store it on the Clipboard. Next, open any graphics program like Photoshop, Paint Shop Pro, or Fireworks, start a new file, and paste the screen shot from the Clipboard.

You can also download a screen capture utility (such as HyperSnap, Snapz Pro, or CameraMan) from the Web. These utilities are fairly inexpensive, about $30, and in some cases, like HyperSnap, they're shareware. These utilities are better than the computer's built-in utilities because they capture mouse-down activities, such as selecting items in pop-up menus.

 ✔ **HyperSnap:** www.hypersnap-dx.com/hsdx/

 ✔ **Snapz Pro:** www.AmbrosiaSW.com/Products/SnapzPro.html

 ✔ **CameraMan:** This software is available online for sale at a variety of sites. The best way to find it is to search for "CameraMan software" with a search engine.

To assemble a proposal for clients, you may need to schedule a conference call with them to brainstorm ideas. After you talk to them, you should have a better idea of what they're looking for. You can then suggest different options and see how they react. With more targeted information like this, you are in a better spot to assemble a winning proposal.

When you create a proposal, you must include the following things:

- ✔ **Project budget.** The most important aspect to include in your proposal is the bottom line: How much is this project going to cost the client? Clients often include a budget range in their RFP. If so, you can work backwards from the budget amount and scale the production effort to fit. When the client does not include such info, you must estimate what the project will cost based on the scope of the work and the schedule in your proposal.

  When estimating, always estimate from 20 percent to 25 percent more than you think that the project will cost. You can always impress the client by billing less, and if you end up needing the additional amount, you'll be thankful that you built in the extra padding. Regardless of how the project goes, asking the client for more money is always bad form unless the client has asked you to increase the scope of the project. Clients expect you to put enough time into the proposal to accurately predict your costs and profit margin.

- ✔ **Outline content and special features.** Create a basic outline of the content and features you propose for the Web site based on both what the RFP states and the brainstorming you've done with the client. For example, if you think that an interactive timeline would be a great addition to the Web site, list it as a special feature and describe how it would work.

- ✔ **Sample navigation ideas.** Along with a list of content and features, you may even go so far as to suggest how you'd organize the interface. For example, you can outline a list of main categories and subcategories and even outline how the interface might work. Will it be a fancy Flash-based navigation system or a standard cross-navigation system?

- ✔ **Visual examples.** Clients usually respond better to visuals than a lot of text. Wherever you can, include diagrams, sample graphic design ideas, and pictures of the client's competing sites.

- ✔ **A production schedule.** Include a section that outlines the production schedule, complete with client sign-off points, your team's milestones, and the client's *deliverables* (tasks that the client is responsible for). A client sign-off point is when the client formally accepts the recent progress (by signing a document to that effect) and knows that they cannot ask for revision without incurring additional costs. It's also important to determine up-front who has sign-off authority for the client. Many times, the client includes a desired due date for the project. In this case, you can work backwards from the date and scale the production effort accordingly. For example, if the client wants the project done in just one month, the scope of what you can accomplish is already limited.

The client's schedule is a very important element in your schedule. Client sign-off points are necessary because they enable you to close one phase of production and move on to the next, knowing that everything up to that point has been accepted.

Client deliverables are tasks the client is responsible for, such as providing you with the necessary images and content. Getting a client's deliverables in writing is critical because that written text is the only leverage you have if the schedule slips due to the client's neglect. By listing both client and team deliverables, everyone agrees to their respective responsibilities up front and avoids surprises later.

✔ **Provide market and competitive analysis.** This may not be necessary for your project. If you are developing a Web site for a commercial enterprise, such as an online store, doing a little research into other similar Web sites to make sure that the design you propose is competitive is helpful.

Winning Clients: A Picture Is Worth a Thousand Words

When you assemble your proposal, you can never include too many images to show clients what you can do. Giving them a lot of text to read about how you'd design the site is not enough: They must *see* how you'd design the site.

Therefore, you should invest some time up front to assemble a few designs for a project — even before you win the contract. Although doing so takes extra time and costs you money, sometimes this is the only way to beat out the competition and win the project.

This tactic can, however, be a double-edged sword. You have to guess the client's design tastes. At this point, you don't want to create the full range of design options; you just want to give clients a sampling of the possibilities. If the client does not like the designs you've included, he or she may reject you as a candidate. On the other hand, the client may love what you did and want the site to look just like the designs in the proposal, thus saving you a lot of extra design work.

For these reasons, you've got to be the judge of what to submit to clients. Instead of showing any design options for the project, you may decide to show designs that you've done for other clients in a sort of portfolio appendix in the proposal. This tactic is especially useful if you cannot present the proposal in person. Often, clients just want you to send the proposal in for their review. If you make the cut, they'll ask you to come in for a meeting.

Knowing What to Charge as an Independent Consultant

Knowing what to charge is always hard. You can use any one of various formulas to arrive at an hourly rate that takes into consideration your annual expenses, profit margin, and salary, but you can arrive at this number through common sense, too.

For example, to come up with an hourly rate for your freelance Web design services, you can do several things:

- ✔ **Ask around to find out what other designers are charging.** This information can give you a good reality check as well as a range of prices. You may find that freelance designers in your area are charging between $50 and $150 an hour.

- ✔ **Be honest with your level of skill and experience.** If you've been around for a while and you've got a range of high-profile sites in your portfolio, you probably know exactly what you should charge for your freelance services, and it's probably towards the top end of the range. If you're new to Web design but are an old hat at print design, your fee may be somewhere in the middle.

- ✔ **Estimate your salary and expenses.** As an independent consultant, you have to calculate what it costs you to run your business each month, how much you want to make, how much time you can honestly bill in each month, and taxes. (As an independent freelancer, you get taxed more than a full-time employee does, but you can also deduct a lot more. Ask your tax professional for guidance here.)

- ✔ **Think of all the things you need to buy in order to run your business.** Electricity, office supplies, computers, software, fonts, Internet connection, trade magazines and organizations, and so on all add up. Think of a monthly budget for all these things, and then think of what you'd like to make on top of that. For example, if it costs you $4,000 a month to run your home office and you want to clear $6,000 a month, you've got to figure out how to make $10,000 a month.

- ✔ **Figure out how many hours you must bill each month.** *Billable time* is all the time you actually spend doing client work. Ideally, this is at least half of your time; but more often than not, checking e-mail, writing proposals, and other activities cut drastically into your available time.

    If you assume that there are 50 workweeks in a year (leaving two for vacation), you've got 4.1 weeks in a month. At 50 percent billable time, that leaves 83.3 hours of billable time. To make $10,000 a month, your hourly rate is $120.00.

I've noticed that a freelance hourly rate oddly corresponds to an annual salary. Notice that $10,000 a month is $120,000 per year, and the hourly rate is $120.00. The same phenomenon occurs in the workplace. For instance, a high-level designer that is paid $150,000 a year in an agency can probably charge about $150.00 an hour for freelance work. Similarly, a junior designer that makes about $50,000 a year for an agency can charge about $50.00 an hour for consulting work.

When you bid on a project, use your hourly rate to come up with an estimate of what the project will cost. I've found that it's better to charge clients a flat per-project fee than to charge them hourly. This way, the client knows exactly what the project will cost, and he or she isn't surprised to receive a series of invoices for your hourly work. Besides, when clients are surprised, the sticker shock seems to cause a delay in their payment processing!

Another reason to charge a flat per-project rate is that if you work fast and zero in on the design quickly, you are paid for the *value* of your work, not just the few hours it took you to knock it out. Make sure that you're paid for using your brain, not your hands!

The hardest part of charging a flat rate is accurately estimating the amount of work and the time it will take you to complete the project. I like to spend a lot of time thinking through the proposal, gauging the work, and adding from 20 to 25 percent to the budget for good measure. I also like to give clients a range (such as $4,500–$5,200) that is contingent on the number of design revisions they request. This tactic also keeps client pickiness to a minimum.

Knowing What to Charge as an Agency

Web design agencies use formulas similar to those used by freelancers for calculating their internal hourly rates. Generally, agencies have different billing rates for each level of designer, from production artists on up to creative directors. The prices that Web design agencies charge clients for these designers, however, are a lot higher than what the agency pays their designers. Although such agencies may pay a junior designer $50,000 a year, they may bill that person out at $100 per hour when they are calculating the costs of a project.

Although such a high price sounds heavily bloated, you must consider that agencies have a lot of overhead expenses to cover. In addition to the normal rent and supply expenses, agencies have a lot of nonbillable, but valuable, support people, such as administrative assistants and accountants. The billable people in the organization pay for the nonbillable people.

The larger the organization gets, the more expensive it must become in order to keep the ship afloat. For this reason, service companies like Web design agencies don't "scale" (grow net revenues) very easily. The profit margin doesn't increase exponentially as you scale up the operation, but at least the cash flow evens out, making it easier to predict monthly budgets.

Because of overhead costs, typically each Web design firm has what is called a "minimum size of engagement." If a client called a big design firm for a project that had a budget of only $50,000, that firm would probably refer the client to a smaller agency. Big agencies simply cannot afford to take projects unless they meet a certain budget range.

Because of an agency's "minimum engagement" budget rule, the independent consultants and the smaller design houses play an important role in taking on the multitude of smaller projects with budgets from $5,000–$100,000.

Managing a Client's Expectations

Above all else, setting and managing a client's expectations before and during a project are among the most important tasks you have as a designer. No two people ever hear or see the same thing. Even when you are explaining a project to a client, the client is thinking one thing when you mean something else. For example, if you require content from the client, make sure that the client knows when and how to deliver it to you. Also make sure that the full range of services you provide and don't provide are clearly outlined in the proposal.

If you have nothing in writing, you'll have a difficult time describing why a certain feature was left out of the project or why the schedule slipped. Whatever goes wrong is always your fault. When assembling the proposal, the best way to protect yourself and ward off any potential conflicts with the client is to be very clear about due dates and what content will be included in the site.

Setting Client Responsibilities for the Project

In the project proposal, one of the most important elements to list is the client's responsibilities. Make sure to discuss these seriously with the client at the beginning of the project and put the fear of you-know-who into them. Clients must understand that the project stops in its tracks if they do not meet their deadlines for delivering content or approvals to you.

For some reason, clients tend to think that they don't have to do a thing after they sign the contract. They don't realize that you can't do your job without getting content from them. For example, when you build the product section of the Web site, you'll need photos and information for each of the client's products. Unless taking new photos and writing new informational copy is part of your proposal, the client must provide this material in a timely manner.

 Just to cover your rear, pad an extra week into the schedule for each client deliverable without telling the client (depending on the size of the project). This way, even if the client slips, you won't, and you can better schedule your team's resources and time.

Getting Clients to Sign Off on Key Milestones

In addition to feeding content and materials to you during the project, clients must also sign off on various key milestones along the way. By getting clients to sign off on key steps in the project, such as the site map, you protect yourself from any future arguments over the scope and quality of the project. At the beginning of the project, it's also very important to establish who has sign-off authority for the client. In some cases, a different person in the client's organization may sign off for different parts of the project.

For example, imagine that you are halfway into HTML production and the client's CEO balks, refusing to pay unless you include a founder's page that every page can access. If you have a signed site map with no founder's page on it, you can clearly state that a founder's page was never part of the scope, and you have so-and-so's authorized signature to prove it.

Aside from protecting you from clients' tendencies to change their minds and demand new features, a sign-off policy also protects the clients. They have signed documents that assure them and their managers that they will get what they're paying for.

Managing the Web Project Workflow

When you're knee-deep in a project, you have the internal challenge of managing people on your team to get the job done. For the most part, if you're working within a larger organization, special project managers or executive producers manage the client and the team members to ensure that all the resources (content, people, and so on) are in place and to ensure that the project keeps on track. This management model enables you, the designer, to focus on what you do well.

If you are on your own, managing the client and the project schedule and doing all the design and production work can keep you working around the clock.

If you're on your own, you might pick one thing that you do well, and that you enjoy, and offer only that service. Doing all aspects of Web site design from creative to programming is difficult enough; *managing* the whole process by yourself is even more difficult. If you do only one thing (such as site map design, Flash animation, or Web creative direction), you must manage only one deliverable. When you are a specialist, marketing your services is easier than if you're a generalist. You can market directly to clients, to design agencies, and even to other freelance designers, and everyone knows exactly where you fit into the project.

Hiring and Managing Subcontractors

As your Web design consulting business expands, you may find that you're getting more work than you can handle. If you're like me, you don't like to say no to more work! One way to handle your growing business is to find able-bodied freelancers like you that you can rely on for expanded project needs.

For example, one client may want you to develop a series of four design directions at the very same time that another client needs work done. In cases like this, you may subcontract another designer to help you create a few of the design directions so you can get everything done on time.

When hiring subcontractors, their rates may often be close to your own rates. Marking up their services by about 15 percent is acceptable, but if you mark up more than that, you're just eating away at the project budget. Ideally, if you know your time will be tight, you'll plan in advance to provide for a subcontracting budget.

Look at your initial client contract to see whether hiring subcontractors raises any legal issues. Often, a client simply signs the project proposal and no other legal agreement. In such cases, you are free to hire and manage subcontractors as needed. If the client, however, asks you to sign a work-for-hire agreement along with the proposal, the agreement usually forbids any subcontracting activity.

As for signing any agreements with your subcontractors, you too may keep your own standard work-for-hire agreement on hand for them to sign — especially for larger projects. For small projects, however, the subcontractor usually just puts a mini proposal together that shows the work to be done and the schedule, and that's enough to go on.

At the end of the project, the subcontractor sends you an invoice. Keep these invoices in a safe place and make sure that they include the following information (you'll need it for tax purposes at the end of the year):

- ✔ First and last name
- ✔ Address
- ✔ Phone number
- ✔ Social Security number or Federal ID number

Like sending out a cynical version of holiday cards, at the end of the year (in the United States) you must send out 1099 forms to every subcontractor to whom you've paid more than $600 throughout the tax year. Total up the amount you've paid them and fill out just one 1099 form for each person. You can find these forms at any office supply store or at your local post office.

You must send the 1099 forms out in the mail by the end of January, or you may not be able to claim the invoices as expenses on your own taxes. Again, talk to your tax professional for the full scoop because the laws seem to change as often as a celebrity's hairdo.

Chapter 17

Ten User Interface-Design Party Tricks to Impress Users

Common questions from print designers entering the Web design field are "How much do the user interface and the visual design overlap?" and "Is the designer responsible for both?" The answer is that the two are intrinsically tied together, and so, like it or not, you as a Web designer must also be pretty handy as a user interface designer.

Every page of a Web site must have some form of navigation. Ideally, the navigation helps to orient people in the site. A random and unique set of links on each page makes the user feel like a mouse in a maze, blindly foraging ahead without seeing the big picture. If, on the other hand, the mouse could see the aerial view of the maze and where he was in it, he'd suddenly have the power to find the cheese at the end. This sort of "You are here" feedback built in to your navigation scheme is a way to boost the usability of your site instantly.

In addition, the visual design of this navigation scheme directly affects how people perceive and interact with it. If, for instance, you design an icon that has no label or no dimensional quality, users may think that it's just part of the page decor and continue to scour the page, looking for "real" buttons.

This chapter consolidates a lot of the user interface conventions and techniques I discuss throughout this book. In this one convenient chapter, you find the top ten user interface design party tricks to keep on hand for the next time you design a Web site.

Use Only Five to Seven Main Categories

Five and seven are magic numbers in life because remembering a list of five to seven things is easy. Any more than that and our brains melt down. Maybe it's because we have five fingers on each hand. We can mentally attach one item to each digit and, if we've had enough strong coffee, can remember a few more items on the next hand.

You may think that I'm joking, but I've heard from psychologists-turned-user-interface-designers that the five-finger phenomenon actually has merit. In Web design, many user interface designers suggest that keeping your list of categories down to just five to seven is best. This strategy keeps users from feeling overwhelmed in your site.

The problem with the five-to-seven rule, however, is that most modern Web sites have a lot more going on, and honing the site down to just five or so areas is difficult. In such cases, I've found that breaking the page down into a few functional areas (no more than five, of course) that each has no more than five to seven navigational items helps. Take a look at the diagram in Figure 17-1. In this design, the top navigation area has five links to the main categories of the site. The side navigation area has another five links, and the bottom footer has seven links. The content in the middle may have a few links too, but they are shortcuts to sections otherwise accessible in the three navigation areas.

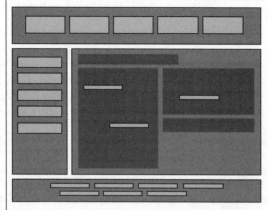

Figure 17-1:
Each of the three functional areas contains five to seven links.

Always Label Your Buttons and Icons

As idiot-proof as you think your icon or illustration may be, I've found that you can never rely on pictures alone to tell users what a button does. Unless you're designing a print function or other common computer task, adding a simple text label to a button or icon is a good idea. After all, no picture could infallibly represent the product catalog section of a site.

By the time you illustrate an icon detailed enough to give users a good idea of what the section is, you have a picture worth framing. You may as well save some space and add a simple text label. I'm not saying to not use icons; they can add a lot of design flavor to a site. Just be sure to supplement them with a label for clarity's sake.

Use Recyclable Materials: Cache Your Buttons

A cool browser feature that you should always take advantage of is the caching feature. After a browser downloads a graphic on a Web page, it stores it in its temporary memory, or *cache*. The next time the browser encounters the same graphic on another page, it redraws it from memory. Redrawing graphics from memory is much faster than downloading them.

Because of this feature, the more you reuse graphics (such as navigation buttons) on subsequent pages, the better your site's performance. The browser has to download only the new content material. Reusing the same graphics also improves the usability of your site because the graphics are consistent.

The consistent use of graphics placed in the same location helps to orient people in your site; it's a visual and functional anchor.

In Figure 17-2, I used a table structure to partition and organize different navigational graphics so that I can cache them effectively. The top row holds the graphic for the Products section. This graphic remains the same throughout the entire Products section, which includes ten or so pages. After the graphic is cached, it redraws quickly on all these pages.

The second row contains the subnavigation choices for the Products section. While the user clicks around in the Products section, only the second row changes to reflect where the user is and to provide access to the other subsections. This means that the browser just has to download the second row. The top row is redrawn from the cache.

Figure 17-2:
With a table,
you can
segment the
navigational
choices for
efficient
caching.

The top row remains constant across multiple pages.

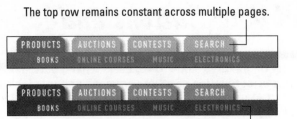

Only the bottom row changes on new pages.

Incidentally, caching is why your browser may crash after loading a lot of Web pages. The browser's cache gets full and loads new pages sluggishly. You can adjust the size of your cache (how many megabytes it will store in memory before it gets sluggish) in the advanced preferences. In Internet Explorer, select Tools⇨Internet Options. On the General tab, click the Settings button. Move the slider labeled Amount of Disk Space to Use to the right to increase the size of your browser's cache (and speed up the loading of pages). In Netscape Navigator, you can choose Edit⇨Preferences and look for the Advanced option. There, choose Cache and enter a higher cache setting.

The browser usually empties the cache upon quitting (unless you changed the default settings), but you can also clear the cache while you work. This is a good idea if you're looking at a lot of pages in the same session. You can clear the cache in the same place that you adjust the cache size. In Netscape Navigator, choose Edit⇨Preferences, find the Advanced option, and then look for a button that screams something like Clear Cache Now. In Explorer, select Tools⇨Internet Options. Make sure you select the General tab and click the Clear History button in the History section.

Light the Path with "You Are Here" Feedback

The navigation system that you design should not only provide access to all the main functional areas of the site, but also give users some sense as to where they are in the Web site. Like a mouse able to see the maze from an aerial view, your navigation system should provide the same sense of orientation and visually show people the size and scope of the site.

In Figure 17-3, a small map of the whole site immediately gives users a view of the site and a quick means to navigate through it. When a user rolls his mouse pointer over each little icon, the icon is highlighted, and a label that tells the user what it represents appears. A breadcrumb trail provides continual feedback of where you are in the site.

Figure 17-3:
This
navigation
system
shows a
miniature
view of the
entire site.

products > cooking > flatware

Make It Easy to Get Back Home

One of the functional items people forget to include most often in Web design is a link back to the home page. People drill down in a site, find the info they need, and then suddenly realize that the only way to get back to the home page is by reentering the URL.

Often, the company's logo at the top of the page is a secret link back to the home page. Seasoned Web surfers usually try to click the logo to get back home, but to a newbie, the logo just looks like a logo.

The best course of action is to include a dedicated link back to the home page as part of your standard set of navigational buttons. You can even treat the home page as a main section of the site, as shown in Figure 17-4, by giving it the same visual importance as any other main functional area of the site. Otherwise, as shown in Figure 17-5, you can give the home page a slightly different appearance and include it next to the main lineup of buttons.

Figure 17-4:
You can
count the
home page
as one of
the main
sections of
your Web
site.

MO●N
Country fresh produce   HOME   MEATS   FRUITS & VEGGIES

Figure 17-5:
You can also include the home link next to the main navigation choices.

MC●N
Country fresh produce
home   check out   search
MEATS   BREADS   FRUITS & VEGGIES

Visually Differentiate Clickable and Nonclickable Things

Although reusing graphics wherever you can to take advantage of the browser's caching ability is tempting, don't use the same graphic as a button on one page and as a decorative headline on another. For example, if you use an icon as a button leading to the About section of the site, don't use the same icon merely as decoration for the headline on that page. Otherwise, people will still think that it's a button. Give the icon a slightly different visual treatment so people know that its function has changed.

You should always treat the visual design of clickable things differently than the design of headlines, images, and other nonclickable things. Design interactive elements to look like their function. For example, buttons should have a raised or three-dimensional quality that invites people to click them. Headlines and other nonclickable things should have a flat appearance.

Picking one or two treatments for interactive stuff and sticking with your choice is also a smart idea. For example, if some buttons are beveled, others have a drop shadow, and still others are flat-looking but have rollover highlights, users may get confused.

"One of These Buttons Is Not Like the Other"

If you've ever watched *Sesame Street,* you may remember the famous skit: "One of these things is not like the other." In this scenario, kids are taught to weed out the objects that don't fit with the rest of the group. This is great preparation for college entrance exams, a bad lesson for the politically correct movement, but an excellent analogy for user interface design.

If you've got a lot of different navigational choices on the page (refer to the diagram in Figure 17-1) and each choice is grouped in different areas, make sure that you group all the items together logically. Assemble a group of buttons that have similar functions.

For instance, group all the buttons together that go to the main categories of the site. Don't include, however, a random link to some legal mumbo-jumbo page. Save that link for another group of links that include other resources, such as credits.

Be Consistent: Don't Change Your Button's Look or Placement

After you go through the trouble of designing a navigational system that works, don't change it! If you do, you create the additional work for yourself of designing a new layout for each page, and you also create a lot of chaos for the user.

The best interfaces are those that remain consistent throughout a site. The user becomes comfortable with the buttons and remembers where to find them. The interface becomes almost transparent, and the user can focus on the content of the page.

If you change the design or placement of a button from one page to the next, users may not find it, or they may think that the button has an entirely different function — even if it has the same text label. They may ignore it and continue to scan the page, searching for the button they just clicked.

Tread Lightly with Real-Life Metaphors

Sometimes clients want to inject a theme into their Web site to make it feel like an everyday object or space. A lot of kids' sites, for example, use interfaces that look like a clubhouse or a TV.

Although real-life themes provide a great way to spice up the design of a site, they can also impose a lot of design constraints on you. For instance, as in Figure 17-6, if you want the interface to look like a digital camera with chrome buttons surrounding a central screen, you've suddenly got a small viewing space for all your content.

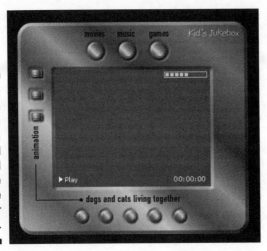

Figure 17-6:
This interface looks like a digital camera and leaves little room in the interior window.

Use metaphors sparingly to give users just a hint of the real-life object you're imitating. Instead of making the interface really look like a digital camera, just use the chrome buttons to hint at the camera metaphor and give yourself a lot more room for content. By doing so, you stay in control of the layout and presentation.

Use Color-Coding Sparingly

Another way to orient people in your Web site is to color-code each of the main sections. Color-coding is especially useful if each section of a site is fairly large. For instance, if the Products section has hundreds of pages, a user may start to feel disoriented, even if the ever-present navigation system has the Products button highlighted. If the entire Products section, however, has a red theme, people feel more grounded — especially if the other sections have their own unique color scheme as well.

If you color-code a Web site, be sure to choose colors that work well together and have similar light and dark values. Don't choose a set of five dark dingy colors and one bright yellow color. Be sure that you can apply the same design standard to each section. For example, a set of dark blue, dark maroon, dark green, and dark purple buttons will all show up well and look nice on a light background, but bright yellow buttons will be lost. Although Figure 17-7 is in black and white, the difference between dark and bright colors on a white background is apparent.

Figure 17-7:
The first
colors have
similar
luminance
values; the
fifth hardly
shows up.

Another caveat is that a color-coded system works well only if you have five to seven categories (which you should have anyway). If you have more categories than that, you may have difficulty choosing a set of colors that work well together and are still different enough from one another. Besides, using too many colors will make your site look like a rainbow gone bad!

Chapter 18

Ten Get-Dangerous, Do-It-Yourself HTML and JavaScript Tips

*E*ven if you're a diehard print designer without a smidge of technical ability, when you start tinkering with HTML coding, you'll find that it's easier and more fun that you thought. Don't worry, you're not turning into a nerd — you're just evolving into a Web designer.

To aid in your tinkering, here I cover ten common functional and layout coding techniques using HTML and JavaScript for you to explore. These techniques range from placing tables inside of other tables in order to achieve minute control over your layout to building rollover buttons with JavaScript. Along the way, I also cover how to spawn new browser windows and how to embed Flash and QuickTime movies into your page.

Shhh . . . Tables Are Nesting

Nested tables are the handiest way to lay out a Web page with fine-tuned control. A *nested table* is one that is placed inside the cell of another table. Each cell of a table is sort of like a mini Web page. Each cell can have its own background tile, background color, text, form elements, and even a whole table within it, as shown in Figure 18-1.

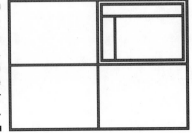

Figure 18-1:
Within each
table cell,
you can
place
another
table.

You can even nest tables multiple levels deep, placing a table within a table within a table! Beyond three or four levels, however, the browser may have trouble drawing the design, so don't get too carried away.

The easiest way to place a table within another table is to use an HTML editor, such as GoLive or Dreamweaver, and just cut and paste it into another table. The table goes between the opening and closing table data tags <td> and </td>, which are shown in bold in the following code:

```
<table width="58%" border="0" cellspacing="0" cellpadding="0"
        height="175">
  <tr>
    <td width="53%" height="78">
      <table width="100%" height="78" border="0"
            cellspacing="0" cellpadding="0">
        <tr>
          <td> </td>
          <td> </td>
        </tr>
      </table>
    </td>
    <td width="47%" height="78"> </td>
  </tr>
  <tr>
    <td width="53%"> </td>
    <td width="47%"> </td>
  </tr>
</table>
```

Notice that the parent table has opening and closing tags (`<table>` and `</table>`) just like the nested table. Nested tables are the only way to get the intricate design illustrated in Figure 18-2. In this layout, the parent table has four cells. Within each cell is another table with its own unique arrangement of colored cells, graphics, and form elements.

This cell contains another table.

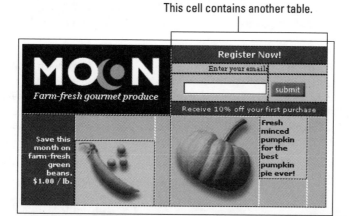

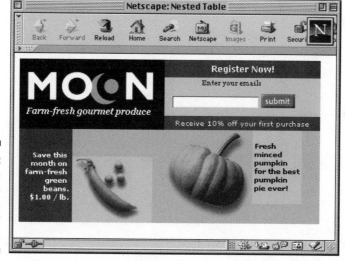

Figure 18-2:
Within each cell of the parent table is another table.

Having Fun with Pop-up Windows

When users click on a hyperlink, a new Web page loads into the browser window, replacing the current page. Instead of replacing the current page with another page, you can open the page in a new browser window. This technique is useful when you have an advertisement link on your page and you don't want people to leave your site when they click it. Or, you may want to use a Web page as a launch page to open a small promotional page or training video in another window.

You can spawn new browser windows in one of two ways: with simple HTML, or with JavaScript. With HTML, you cannot control the size of the new window, and the standard array of browser buttons is included along the top, as shown in Figure 18-3. If you use JavaScript, you can control the exact size of the window and whether it has scrollbars. Also, a window created in JavaScript has no browser controls at the top, as shown in Figure 18-4.

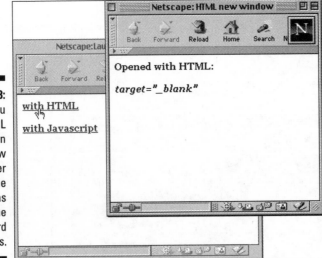

Figure 18-3:
When you use HTML to open a new browser window, the window has all the standard buttons.

To make a link open a page in a new browser window, simply add a little bit of code to the standard `<href>` link tag, like this:

```
<a href="window1.htm" target="_blank">with HTML</a>
```

The `target="_blank"` addition to the link tells the browser to open the page window1.htm in a new browser window.

Figure 18-4:
With
JavaScript,
you can
control the
size of the
new
window.

To make a link open a new window that is a specific size, you must use JavaScript. To make the JavaScript work, you need code in two places: the function itself described up at the top of your HTML document (right before the closing `</head>` tag), and the JavaScript added to the link itself. Here's the set-up code that you should include at the top of your document to describe the function:

```
<script language="JavaScript">
<!--

function openPopUpWindow(url) {
popupWin = window.open(url, "PopUp",
        "width=575,height=450,left=0,top=0,toolbar=no,menu
        bar=no,location=no,scrollbars=yes,resizable=yes");
}
// -->

</script>
```

The first few lines of code name the new function `openPopUpWindow`. You can then describe a number of attributes for the new window, such as its height and width in pixels and whether it has scrollbars. After the JavaScript function is described, you then reference the function in your standard link like this:

```
<a href="javascript:openPopUpWindow('page2.html');">with
        JavaScript</a>
```

After its name, you tell the browser what page to put in the new window, such as page2.htm.

Embedding QuickTime and Flash Movies

To place media such as QuickTime and Flash movies in your Web page, use the `<object>` and `<embed>` tags. The process is similar to placing an image in your Web page. List the name of the media object (such as myflashmovie.swf) and a few attributes (such as its height and width). You can center it or place it inside a table cell or CSS layer just as you would any other Web page element.

Here's what the code looks like to place a Flash movie called movie.swf (the `.swf` extension after the name is the standard file extension for Flash movies):

```
<object classid="clsid:D27CDB6E-AE6D-11cf-96B8-444553540000"
        codebase="http://download.macromedia.com/pub/shock
        wave/cabs/flash/swflash.cab#version=4,0,2,0"
        width="500" height="350">
<param name=movie value="movie.swf">
<param name=quality value=high>
<param name="loop" value="false">

<embed src="movie.swf" quality=high
       pluginspage="http://www.macromedia.com/shockwave/d
       ownload/index.cgi?P1_Prod_Version=ShockwaveFlash"
       type="application/x-shockwave-flash" width="500"
       height="350" loop="false">
</embed>

</object>
```

The sprawling stuff in the opening `<object>` tag tells the browser what kind of object you're embedding, along with a link to find the necessary plug-in to view. The same information is also found in the `<embed>` tag. You need both the `<object>` and the `<embed>` tag because on a Mac, Netscape and Internet Explorer understand the `<embed>` tag. On Windows, Internet Explorer looks at the `<object>` tag and Netscape looks at the `<embed>` tag. Such discrepancies between browsers and platforms can be confusing, but basically, when in doubt, use both tags. The browsers ignore the tag that they don't understand.

In addition to the movie's name, you should enter a height and a width attribute and a loop value (if you want the movie to repeat). In the previous code sample, I make these parameters appear in boldface type so that if you want to steal this code, you know which parts to customize for your own Flash movie.

The code to embed a QuickTime movie is quite similar. In this case, the movie's name is movie.mov. The movie's display space is 640 x 496 pixels, and it begins to play as soon as the page loads:

```
<embed src="movie.mov" width="640" height="496"
        bgcolor="000000" controller="true" autoplay="true"
        pluginspage="http://www.apple.com/quicktime/downlo
        ad/">
</embed>
```

Making Jump Menus

A *jump menu* is a pop-up list of options that each takes the user to a different Web page. Jump menus built in JavaScript are similar to select menus that you can build in HTML. Both jump menus and select menus expand when the user clicks them. On a jump menu, after users make a selection, they immediately jump to that new page. On a select menu, after users make a selection, they must click a Submit button in order to carry out the command.

You must write additional code in either JavaScript or another programming language to make the HTML select menu and Submit button set work together. As illustrated in Figure 18-5, both take up very little room on the screen when not in use, but can offer a lot of navigational (nav) choices as shown in Figure 18-6.

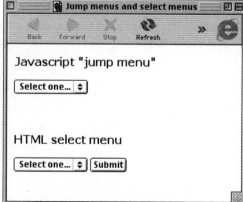

Figure 18-5:
Both jump menus and select menus offer a number of nav choices in a small space.

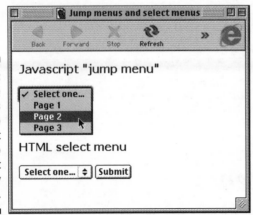

Figure 18-6:
When the
user clicks
the jump
menu, it
opens to
reveal a list
of nav
choices.

To make a JavaScript jump menu you need two things: the JavaScript function defined in the top section of your HTML page (before the closing </head> tag), and the instructions to place the menu in the <body> section of the page. Software programs such as Dreamweaver enable you to create these quickly by clicking on an icon and filling out a form. The CD that accompanies this book contains a free trial version of Dreamweaver so you can follow this exercise. To make a jump menu in Dreamweaver, follow these simple steps:

1. **Launch Dreamweaver and create a new Web page.**

   Dreamweaver usually starts you off with a new blank page automatically. If not, choose File⇨New from the menu.

2. **Switch to the Forms toolbar.**

   In the Objects panel (the main toolbar), click the top title to reveal a drop-down menu of choices. From the list, click the Forms panel option, as shown in Figure 18-7.

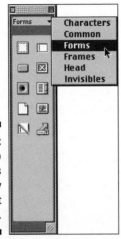

Figure 18-7:
Switch to
the Forms
toolbar by
choosing it
from the list.

3. **Insert a jump menu by clicking the Insert Jump Menu icon in the Forms panel, as shown in Figure 18-8.**

   The Insert Jump Menu window appears.

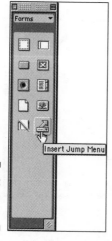

Figure 18-8:
Insert a jump menu.

4. **Assemble the jump menu from the Insert Jump Menu window.**

   Here you find the options needed to steer you through the process of building the jump menu. Check it out in Figure 18-9.

   From the Menu Items list, click Select One and then click the plus icon (above this list) to add it to your list. This is the text that will appear on your jump menu before the user clicks it.

   To add to your list, type **Page 1** in the Text field box.

   Below this, type **page1.html** in the When Selected, Go To URL text field.

   Then click the plus icon to add these to your jump menu. These are options that display after the user clicks the menu.

   Continue to enter a few names of your list items in the Text field and their links in the When Selected, Go To URL field.

   When you're finished, click OK. The jump menu editor window closes, and you return to your Web page layout where your new jump menu appears.

   You should now have a perfectly good jump menu as shown in Figure 18-6, ready for testing in a browser. To try it out, save your file in Dreamweaver.

Click the plus icon to add it.   Enter the name for the list item.

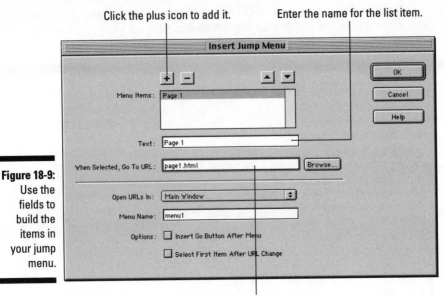

Figure 18-9:
Use the
fields to
build the
items in
your jump
menu.

Enter the link for the item.

5. **From the File menu, choose Save to name and save your file.** Make sure you save the file with the `.html` extension after its name and place it on your desktop or in a place where you can easily find it again. To view in a Web browser, launch the browser and choose File⇨Open File (in Netscape) or File⇨Open (in Explorer) to open your newly created page.

Designing Custom Submit Buttons

When you build a form, the user must click some sort of button to process the data. For example, when users fill out their name, address, and credit card information to purchase something online, they must click some button to send all the data to the server so that they can place their order.

You can either use a standard ugly HTML Submit button like the one shown in Figure 18-10, or you can really let users click in style by making your own custom-designed button like the one in Figure 18-11.

Figure 18-10:
Standard
HTML
Submit
button.

Figure 18-11:
Use any
graphics
program to
make your
own
buttons.

You can use any graphics program, such Photoshop or Fireworks, to create your own Submit buttons. They can be any size or shape, but keeping them about the same size as the other elements in your form is a good idea. Otherwise, they'll dwarf the form!

Save the graphic you create as either a GIF or a JPEG image just as you would any other image for your Web page. To use your custom graphic as the Submit button, use the following HTML code:

```
<input type="image" border="0" name="registerbutton"
        src="register.gif" width="64" height="31">
```

In this code, the key is `input type="image"`. This code turns an ordinary graphic into a button. Within the `<input>` tag, you include the name of the graphic, in this case, and its dimensions.

As Figure 18-12 shows, a Submit button doesn't always have to read *Submit*. You can choose *Find it*, *Continue*, or just about anything else that makes sense for its function.

Figure 18-12:
Customize a
form's look
by using
your own
graphic for
the Submit
button.

Background Tiles

To add visual interest to your Web page and to create the illusion of intricate overlapping design elements, you can design a custom background tile. You can use any graphics program to build a tile and save it as a GIF or JPEG image.

Just keep in mind that the tile will repeat. If you have a small tile with a pattern, be sure that the tile's right edge looks good next to the tile's left edge, and that the top edge looks good next to the bottom edge. Otherwise, you see stark lines in between each tile, as in Figure 18-13.

Figure 18-13:
Nonmatch-
ing tile
edges (left)
leave visible
lines;
matching
edges
(right) are
seamless.

Making the pattern look smooth takes some creative tinkering. The best way is to use a program such as Photoshop to doctor up the edges so that they match.

Instead of using small tiles that repeat (and worrying about their edges matching up), you can use a large tile that is much bigger than the standard browser window. If you make your tile 1,500 x 1,000 pixels, users will probably never see it repeat. Making your tiles large also gives you a lot more design flexibility — you can make any sort of design that you like and not have to worry about matching up the edges.

Adding Empty Space in Your Web Page

Sometimes you need to insert empty white space around graphics or in between forms to control the look of your Web page layout. (For more on adding space around graphics, see Chapter 14.) You can add such space in one of two ways:

- **Non-breaking spaces.** A non-breaking space is an invisible HTML character that is like using the space bar on your keyboard — it inserts a small gap in between two words, letters, or images. When you add text to your Web page, HTML honors only one space made with the space bar. To add any extra space, therefore, you must use the non-breaking space character:

  ```
   
  ```

  You can use a number of non-breaking spaces in a row to create a larger space, but remember that they only work only horizontally. To create a big vertical space, you should use a transparent GIF shim.

- **Transparent shims.** A *shim* is a transparent, 1 x 1 pixel GIF that you can build in any graphics program. (See Chapter 14 for building instructions.) Place a shim in your Web page just like you place any other image. Because it's transparent, however, you can resize it in the HTML image tag to be whatever size you need without fear of distortion:

  ```
  <img src="shim.gif" width="50" height="100">
  ```

Adding Background Music to Your Page

Your Web page doesn't have to be like an old-time silent movie. You can liven it up by adding a background soundtrack. You can add sound to your page in a number of ways:

- `<bgsound>` tag. Use this tag to specify a background music file for a Web page and set it to loop a number of times. Background sounds play automatically when the page loads. To add them to your page, you use the following `<bgsound>` tag:

  ```
  <bgsound src="beat.aif" loop="10">
  ```

The problem with this tag, however, is that is specific to Internet Explorer. Netscape simply ignores it.

✔ `<embed>` tag. You can also use this tag to insert music in your page. When you use the `<embed>` tag, you have additional options, such as including volume, play, and stop controls (highlighted in bold). Here's the code to make the sound play automatically with no visible controls, like background sound:

```
<embed src="sound.wav" autostart="true" LOOP=10
        controls=false volume="50%"></embed>
```

Notice that in this example, the volume is set to 50%. This setting automatically plays the audio at 50% of the user's sound capability regardless of how their audio level is set. To embed the sound with onscreen controls and to make it start only when the user clicks a play button, as in Figure 18-14, use this code:

```
<embed src="sound.wav" height="60" width="145"
        autostart="false" LOOP=10 volume="50%"></embed>
```

In this example, because `<autostart>` is false, the sound does not play unless the user clicks a button to start it. A controller bar with play and stop buttons automatically appear if you assign height and width attributes (in bold in the code above). These dimensions become the height and width of the controller bar.

Figure 18-14:
The sound control appears automatically in the browser at the specified position.

Auto-Timing Your Web Page

One of the coolest and simplest things that you can do as a Web designer is to make a page last only a few seconds before it automatically goes to a new page. This technique is useful, for instance, if you want to have a brief intro-duction message or design that appears a few seconds before the main page loads.

This technique is most widely used, however, to automatically redirect people to a new Web address or page if the site has moved. It works by adding a <meta> refresh tag (there are different kinds of meta tags) at the top of your document inside the head section, like this:

```
<html>
<head>
<title>automatic timer</title>
<META HTTP-EQUIV="refresh"; content="5; url=page2.html">
</head>
```

The important parts of the meta tag for our auto-timing purposes are the content and url attributes. The content attribute specifies in seconds how long the page pauses (in this case, five seconds) before moving on to the URL (in this case, page2.html).

Creating Rollover Buttons . . . Yikes!

My final HTML and JavaScript tip is how to make rollover buttons. *Rollover buttons* are buttons that change their appearance as the mouse pointer rolls over them. This change helps to identify the button as clickable.

By far, the best way to make these is to use a graphics program, such as ImageReady (Photoshop's interactive counterpart) or Fireworks. These pro-grams make creating a rollover so easy that you'll never write JavaScript code for this again. (Like I ever did in the first place!) Here's how to make a simple rollover button in Fireworks:

1. **Launch Fireworks and start a new file by selecting File⇨New.**

2. **In the New Document window, set the file dimensions to 220 x 200 pixels and keep the resolution at 72 ppi.**

   Enter **200** in the Width text field and **200** in the Height text field, as shown in Figure 18-15. This size will give you enough room to work as you create your button.

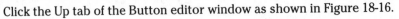

New Document

Canvas Size: 156.25 K

Width: 200   Pixels   W: 200

Height: 200   Pixels   H: 200

Resolution: 72   Pixels/Inch

Canvas Color:
- ● White
- ○ Transparent
- ○ Custom

Cancel   OK

Figure 18-15:
Make a new file that's 200 x 200 pixels.

3. **Insert a new button in your new document by choosing Insert⇨New Button from the menu.**

   A Button editor window (like the one in Figure 18-16) appears. Here you build your rollover button.

4. **First build the Up state of your button.**

   Click the Up tab of the Button editor window as shown in Figure 18-16.

   The *Up state* of a button is its resting state that users see before they roll over it with a mouse or click it.

   Draw the Up state of the button by clicking the Rectangle tool in the toolbar (it looks like a white square with a black border) and dragging a simple rectangle shape for the Up state.

   After you draw the rectangle shape, it will automatically be selected. While the rectangle is selected, click the Fill and Stroke buttons in the toolbar to change the background (Fill) and border (Stroke) colors of the rectangle. When you click the Fill or Stroke color swatches, a pop-up palette appears where you can select a new color. For this example, I chose a medium-valued fill color and no stroke.

   You can also add a text label by selecting the Text tool and clicking once on the button that you drew. In the Text Editor window that appears, type a label and apply desired settings for font, point size, and color.

The Text tool

The Pointer tool | The Up state tab

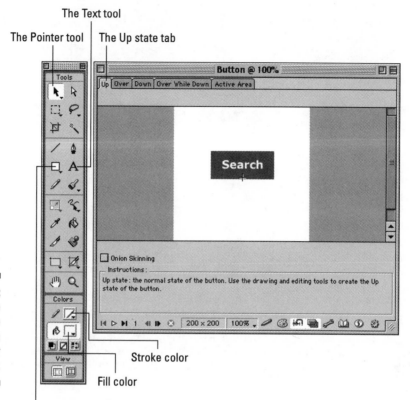

Figure 18-16:
The Up state
tab of the
Button
editor
window.

Stroke color

Fill color

The Rectangle tool

5. **Build the Over and Down states of the button.**

The Over state defines what users see when they roll their mouse over the button.

Click the Over tab of the Button editor window and then click the Copy Up Graphic button, as illustrated in Figure 18-17. This copies the graphic that you create from the Up tab to the Over tab.

After you copy this, click the Pointer tool in the toolbar (refer to Figure 18-16 to identify this tool). Click once on the rectangle you drew to select it, and change its fill color in the toolbar to a lighter shade. I should mention that changing the color of the Over state is just one way to highlight it. You could also add an effect to it like a drop shadow or change its size.

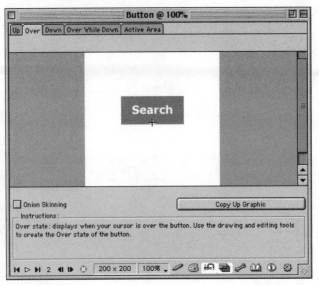

Figure 18-17:
Build your
button by
copying
from the
previous
state and
making
modifi-
cations.

Repeat the same process to build the Down state of the button.

The *Down* state defines what users see when they click the button. In the Button editor window, click the Down tab. In the Down tab, click the Copy Over Graphic button. Select the rectangle with the Pointer tool and change its fill to a darker shade.

6. **Test the rollover effect of your new button.**

Close the Button editor window. You can see your new button placed in your document.

To preview the rollover effect, click the Preview tab located at the top of the document window and try rolling your mouse over the button to watch it highlight, as shown in Figure 18-18. When finished previewing, click on the Original tab at the top of your document to return to normal editing mode.

Figure 18-18:
Check out
your rollover
effect by
clicking the
Preview tab.

7. Before exporting your new button, trim the canvas size to fit your button.

When you first started this document, you entered **200** pixels for both the height and width of the "canvas" (document size). Because you don't need this much space for the button, you can trim the canvas to match its size.

From the Modify menu, choose Modify⇨Trim Canvas.

8. Export your new button by choosing File⇨Export.

The Export window opens.

In the Export window, name your file. In this example, I named mine rollover.htm.

Be sure that you select HTML and Images from the Save As options, as shown in Figure 18-19. Locate a place on your hard drive where you can find the file again once exported and click the Save button.

After clicking Save, you return to your document where you can continue working. If you're finished working, you can save the file in the native Fireworks PNG format by choosing Save from the File menu.

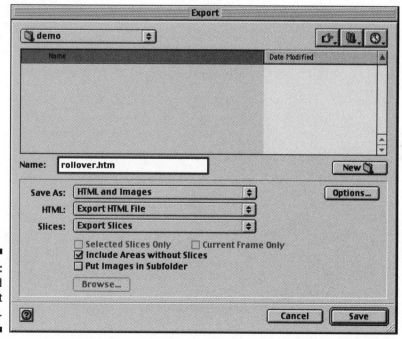

Figure 18-19:
Save and
Export
your file.

9. View your handiwork.

After you export your file (it will export as a series of graphics for the rollover states and one HTML file), open the HTML file in any Web browser to view it. If you're curious to sneak a peek at the JavaScript behind your button's functionality, open the HTML file in any text editor, such as Notepad. Or, while previewing the button in the browser, choose View➪Page Source.

For more in-depth lessons on making a whole interactive rollover navigation system in Fireworks, don't miss the free tutorials on the CD included with this book.

Chapter 19

Ten Things That Can Go Wrong

● ●

In This Chapter

▶ Managing project scope creep

▶ Making time for a site map

▶ Presenting design options that you can live with

▶ Including user tests in your proposals

▶ Keeping technology tinkering under control

▶ Planning for international localization

▶ Keeping up with database-driven sites

▶ Developing a marketing plan for a site

● ●

*Y*ou may know how to initiate a project with a client, build a site map, create design directions, and make technology choices, but you must know one more thing to be a successful Web designer: contingency planning. Anticipating the worst that can happen in the course of a project and how to deal with it is the last step towards becoming a full-fledged Web designer. In this chapter, I list the top ten things that can go wrong, why they happen, and how you can respond to keep a project on track.

"Can We Add Just One More Thing?"

When clients first come to you, they often don't know what is possible with Web technologies. They don't know what you can and can't do or how much anything really costs, so they don't ask for it in their Request For Proposal (RFP). After a project is underway, however, and clients start to see the site take shape, their eyes tend to grow wider and wider with all the cool possibilities.

As clients become familiar with the Web development process, they may often ask you to "throw in" an extra Flash movie here, a personalized greeting there, and all manner of extra features to liven up the site. In Web design circles, these little additions to the project are called *scope creep*. If you give in to these little client requests, the scope of the project can slowly creep upwards until you are basically working for free — or worse, going into debt!

Identifying and resisting scope creep whenever it happens are critical. Aside from loosing your shirt financially, scope creep causes two other huge problems:

- **The ripple effect.** Although a change may seem small at first, you must look at how it affects production of the rest of the site and the ongoing maintenance of the site. Sometimes just by changing one little thing, you break something elsewhere in the site because it was never planned for in the first place. Or, you cause unforeseen technical or customer support issues in the future. For example, adding a simple survey requires a live human on the client's end to assess the incoming data.

- **Production efficiency.** Because scope creep can come at any time in the Web design process, you cannot implement the new feature without causing production inefficiencies. Adding a new feature midstream causes the team to stop what it's doing, redo tasks already completed, and refocus on the addition. Start-to-finish, midstream changes take more time to implement than they would if they were in the initial plan.

Still, scope creep happens and, because you're the customer service type, you find it tough to say no. Here's how to gracefully manage scope creep:

- **Get everything in writing.** Before you begin work on a project, make sure that your proposal clearly states the scope of the project — what you will include, what the client must provide, and what the project does not include. Also make sure that your site map is detailed enough to show how all the proposed content works together.

  If everything is in writing, no one can question what was included in the original deal.

- **Share the budget ramifications.** When a client asks you to insert a little something in the site, say, "Sure, I'd be glad to! Let me come back to you with what that would cost and how much time it would add to the project."

  Need I continue? Sharing the realities of an expanded budget and time schedule often quickly turns a client around. If your client decides to move forward with the addition, at least you and the client have clear expectations about how it impacts the project.

"We Don't Have Time for a Site Map!"

Often, clients come to designers at the very last moment and ask for an entire site designed and delivered within a ridiculous timeframe. The client insists on a crazy schedule, usually to try to meet an important conference or meeting on a hard date.

In situations like these, you may be tempted to dispense with the proposal and the site map so that you can dig right into the design directions. The problem with rushing in, however, is that neither you nor the client will have a road map to guide you. Without a road map, you have no idea what to include in the design directions — you plod in the dark, wasting time as the deadline slowly ticks closer.

Even worse, when you dispense with the planning phase, you set yourself up for disaster in terms of client expectations. The client may be thinking one thing, and you may be thinking another. Midway through the project, the client may not see what he expected to see, and panic follows.

Ironically, the most time-efficient way to proceed is to invest a little time up front creating a proposal that clearly outlines the content and goals of the site and to follow that with a site map that shows how you plan to arrange the content. You can do both these things in just one to two days of working closely with the client. With a clear plan in hand, you can knock out the design directions and produce a site that the client loves with plenty of time to spare.

"The Clients Want THAT Design?!"

When you are presenting design directions to a client, you may be tempted to shower them with a ton of options to choose from. Offering them lots of options gives them the impression that you've spent a lot of time thinking about their project, and it gives them a lot of ideas to consider.

The problem with this logic, however, is that it's difficult to come up with more than four to six directions that are distinctive and that you like. You always have a favorite and a least favorite design. For some reason unknown in the cosmos, clients have a knack for falling in love with your least favorite design. Therefore, never present a design that you can't live with.

To assemble a good group of designs to present, have a few different designers each come up with one or two designs. This way, you're sure to get an assortment of unique designs. From these, choose the top four to six designs that you feel good about presenting to the client.

If you are an independent consultant and don't have a staff of designers, try finding a few like-minded independent designers to help you develop design directions for each project.

"Who Needs Usability Testing When You've Got Me?"

You may laugh, but I've heard the sentiment, "Who needs to test when you've got me?" expressed by more than one Web designer. Often, designers find that they simply don't have enough time or money to organize a formal user test for a new Web site — many times because the designers never planned for testing in the first place. All too often, testing is considered an unnecessary expense in the budget — even by the clients.

For large projects, a client can end up spending a lot of money on a project that simply doesn't work. Without testing, no one knows about problems until the site is live on the Web and the negative customer feedback starts rolling in. On the Internet, location is irrelevant. Potential visitors find it just as easy to type in one URL as the next. After a user has a bad experience at a site, a second visit is not likely. Testing is crucial.

For large sites, planning and budgeting for formal user tests are imperative. For small- to medium-sized sites, you can still plan for user testing, but you don't have to go all out with the formal, expensive, time-consuming procedures. Organize small, informal testing intervals along the way using friends, colleagues, and even the clients themselves.

"But I'm Sure I Can Make This New Technology Work!"

As you wade knee-deep into production, the programming folks working around the clock can very easily lose track of the time schedule. Most programmers and HTML people that I've met love the challenge of solving problems and doing what others say can't be done.

The relentless pursuit of solving problems, however, can quickly become a drain on the project's schedule. The project manager must keep a close eye to ensure that the technology team stays on track and doesn't spend more than the allotted time on any one technical issue.

Tinkering is not limited to just the technology team: Designers are also known to push pixels around for hours until they get the perfect design. To keep a project on schedule, the project manager must stay on top of the milestones and where the team lies in the process.

"Oh . . . It Needs to Be Translated?"

Although most sites on the Web are in English, a growing number of companies are localizing their sites to cater to the needs of the international marketplace. *Localizing* entails translating the Web site into new languages and, in many cases, hosting the site in countries abroad.

If the Web is a global medium, why would you need to host a site in another country? If you've ever tried loading a Web site from across the world, you've probably noticed that the performance is pretty bad. A site hosted on a far-away server may be lean in terms of file size, but its sheer distance from you makes it load slowly. If you look at it from the European perspective and consider that most Europeans pay per minute of Internet usage and view Web sites that are hosted in the United States, you realize that a lot of European customers pay a premium for slow service.

Along with hosting a site abroad for better performance, you may also consider translating the site into a number of languages. I've found that up to 50 percent of a Web company's business can come from overseas. The problem, however, is that this 50 percent is spread across six or so languages, from German to Japanese.

When designing a Web site (in English), the guideline is to allow 30 percent more space for text to accommodate the longer word and sentence structures of other languages. Take a look at Figures 19-1 and 19-2. These figures show the same page from an online course in both English and German. A line-by-line comparison from the headline to the bulleted list shows how much more space the German language takes up on the page. If you are not careful in your initial planning, translating a site into another language may significantly alter the page layout.

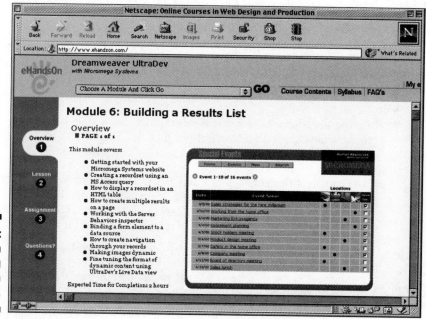

Figure 19-1:
A page from a training course in English.

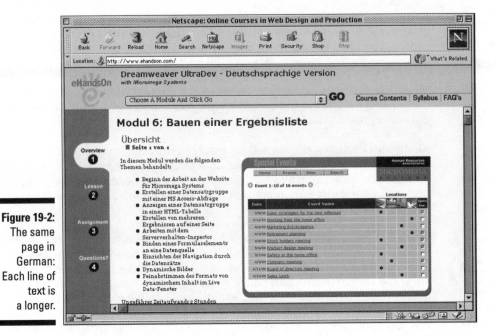

Figure 19-2:
The same
page in
German:
Each line of
text is
a longer.

"The Site Needs to Work on Windows?"

Face it: Most designers and creative types work on Macs, and most tech-heads work on PCs. Although most graphic design software tools these days look and function the same on both Mac and Windows, the long-standing tradition in the creative community to use a Macintosh still exists. (Mac fans will be happy to know that this book was written on my trusty ol' G3.)

Because most people creating Web graphics use a Mac, however, a lot of graphics look great on a Mac but not on a PC. The two biggest design factors when designing cross-platform Web graphics on a Mac are

- ✔ **Gamma differences.** Macs and PCs have different monitor brightness and color display settings. A Mac's display is much lighter and less saturated than a PC's. Therefore, graphics with dark colors and subtle color variations often appear solid black when viewed on a PC.

  If you develop Web graphics on a Mac, always test out your graphics on a PC before you include them on the site. Also, some software programs, such as Fireworks, have a Windows gamma preview feature that enables you to see how your work looks on a PC.

  The reverse is true for those of you renegade designers building graphics on a PC. Always test out your graphics on a Mac, or use a graphic program's gamma preview function to make sure that your graphics look right on both platforms.

> ✔ **Font size differences.** When you mock-up a Web page on a Mac — complete with dummy text that will ultimately be replaced with HTML text — the text looks smaller than you intended when viewed on a PC. This is because PCs usually have a 96 dot per inch (dpi) display, which is a finer dot size than the Mac's 72 dpi.
>
> For mock-up purposes, try bumping up your font sizes by 1 point. For instance, instead of 10 point Times for the body text, use 11 point. If you're building graphical headlines, try making them slightly larger than you think they should be. Finally, always take a peek at your work on a PC before you send it off to the production team.

"Uh . . . It Needs to Work on a Mac?"

Because programmers and HTML slingers mainly work on PCs, they can easily assemble Web pages that look perfectly fine when viewed on a PC but are a mess on the Mac. Mainly, the problem is the browser. The same version of Internet Explorer and Netscape Navigator on a Mac and on a PC are completely different browsers. Usually, the Mac versions are a little behind in their capabilities.

Although Mac users comprise a much smaller segment of the Web-viewing public, they are still an important audience that no self-respecting Internet company can ignore. Technical solutions don't always work the same on Macs as they do on Windows machines.

Before building a Web site, you and the client must decide which browsers and what versions of them that the site should support. Then, as you get into production, make sure the development team has access to these browsers on Macs and PCs to make sure that the site looks and behaves correctly.

"We'll Just Make the Whole Thing Database-Driven!"

If you read about all the cool technologies you can use to automate and scale a Web site that I discuss in Chapter 15, you may be tempted to make the whole site reliant on a database. After all, the database can populate each page of the site on the fly, so all you have to do is create a few template pages and voilà!: an instant, automated Web site. To update the site's content, you need only to make changes to the online database and, presto, the whole site updates instantly.

Although such programming technologies and databases streamline the creation and maintenance of a Web site, they are not without their own special requirements:

✔ **A dedicated team.** To keep the technologies and databases kicking, the client needs a serious team of propeller-heads on staff around the clock to make sure nothing goes wrong. If the database gets corrupted (which happens more often than you might think) or if the database server goes down, the whole site goes down in flames and your client ends up on the front page of the local newspaper.

✔ **Souped-up servers.** If a good portion of the site relies on database technologies, you're putting strain on the servers and increasing the chances that they will give out. Remember, each time that someone visits a page, that visitor accesses the database. With hundreds of visits each day to multiple pages, you're looking at a lot of server activity!

If a significant portion of the Web site relies on database technologies, make sure that the client has a "hot" backup system in place. This is a redundant server with a copy of the database (backed up every 30 minutes or so) that can come online in a pinch if the main server goes down.

Another tactic is to have a different server housing each major database. This configuration mitigates the strain on each individual server and helps to isolate problems.

"If We Build It, They Will Come"

What worked in the movie *Field of Dreams* won't work for a Web site marketing plan. With so many Web sites on the Internet, getting people's attention and drawing them to your site is very difficult. You cannot launch a site anymore and expect people to just find it or even care about your offerings. That's why you and the client must build a solid marketing plan and start executing it even before the site is live on the Web.

The best marketing plan for a Web site is one that involves a combination of traditional offline marketing and public relations techniques with online tactics. By offline, I mean every advertising medium that is not the Web: radio, trade shows, direct mail, billboards, print ads, and (heaven forbid) TV commercials. (Expensive TV ad time can quickly eat up the financing of young Web companies and lead to "dot com-bustion.") Online techniques can be much less expensive or free and just as effective. Some ideas include

✔ **Swapping banner ads or purchasing banner ad space.** Identify a number of Web sites that have a similar clientele and offer to swap ad banners. Often, to accommodate the disparity between the amount of traffic between your site and your partner's, you can work out additional forms of compensation. For example, if the partner's site has heavier traffic, you could sweeten the deal by offering a special discount on your products to that company's visitors.

As a last resort, you can always purchase banner space, but I recommend avoiding this because banners are expensive relative to the amount of traffic that they generate.

✔ **Co-promoting with other companies.** Another effective marketing tactic is to partner with other online companies with customers who can benefit from your offerings. For example, if your site sells custom reading glasses, try partnering with a book club site and running a promotion such as, "Sign up today for the book club and receive 10% off ACME custom reading glasses."

With this approach, you can have a much greater presence on the partner's Web site than with a banner ad, and your partner may even actively promote you in its online and offline marketing campaigns.

✔ **Using <meta> tags to help search engines find a site.** When people use a search engine such as www.google.com to look for a Web site, they enter a series of key words and phrases such as "horse, sale, dutch warmblood" into a search field. To find Web sites that match these keywords and phrases, search engines look through not only the text of Web pages, but also the <meta> tags contained in their HTML code. When you build a site, you should include as many keywords and phrases as you can think of that relate to the content of your site and include them in each page's <meta> tags.

Appendix

About the CD

• •

*B*efore I hand out any Web design wings, you've got to dig in and get some practice with some of the standard-issue Web software tools. On the CD that's included with this book is an assortment of free software trials.

On the CD-ROM:

- Fireworks 4 free 30-day trial
- Dreamweaver 4 free 30-day trial
- Flash 5 free 30-day trial
- Photoshop 6 trial
- Inspiration 6 trial

System Requirements

Make sure that your computer meets the minimum system requirements listed below. If your computer doesn't match up to most of these requirements, you may have problems using the contents of the CD.

- A PC with a 133 MHz Pentium or faster processor, or a Mac OS computer with a Power PC processor.
- Microsoft Windows 95 or later, or Mac OS system software 7.5 or later.
- At least 32MB of total RAM installed on your computer. For best performance, we recommend that Windows 95-equipped PCs and Mac OS computers with PowerPC processors have at least 64MB of RAM installed.
- At least 400MB of hard drive space available to install all the software from this CD. (You need less space if you don't install every program.)
- A CD-ROM drive — double-speed (2x) or faster.
- A sound card for PCs. (Mac OS computers have built-in sound support.)

✔ A monitor capable of displaying at least 256 colors or grayscale.

✔ A modem with a speed of at least 14,400 bps.

✔ Internet connection

✔ Internet Explorer or Netscape 4.0 or higher

Using the CD with Microsoft Windows

To install the items from the CD to your hard drive, follow these steps.

1. **Insert the CD into your computer's CD-ROM drive.**

2. **Open your browser.**

3. **Click Start⇨Run.**

4. **In the dialog box that appears, type D:\START.HTM.**

5. **Read through the license agreement, nod your head, and then click the Accept button if you want to use the CD — after you click Accept, you'll jump to the Main Menu.**

6. **To navigate within the interface, simply click on any topic of interest to take you to an explanation of the files on the CD and how to use or install them.**

7. **To install the software from the CD, simply click on the software name.**

In order to run some of the programs and files on the *Web Design For Dummies* CD-ROM, you may need to keep the CD inside your CD-ROM drive. This is a Good Thing. Otherwise, the installation program would require you to install a very large chunk of the program to your hard drive, which may prevent you from installing other software.

Using the CD with Mac OS

To install the items from the CD to your hard drive, follow these steps.

1. **Insert the CD into your computer's CD-ROM drive.**

   In a moment, an icon representing the CD you just inserted appears on your Mac desktop. Chances are, the icon looks like a CD-ROM.

2. **Double click the CD icon to show the CD's contents.**

3. **In the window that appears, double click the START.HTM icon.**

4. Read through the license agreement, nod your head, and then click the Accept button if you want to use the CD—after you click Accept, you'll jump to the Main Menu. This action displays the file that walks you through the content of the CD.

5. To navigate within the interface, simply click on any topic of interest to take you to an explanation of the files on the CD and how to use or install them.

6. To install the software from the CD, simply click on the software name.

After you are done with the interface, simply close your browser as usual.

After you have installed the programs you want, you can eject the CD.

What You'll Find

Here's a summary of the software and utilities on this CD arranged by category. If you use Windows, the CD interface helps you install software easily.

If you use a Mac OS computer, you can take advantage of the easy Mac interface to quickly install the programs.

Web Design Software

Dreamweaver 4, from Macromedia Inc.

For Windows 95/98/NT and Mac OS. 30-day trial version. Like a cross between a word processor and a graphics program, Dreamweaver allows you to build HTML pages visually. It's also a great tool to learn HTML because you can see the HTML code in one window as you build the page with graphical tools in another window. Dreamweaver is also a great tool for managing and uploading a whole Web site to a remote server.

Fireworks 4, from Macromedia Inc.

For Windows 95/98/NT and Mac OS. 30-day trial version. Build Web graphics from the ground up and churn out interactive pages ready for the Web or further customization in an HTML editor like Dreamweaver or GoLive.

Flash 5, from Macromedia Inc.

For Windows 95/98/NT and Mac OS. 30-day trial version. Flash enables you to build amazing, interactive, twirling animations that leverage the tight file sizes and scalability of vector graphics. In addition, its robust programming language, ActionScript, is some pretty serious stuff — it has the power to build software-like applications for the Web.

Inspiration 6, from Inspiration Software, Inc.

For Windows 95/98/NT and Mac OS. 30-day trial version. Inspiration is a great software tool for building professional-looking site maps. Its easy-to-use interface helps you quickly sketch out shapes to represent pages of a site and link them together with arrows.

Photoshop 6, from Adobe

For Windows 98/NT and Mac OS. Trial version. Try your hand at photo-manipulation, illustration, and designing Web graphics with Photoshop, the most powerful bitmap editing software around.

If You've Got Problems (Of the CD Kind)

I tried my best to compile programs that work on most computers with the minimum system requirements. Alas, your computer may differ, and some programs may not work properly for some reason.

The two likeliest problems are that you don't have enough memory (RAM) for the programs that you want to use, or you have other programs running that are affecting installation or running of a program. If you get error messages, try one or more of these methods and then try using the software again:

- **Turn off any antivirus software that you have on your computer.** Installers sometimes mimic virus activity and may make your computer incorrectly believe that it is being infected by a virus.

- **Close all running programs.** The more programs you're running, the less memory is available to other programs. Installers also typically update files and programs; if you keep other programs running, installation may not work properly.

- **In Windows, close the CD interface and run demos or installations directly from Windows Explorer.** The interface itself can tie up system memory, or even conflict with certain kinds of interactive demos. Use Windows Explorer to browse the files on the CD and launch installers or demos.

✔ **Have your local computer store add more RAM to your computer.** This is, admittedly, a drastic and somewhat expensive step. However, if you have a Windows 95 PC or a Mac OS computer with a PowerPC chip, adding more memory can really help the speed of your computer and enable more programs to run at the same time.

If you still have trouble installing the items from the CD, please call the Customer Care phone number: 800-762-2974 (outside the U.S.: 317-572-3993).

Index

• H •

• *I* •

• U •

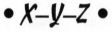

Wiley Publishing, Inc.
End-User License Agreement

READ THIS. You should carefully read these terms and conditions before opening the software packet(s) included with this book "Book". This is a license agreement "Agreement" between you and Wiley Publishing, Inc. "WPI". By opening the accompanying software packet(s), you acknowledge that you have read and accept the following terms and conditions. If you do not agree and do not want to be bound by such terms and conditions, promptly return the Book and the unopened software packet(s) to the place you obtained them for a full refund.

1. **License Grant.** WPI grants to you (either an individual or entity) a nonexclusive license to use one copy of the enclosed software program(s) (collectively, the "Software" solely for your own personal or business purposes on a single computer (whether a standard computer or a workstation component of a multi-user network). The Software is in use on a computer when it is loaded into temporary memory (RAM) or installed into permanent memory (hard disk, CD-ROM, or other storage device). WPI reserves all rights not expressly granted herein.

2. **Ownership.** WPI is the owner of all right, title, and interest, including copyright, in and to the compilation of the Software recorded on the disk(s) or CD-ROM "Software Media". Copyright to the individual programs recorded on the Software Media is owned by the author or other authorized copyright owner of each program. Ownership of the Software and all proprietary rights relating thereto remain with WPI and its licensers.

3. **Restrictions On Use and Transfer.**

    (a) You may only (i) make one copy of the Software for backup or archival purposes, or (ii) transfer the Software to a single hard disk, provided that you keep the original for backup or archival purposes. You may not (i) rent or lease the Software, (ii) copy or reproduce the Software through a LAN or other network system or through any computer subscriber system or bulletin- board system, or (iii) modify, adapt, or create derivative works based on the Software.

    (b) You may not reverse engineer, decompile, or disassemble the Software. You may transfer the Software and user documentation on a permanent basis, provided that the transferee agrees to accept the terms and conditions of this Agreement and you retain no copies. If the Software is an update or has been updated, any transfer must include the most recent update and all prior versions.

4. **Restrictions on Use of Individual Programs.** You must follow the individual requirements and restrictions detailed for each individual program in the "About the CD" appendix of this Book. These limitations are also contained in the individual license agreements recorded on the Software Media. These limitations may include a requirement that after using the program for a specified period of time, the user must pay a registration fee or discontinue use. By opening the Software packet(s), you will be agreeing to abide by the licenses and restrictions for these individual programs that are detailed in the "About the CD" appendix and on the Software Media. None of the material on this Software Media or listed in this Book may ever be redistributed, in original or modified form, for commercial purposes.

Notes

Notes